'Because we are poor':
Irish Theatre in the 1990s

'Because we are poor':
Irish Theatre in the 1990s

Victor Merriman

Carysfort Press

A Carysfort Press Book

'Because we are poor': Irish Theatre in the 1990s
by Victor Merriman

First published as a paperback in Ireland in 2011 by
Carysfort Press Ltd
58 Woodfield
Scholarstown Road
Dublin 16
Ireland

ISBN 978-1-904505-51-8

Typeset by Carysfort Press Ltd

Printed and bound by eprint limited
Unit 35
Coolmine Industrial Estate
Dublin 15
Ireland

Cover design by eprint

This book is published with the financial assistance of
The Arts Council (An Chomhairle Ealaíon) Dublin, Ireland

To my parents, Colette and Victor, with love and gratitude

Do Niamh, le grá agus ard-mheas i gcónaí

Table of Contents

Acknowledgements

These responses to Irish theatre owe a great deal to Michael D. Higgins's invitation to me to serve as a member of An Chomhairle Ealaíon/the Arts Council (1993-1998). Council chairman Ciarán Benson's decision to undertake a full review of theatre provision in Ireland (1995-1996), and to ask me to chair it, was of great importance in broadening and grounding my understanding of the dynamics at work in the art form, at a time of extraordinary energy and development. I recall with respect and affection the indefatigability of the members of the Review Steering Committee, Páraic Breatnach, Mary-Elizabeth Burke-Kennedy, Eithne Healy, Phelim Donlon's expertise, integrity, and wise counsel, and Patrick Murray's unfailing good humour.

One of the significant advantages which Irish theatre scholarship enjoys is the enthusiasm of Irish theatre artists for critical debate. The extent of my debt to a range of makers of, and thinkers about Irish theatre will be readily apparent to the reader. This book is also informed by, and indebted to a range of personal and professional relationships. The doctoral studies out of which the shape of the project emerged were encouraged by Erica Carter, Peter Middleton, and Lizbeth Goodman, and were completed under the inspiring supervision of Shaun Richards. Awam Amkpa and Tim Prentki have been constant personal and scholarly companions since we first worked together twenty years ago, and with David Lloyd, Tom Hall, Aidan Arrowsmith and Chris Morash, read draft chapters in a spirit of provocative fellowship. What became Chapter Seven was afforded a first outing in research seminars at The Drama Centre, University College Dublin. I am grateful also to Chris Murray and Tony Roche for their encouragement of my work during their service as editors of the *Irish University Review*.

The manuscript benefited from the comments of anonymous readers, and the editorial team at Carysfort Press, Dan Farrelly, Eamonn Jordan and Lilian Chambers, supported this project throughout, and have ensured a smooth production process. Mairéad Delaney made the resources of the Abbey Archive available during the research phase, and provided the cover image for the book. Sections of this book appeared in earlier versions in the following publications: *Irish University Review, Modern Drama, The Cambridge Companion to Twentieth-century Irish Drama*, and *Beckett and Ireland* (Cambridge University Press, 2010). I thank the editors and publishers for permission to reprint. I am especially grateful to Reverend Professor Kenneth Newport, Pro-Vice-Chancellor (Research and Staff Development), Liverpool Hope University for the support provided by Hope's research funds toward this publication.

Finally, it remains proudly true that research and scholarship in the Arts and Humanities is a gift economy, not a cash economy. The riches it produces are negotiated in free and mainly disinterested exchange, and circulate freely as contributions to knowledge and understanding. It is for this reason, above all, that I value so highly the encouragement and generosity of colleagues and students with whom I have worked since my first appointment in higher education, in 1990.

For forty years Ireland has been free, and for forty years it has wandered in the desert under the leadership of men who freed their nation, but who could never free their souls from the ill-effects of having been in slavery. To that slave-born generation it has always seemed inevitable and right that Anglo-American plutocracies, because they are rich, should be allowed to destroy us because we are poor – destroy us root and branch through mass emigration.

M.J. Molloy, 'Preface to *The Wood of the Whispering*', ed. Robert O'Driscoll, *Selected Plays of M.J. Molloy* (Colin Smythe, 1998): 111.

1 | Introduction: 'Because We Are Poor'

> Postcolonial writing ... is initiated at that very moment when a native writer formulates a text committed to cultural resistance.[1] *Declan Kiberd*

> Irish culture cannot express, reflect, embody – or any of the other favoured metaphors – the decolonizing nation until it is so constituted by an enabling metadiscourse: criticism.[2] *Gerry Smyth*

The 1990s is a moment of exceptional interest in the development of Independent Ireland, the nature of its drama, and its theatre practices. It is the decade of Mary Robinson (President of Ireland 1990-1997), and of the first ever department of state for Arts and Culture, under the visionary direction of Michael D. Higgins (1993-1997). It opens with the extraordinary international success of Brian Friel's *Dancing at Lughnasa* (1990) and ends with stirrings of concern about the impact of global success on the theatre/Ireland relationship. Scholarship in Irish Studies develops at an impressive pace, and across a considerable range of interests, during the period. In 1989 J.J. Lee's compendious *Ireland 1912-1985*[3] appears, and in 1990, Breen et al's *Understanding Contemporary Ireland: State, Class and Development in the Republic of Ireland*[4] is published. In the broad field of Irish Studies, the challenge to map the contours of debate on cultural production has been vigorously taken up, since the publication of David Cairns and Shaun Richards's landmark study, *Writing Ireland: Colonialism, Nationalism and Culture*.[5] Declan Kiberd's *Inventing Ireland*[6] is a work every bit as commanding as that of J.J. Lee, with a specifically cultural focus, and there are the compelling Field Day essays on culture, nationalism and politics, by critics such as Fredric Jameson, Terry

Eagleton, Edward Said and Seamus Deane.[7] Recent work includes the welcome updating of Terence Brown's *Ireland: A Social and Cultural History (1922-2002)*, and monographs and collections of essays by Joe Cleary, Luke Gibbons,[8] and David Lloyd.[9]

The range and volume of scholarship in the field of Drama and Theatre Studies illustrates, in one discipline, the validity of Lee's comments on the vigour of critical debate on Ireland in general, from the 1980s.[10] Adrian Frazier argues that

> Irish theatre scholarship is prolific and high quality. It is distinctive in its adeptness with a historical, archival approach; its theoretical curiosity about linkages between theatre, culture and politics.[11]

For Christopher Morash, the period is one of sustained engagement with drama as cultural production, in ways which seek to produce new readings of the past, and the present, as part of a felt need for social transformation.[12] Those who produced significant critical works over a decade or so from 1993 include Nicholas Grene,[13] Margaret Llewellyn-Jones,[14] Christopher Morash,[15] Christopher Murray,[16] Lionel Pilkington,[17] Anthony Roche,[18] and Robert Welch.[19] There have been a number of collections of critical essays, and *irish theatre magazine*[20] emerged as an important organ of debate. The titles and concerns of the works cited suggest that Joseph Lee's summary of the task of the contemporary historian as one of evaluating 'the performance of a sovereign people'[21] was one with which many felt the need to engage. For Lee, that project involves the historian in 'seeking to reveal the range of relevant linkages between the activities with which he is concerned'.[22]

Lionel Pilkington identifies a 'need for a cultural history of Ireland that accounts for Irish theatre's complex relationship to colonialism and modernity.'[23] In that spirit, this book offers critical readings of a selection of plays staged in the Republic of Ireland during the period from 1983, alongside readings of continuities and upheavals in culture, society and the state during that period. I attempt to intervene in an area in which little or no work has been done: the potential and responsibilities of artists, intellectuals and other cultural workers in relation to a national project of decolonization. My engagement with 1990s theatre began as an effort to comprehend what Irish theatre might reveal about Irish society, moved away from a 'theatre/society' relationship towards a series of questions focused more on relationships between theatre practices and the Irish state, and has reached a point of pondering what role, if any, theatre might play in enabling a 'second republic'.[24] The book takes advantage of the conceptual elasticity offered by Eric Hobsbawm's construct of a 'long' eighteenth century, and a 'short' twentieth century, to enable inclusion of a seminal production from 1983. The plays discussed include the following, listed with production company, venue and year of performance:

> **1983**: M.J. Molloy, *The Wood of the Whispering* (Druid Theatre Company, Douglas Hyde Gallery, Dublin);
> **1989**: Dermot Bolger, *The Lament for Arthur Cleary* (Arthur Cleary Productions, Dun Mhuire, Wexford, touring);
> **1990**: Brian Friel, *Dancing at Lughnasa* (The Abbey Theatre);
> **1993**: Tom Murphy, *Famine* (The Abbey Theatre);
> **1994**: J.M. Synge, *The Well of the Saints* (The Abbey Theatre); Dónal O'Kelly, *Asylum! Asylum!* (The Peacock Theatre);
> **1995**: W.B. Yeats and Augusta Gregory, *Cathleen Ní Houlihan* (The Peacock Theatre); W. B. Yeats, *Purgatory* (The Peacock Theatre);
> **1996**: Samuel Beckett, *Waiting for Godot* (Gate Theatre Production at Watergate Theatre, Kilkenny, touring);
> **1997**: Martin McDonagh, *The Leenane Trilogy* (Druid Theatre Company, Town Hall Theatre, Galway); Charlie O'Neill, *Rosie and Starwars* (Calypso Productions, Meeting House Square Marquee, Dublin, and Granary Theatre, Cork, touring); *Asylum! Asylum!* (Granary Theatre, Cork)
> **1998**: Marina Carr, *By the Bog of Cats ...* (The Abbey Theatre); Cork Travellers' Visibility Group, *An Unsettled Country* (Granary Theatre, Cork); Dónal O'Kelly, *Farawayan* (Calypso Productions, Olympic Ballroom, Dublin)

Late twentieth-century/early twenty-first-century Independent Ireland – the successor state to the colonial province – has seen extraordinary changes: the emergence of a political settlement in Northern Ireland, the technologically-driven acceleration of processes of globalization, and the emergence and collapse of the most hyperactive environment for capitalist accumulation in Europe, to name but three. I take it as axiomatic that fictional stage worlds are intimately implicated in the actual worlds from which they emerge, and in those into which they play. It follows that no credible attempt to understand a fictional world can take the nature and dynamics of actual worlds for granted, or as read. In short, understanding actual worlds is as vital to critical practice in drama as understanding fictional worlds. I argue that the actual Ireland into which these plays were performed, is a site of continuing contest and negotiation of enduring contradictions rooted in its colonial history, and active in a state which has postponed decolonization. For that reason, it is most productively analysed from a postcolonial critical perspective.

One of the features of contemporary Irish Studies is the central contribution of postcolonial theory to its development. Critical projects such as Field Day and *The Crane Bag*,[25] for instance, intersect around the concept of a 'fifth province', a potent postcolonial metaphor for the utopian imaginary. Among scholars engaged with Irish drama and theatre studies, the term 'postcolonial' was, by the late 1990s, commonplace. It was applied inconsistently, and with considerable variation of intent, hence my attempt here to argue for its fecundity as a progressive discourse focused on transformative critique. By contrast, Christopher Murray's main concern is the elaboration of an Irish dramatic canon, and he treats postcoloniality as a phenomenon of a particular moment:

> For the most part, Irish plays of the 1940s and 1950s are now of interest predominantly as cultural documents. They reflect the values, artistic and moral as well as socio-economic and political, of a people struggling to establish firm contours of identity in a postcolonial phase ... We are dealing with plays of a particular, transitional but nevertheless formative time in Irish history. It was, essentially, the De Valera era.'[26]

Murray's view that there was a postcolonial moment, and that it has passed, is consistent with his assumption that the events of 1958-59 amounted to a genuine historical break: 'Audiences were not looking for any real manifestation of evil in the age of de Valera; society had its eyes shut tight. They didn't open them again until the 1960s.'[27] I support Murray's intuition of a transitional quality in the 1940s and 1950s, but I differ from him in his over-reliance on periodization, and on critical tropes such as 'authorial talent',[28] which limit the effectiveness of his declared critical project.[29] Accordingly, my readings of Beckett and Molloy, which follow, situate their works, and the period in which they were written, among quite different critical conversations than those enabled by Murray's scholarship.

Nicholas Grene seems wary of the postcolonial turn in Irish Studies, as applied to drama. He alludes to the ubiquity of 'a postcolonial orthodoxy in which the colonial connection is seen retrospectively as a 'doom', vitiating everything and everyone, colonizer and colonized alike.'[30] Grene makes rewarding connections and offers significant insights into the 'special intertextual lines of descent'[31] of 'a notably cohesive'[32] Irish dramatic tradition 'constituted around its Irish subject and setting'.[33] He is prepared to acknowledge that Ireland's colonial past had some measure of impact on Irish consciousness, and that it continues to exert material influence: 'No doubt a large part of the anxious obsession with self-representation in the Irish dramatic tradition originates with the colonial and postcolonial condition of the country.'[34] What he seems reluctant to concede is the neo-colonial/postcolonial dynamic I identify as the dominant feature contextualizing cultural production in Independent Ireland. In concluding his argument, he comes tantalizingly close to acknowledging the fact of postponed decolonization as a critical determinant of Irish experience rendered in dramatic form: 'The disposition within the drama to represent in Irish life what is symptomatic of Irish life can be attributed in general terms to the colonial/postcolonial consciousness which leaves the question of national identity always an issue.'[35] Grene hesitates to engage in any sustained way with the central concerns of postcolonial theory, and the debates to which they give rise, and most notably resists the idea of Independent Ireland as a neo-colonial state. In phrases such as 'anxious obsession' and 'symptomatic of Irish life', he suggests that critical and artistic concerns with the nation are a form of pathology – a standard manoeuvre in revisionist discourse. He asserts this pejorative view while nonetheless acknowledging: 'The long-promised Utopia of national liberation provoked comparison with the reality achieved in the actual Free State with all its limitations.'[36]

No critical position is innocent of intellectual indebtedness or ideological interestedness, and I would like to contextualize my use of postcolonial theory in relation to three points: firstly, the validity of postcolonial perspectives on Ireland has been hotly disputed;[37] secondly, there are indications in some recent work on theatre that the moment of globalization and the recognition by the academy of interdisciplinary performance studies offer ways of 'moving beyond' postcolonial critique; thirdly, the postcolonial lens appears to me to offer the best means of developing what Seamus Deane refers to as 'an enabling criticism' (in fact, this is a declared aim of postcolonial studies). Points one and two are obviously linked. Both Joe Cleary[38] and David Lloyd[39] acknowledge that some of those antagonistic to the postcolonial have inspired postcolonial theorists to illuminate their practices, while others have tended to generate more in the way of heat. I will not rehearse the details of the salient arguments involved, as the interested reader will find a comprehensive survey of positions taken in the essays mentioned.[40] Of more immediate interest here, is the emergence, in Drama and Theatre Studies, of a body of work building on Nicholas Grene's obvious impatience to move beyond the idea of the postcolonial.[41] This view is summarized – but, tantalizingly, not grounded in the analysis of specific works – in Fricker and Singleton's reference to what they see as a pervasive tendency for the academy 'to pursue national identity as the drive of both theatre and criticism and to trap Irish theatre in a narrow postcolonial framework.'[42]

What seems to be at work both in Grene, and Fricker and Singleton is a conflation of postcolonial studies with nationalist identity politics. This needs to be challenged, because postcolonial criticism actually privileges critical consciousness and agency, and is explicitly dedicated to exposing the actual and representational frauds and negations of colonial and anti-colonial nationalisms, and the redeployment of their rhetorical tropes in the official nationalism of neo-colonial successor states. Patrick Lonergan suggests that criticism concentrate instead on the phenomenon of globalization,[43] but carefully, lest 'we' 'will merely be rebranding the postcolonial theory, presenting "new and improved" critical terms that will do little to elucidate the actual terms under which theatre is made and received.'[44] In light of his concern with conditions of production and reception, his work contains an unfortunate lacuna: the role of the state in either the global economy or in the cultural economy within which Irish theatre is made and circulated – almost all Irish theatre is subsidized by public money – is barely mentioned. This seriously disables his analysis of the problems of the Abbey Theatre, for instance, in a period which has seen it leave behind its national character in pursuit of global brand development.[45] In short, Lonergan's approach to globalization is thoroughly depoliticized, boiling down to a call for 'an awareness of how plays mean different things, to different audiences, in different parts of the world.'[46] There is no denying the importance of understanding contemporary globalization, but it is important in and of itself, and not because it can re-colonize intellectual space ceded to 'the postcolonial franchise that has dominated Irish Studies in recent decades.'[47]

Whatever its shortcomings in an Irish context, notably its enthusiasm for neo-liberal business discourse,[48] Lonergan's approach does appear to chime with a broader 'post-theoretical' campaign for a kind of transnational theatre without tears, comfortable with commerce, and too cool for critique. Introducing Dan Rebellato's *Theatre & Globalization*, Mark Ravenhill flippantly dismisses critical scepticism common to poststructural and postcolonial theory: 'Marxism and postmodernism had sent so many words to the naughty step.'[49] Around the same time comes news of an exciting series of rattling yarns from a generation of young historians which has 'sprouted up to fill the vacuum left by the departure of theory – or the "-isms" – from mainstream academic life.'[50] Two observations: firstly, in evaluating warnings on the narrowness of postcolonial theory, Edward Said's conclusion on the merits of Irish engagements with and contributions to postcolonial studies, is worth bearing in mind: 'One of the main strengths of postcolonial analysis is that it widens, instead of narrowing, the interpretive perspective, which is another way of saying that it liberates instead of further constricting and colonizing the mind.'[51] Secondly, the point of academic research, is to understand, address and disseminate critical perspectives as a contribution, not only to intellectual life, but to the public good. It is sobering, therefore, to consider recent contestation of the political engagement of postcolonial critical practice in terms of Peadar Kirby's finding that 'far too much academic output in Ireland is functional to the persistence of a highly inequitable society and to the requirements of the elites who benefit from it.'[52] Gerry Smyth suggests that this is no recent phenomenon:

> The NUI's (National University of Ireland)[53] overall research performance – and specifically within the area of Irish-related literary criticism – is complicit with a form of censorship in which the state attempts to control the kind and number of spaces in civil society where potentially dangerous issues of national identity can be debated; as such it is complicit in the 1950s with the deferral of modes of discourse in which such issues might be foregrounded rather than elided or ignored.[54]

Half a century on, Pádraig A. Breatnach provides examples of direct intervention by the state in Irish universities, with foreseeable consequences for the forms and limits of intellectual activity.[55] These examples validate Luke Gibbons's inclusion of Ireland among 'cultures with an eloquent creative heritage but strong anti-intellectual traditions.'[56] More than this, they testify to the reality that universities are being included in an overall strategy of remodelling civil society in Ireland along a neo-liberal service model. This model is narrow and coercive, and its forceful imposition by the state has accelerated since 2002.[57]

It is neither my premise nor my argument that Irish academic life is either stupid or venal: there is no conspiracy. There is some evidence, however, of a consensus between the academy, 'business' – including private and corporate communications media – and the state,[58] which is altering the landscape at the expense of outcrops, or boltholes, of dissent. In the spirit of what used to be accepted as healthy scepticism, I suggest that a condition of Irish academic activity critiqued by Kirby has become more acute. This is not only a feature of the cult of managerialism in institutions of higher education, although this is highly significant,[59] but of a turn away from engaged critical analysis in more general terms. Attempts to steer away from critique – including, at times, especially, postcolonial analysis – in favour of a less "obsessively local" engagement with culture are clearly in tune with the failed Celtic Tiger project of repositioning Independent Ireland as the leading EU exemplar of a radically globalized capitalist economy. In Drama and Theatre Studies, the logic of that project plays out in critical ploys which purport to find in depoliticized readings of globalization an escape route from engaged critical practice.

Academic disengagement from public critique is associated, for Kirby, with the successor state's failure to decolonize, as it exemplifies 'the weak relationship between state and civil society inherited from colonial times.'[60] This weakness is highly significant, as, for Kirby, 'the terrain of civil society (has the) potential for setting a different developmental direction for the Irish state.'[61] It is on this terrain that 'the social struggle to gain the power to define the developmental project'[62] will be resolved. Kirby's favoured outcome envisages civil society as a transformative agent 'integrated fully with the state and the market in a vigorous democratic experimentalism.'[63] From my own perspective, civil society is the location of cultural work, and critical academic projects – Field Day is an outstanding example[64] – have made significant contributions to public self-awareness. Such contributions are acutely necessary in an Independent Ireland that, for much of the twentieth-century, was 'a sluggish society',[65] with 'little sense of history.'[66] In short, academic work can help to nuance public understanding of matters of which, as will be seen, for too long only economic questions have been asked.

By way of more particular accounting for my choice of the postcolonial as an enabling discourse, I draw attention to an ongoing dialogue with the work of Awam Amkpa, begun when we taught courses together (1990-1994) and, happily, ongoing. Amkpa's 'Drama and the Languages of Postcolonial Desire' was first presented as a paper to *The Shaw Arts Festival*, which I convened at Dublin Institute of Technology in April 1999. Anthony Roche chaired a public discussion of matters arising from that paper, and subsequently invited myself and Amkpa to formalize our dialogue in the pages of *The Irish University Review*. It was while responding to that invitation that I recognized the critical fecundity of postcolonial analysis for my own project. This was evident, not least because it enabled central insights on the neo-colonial quality of Independent Ireland, and its historical suspension in a postponement of decolonization. My dialogue with Amkpa situates Declan Kiberd's comment on postcolonial writing, and extends its application to conditions which emerge post-independence. To put it plainly, the need for critical artefacts and cultural practices is at least as acute in a successor state as it ever was in a colonial province. Accordingly, I set out here to expose and account for Irish theatre's staging of the radical otherness of lived experiences of Independent Ireland to official narratives of nation, subjectivity and agency. Viewed through a postcolonial lens, Ireland's dramas during the long 1990s are revealed as sites of dissent, resistance and aspiration to transformation, which exemplify the playing out, in one small place, of a dynamic between modernity's 'delusion of universality and the multiple and different social imaginaries at work in colonized cultures.'[67]

Research and critical practice in Drama and Theatre Studies produces ways of knowing which enrich the quality of conclusions drawn from economic and social research, precisely by foregrounding the possible emergence of dynamic and egalitarian human worlds. It may well be that 'historians cannot be expected to write about what might have been',[68] but, in theatre scholarship, because of the constitution of the artefact in performance, itself the result of deliberate selection from a range of representational choices, it becomes a duty. And this resonates strongly with decolonization: a programme of liberation that needs the critical participation of the individuals and groups which constitute the communities in which reside the developmental potential of the decolonizing state which gives integrity and meaning to the aspiration to a nation.[69]

I argue that engaging with Irish neo-colonialism as, in important respects, a recapitulation of colonial relations, sharpens the focus of critical practice in drama. Failure to do so disables efforts to understand the terms of theatre's engagement, or lack of engagement with social contradiction. Grene's reluctance in this respect reduces sites of cultural contestation such as identity, and postcolonial conditions to categories, concerns and practices which may be ignored by the critical gaze, at little cost. The political, economic and developmental questions confronting Independent Ireland in the 1990s give rise to complex issues which will be teased out in Chapter 2. The complexity of their interplay with questions of cultural production and reception (Chapter 3), produces a necessity for insights enabled by a broader account of postcoloniality as a set of practices alert to the significance, in human relations, of utopian desiring. It enables questions of subjectivity, belonging, and agency for instance, to be situated in radical integration with issues of representation and interpretation, and with what Lionel Pilkington refers to as 'the libidinous physicality of performance.'[70] The fruits of such an engagement are potentially very significant,[71] and Pilkington's own work on theatre and the state produces both a rich contextualization of Yeats, Gregory and Synge among the concerns of their own class, and a rewarding examination of drama's relationship with ongoing cultural and political struggles in Northern Ireland.

My focus is on theatre and Independent Ireland in the 1990s, the art form and the national state as intertwining systems of representation and interpretation. In Chapter 2 I set out my particular position on postcolonial theory, by means of a dialogue with ideas put forward in Amkpa's influential essay, 'Drama and the Languages of Postcolonial Desire.'[72] I go on to outline a view of Independent Ireland, not as a new entity innocently born in 1922, but as a successor state to a colonial province of long standing. I do so in order to establish the explicitly neo-colonial nature of a state that has systematically postponed decolonization, and denied space to any alternative proposed to a series of coercive *pensées uniques*.[73] I draw on Lee, and Breen et al., specifically because their analyses are contemporaneous with the historical moment on which I concentrate. I go on to review Peadar Kirby's writings on the nature and impact of developmental options pursued in Independent

Ireland. Kirby considers the question of development in relation not only to the state, but to civil society and, in light of questions raised by David Lloyd, I refine my sense of civil society's transformative potential.

Chapter 3 draws on insights from artists and critics to develop a view of cultural work in light of my analysis of the successor state in Chapter 2. I reflect not only on the creation of artefacts, but on their circulation, and on questions raised by assumptions underpinning Irish critical practice, journalistic and academic. I identify exemplars of postcolonial intent in scenes from M.J. Molloy's *The Wood of the Whispering*, and Tom Murphy's *Famine*, and point to aesthetic strategies contesting not only social conditions, but audience assumptions about the nature and purpose of the artform itself. This chapter offers an overview of the significance of the plays to be discussed which, I will argue, lies in their provenance in postcolonial desires. My analysis of Independent Ireland (Chapters 2 and 3) suggests that, politically, economically, socially and culturally, the successor state's neo-colonial dynamics are most visible when its homogenizing fantasies encounter actually existing difference. It is in contesting official narratives of belonging that subjectivity is struggled for; the commitment to assign public value to differentiated subjectivities by means of multiple narratives is a project of becoming, which is at the heart of social and cultural agency. This informs the readings of plays considered in Chapters 4 to 8.

Chapter 4: 'Intranational Problematics: Staging the Anti-colonial Moment' is the first of five chapters of detailed analysis of the significance of dramatic action, in light of the political, social and cultural framework set out. I read productions of Yeats and Gregory's *Cathleen Ní Houlihan*, Synge's *The Well of the Saints*, and Yeats's *Purgatory* as dramas, both historical and prophetic, which speak critically to the actual conditions of 1990s Ireland. Chapter 5: 'Hope deferred: Neo-colonial relations on Ireland's stages' considers the dramatic worlds of *Waiting for Godot* and *The Wood of the Whispering* as sites of transition, differentiated around an idea of theatre as public witnessing. Chapter 6: 'Them and Us: Dramas of a Rising Tide' looks in detail at two plays by Tom Murphy, his first, *On the Outside*, with Noel O'Donoghue, and his most remarkable, *Famine*. These plays see the emergence of a radically discontented voice as Independent Ireland commits wholly to a project of modernization within the terms of a model of dependent development.

The small-town provenance of that refusing voice enables the oppositional urban dramas addressed in Chapter 7: 'Countering Hegemonies'. The projects of Wet Paint Arts and Calypso Productions are among the clearest examples in the twentieth-century of Irish cultural workers engaging in explicit confrontation with the betrayals and silences of the state, and the national bourgeoisie. Significantly, both companies actively sought to engage with new audiences, and their works were rarely seen on main stages. What was taking place on those stages, in the works of Martin McDonagh and Marina Carr, concerns Chapter 8: 'Contested Spaces, Competing Voices'. I argue that the enthusiastic consumption by the national bourgeoisie of grotesque figures drawn from an Ireland apparently past is, during the late 1990s, in tune with the state's refusal of the importance of social solidarity at a time of extraordinary change. Chapter 9: 'Re-presenting the nation: theatre, utopia and decolonization', offers concluding comments on pressing issues for Independent Ireland, and on the contribution cultural workers – specifically those involved in Irish drama – might make to addressing them. Postcolonial critical practice has a utopian accent; it is not a technocratic discourse, and is not cowed by pragmatism, though it espouses a thoroughly practical *raison d'être*. In this, it is not unlike those creative works which dreamed a better Ireland into being on Irish stages during the convulsive experiences of the twentieth-century.

---

[1] Declan Kiberd, *Inventing Ireland* (Vintage, 1996): 6.

[2] Gerry Smyth,, *Decolonisation and Criticism* (Pluto Press, 1998): 52.

[3] J.J. Lee, *Ireland 1912 – 1985: Politics and Society* (Cambridge University Press, 1990).

[4] Richard Breen, Damian Hannan, David B. Rottman, Christopher T. Whelan, *Understanding Contemporary Ireland: State, Class and Development in the Republic of Ireland* (Gill & MacMillan, 1990).

[5] David Cairns and Shaun Richards, *Writing Ireland: Colonialism, Nationalism and Culture* (Manchester University Press, 1988).

[6] Kiberd (1996).

[7] Seamus Deane, ed., *Nationalism, Colonialism and Literature* (University Of Minnesota Press, 1990)

[8] Luke Gibbons, *Transformations in Irish Culture* (Cork University Press, 1996).

9 David Lloyd, *Anomalous States: Irish Writing and the Post-Colonial Moment* (Lilliput, 1993). Also, Lloyd, David, *Ireland After History* (Cork University Press, 1999).

10 By 1990 Lee acknowledges 'a marked increase in relevant published work, not only by historians, but by scholars in cognate disciplines.' Lee (1990): xi.

11 Adrian Frazier, 'Introduction: Irish Theatre Scholarship' in *The Irish Review*, No. 29 (2002): 9.

12 See Christopher Morash, *A History of Irish Theatre 1601-2000* (Cambridge University Press, 2002): 255-6

13 Nicholas Grene, *The Politics of Irish Drama: Plays in Context from Boucicault to Friel* (Cambridge University Press, 1999).

14 Margaret Llewellyn-Jones, *Contemporary Irish Drama and Cultural Identity* (Intellect, 2002).

15 Morash (2002).

16 Christopher Murray, *Twentieth-century Irish Drama: Mirror up to Nation* (Manchester University Press, 1997).

17 Lionel Pilkington, *Theatre and State in Twentieth-century Ireland* (Routledge, 2001).

18 Anthony Roche, *Contemporary Irish Drama: from Beckett to McGuinness* (Gill & Macmillan, 1994).

19 Robert Welch, *The Abbey Theatre 1899-1999: Form & Pressure* (Oxford University Press, 2003).

20 irish theatre magazine's inaugural issue was published in 1998.

21 Lee (1990): xiii.

22 Ibid. xii.

23 Lionel Pilkington, 'Recent Developments in Irish Theatre History', *Modern Drama XLVII. 4* (Winter 2004): 728.

24 Peadar Kirby, *Village Magazine*, May 2009.

25 A critical journal of ideas, published from 1977-1985.

26 Murray (1997): 138.

27 Ibid. 10.

28 See his discussion of the 'second renaissance of Irish Drama' in the 1960s in Murray (1997): 162.

29 'To date, no study of Irish drama has looked in detail at the interrelations of history, politics and performance in the way I find rewarding.' Ibid. 11.

30 Grene (1999): 43.

31 Ibid. 2.

32 Ibid.

33 Ibid.

34 Ibid. 267.

35 Ibid.

36 Ibid.

37 Clare Carroll and Patricia King, eds, *Ireland and Postcolonial Theory* (Cork University Press, 2003) contains a series of essays that

critique arguments for and against the applicability and usefulness of postcolonial theory to Irish experience.

38 Joe Cleary, '"Misplaced Ideas"?: Colonialism, Location and Dislocation in Irish Studies', Carroll and Patricia King eds (2003) 16-45.

39 David Lloyd, 'After History: Historicism and Irish Postcolonial Studies', Ibid. 46-62.

40 Edward Said refers to Joe Cleary's essay as a 'magisterial overview'. Edward Said, 'Afterword: Reflections on Ireland and Postcolonialism', Ibid. 178.

41 Grene (1999): 267

42 Karen Fricker and Brian Singleton, 'Irish Theatre: Conditions of Criticism', *Modern Drama XLVII. 4* (Winter 2004): 565.

43 Patrick Lonergan, *Theatre and Globalization: Irish Drama in the Celtic Tiger Era* (Basingstoke: Palgrave Macmillan, 2009).

44 Ibid. 223.

45 Annette Clancy, , Facing Forward: A document commissioned by The Abbey Theatre in partnership with The Arts Council for abbeyonehundred (Dublin: Abbey Theatre, 2005) reveals a lust for international distribution of Brand Abbey/Brand Ireland, at the expense of anything that might be described as a primary role in the social and cultural well-being of the nation. This is tellingly illustrated in a comment attributed to an unidentified playwright, 'You get the impression that (a new play) has to be a home run – a Tony award winner for anyone to take any notice.' See my critique of this turn in Third Text: Ireland Special Issue 19.5, ed. Lucy Cotter (Routledge, Taylor Francis, 2005).

46 Ibid.

47 Lonergan (2009): 30.

48 Lonergan's discussion centres on producing a series of exemplary productions, which support his view that 'practices in business and theatre are becoming convergent.' Ibid. 15.

49 'Marxism and postmodernism had sent so many words to the naughty step.' Mark Ravenhill, Foreword *Theatre & Globalization* by Dan Rebellato (Palgrave Macmillan, 2009): xi.

50 One of the featured group avers, 'I think writing your books with specific political aims in mind is an old-fashioned approach. It's not particularly helpful. I think if you produce a good narrative history, which convincingly creates the world you're writing about, then people will read it and draw their own conclusions.' Marre, Oliver, 'They're too cool for school: meet the new history boys and girls: Theory is a thing of the past for these hip young historians', *The Observer*, 28 June 2009.

51 Edward W. Said, Afterword, Carroll and King eds (2003): 179.

52 Peadar Kirby, *The Celtic Tiger in Distress: Growth with Inequality in Ireland* (Palgrave, 2002): 204.

53 The National University of Ireland, with constituent colleges at Cork, Dublin, Galway and Maynooth.

54 Smyth (1998): 162.

55 Pádraig A. Breatnach, 'Crisis in our Universities: the impact on the Humanities', *Studies: An Irish Quarterly Review*, (Vol. 96, No. 384, 2007): 391-406.

56 Luke Gibbons, 'Alternative Enlightenments', ed. Mary Cullen, *1798: 200 years of resonance* (Irish Reporter Publications, 1998): 81.

57 See Deiric Ó Broin and Peadar Kirby eds, *Power, Dissent and Democracy: civil society and the state in Ireland* (Dublin: A&A Farmer Ltd., 2009).

58 See Breatnach (2007).

59 Breatnach argues that the view taken by the state in the early years of the twenty-first century, is that, 'for the future, universities could be made to function as instruments of policy on behalf of the state.' Ibid. 393.

60 Peadar Kirby, *Poverty Amid Plenty: World and Irish Development Reconsidered* (Trócaire, 1997): 199.

61 Ibid. 202.

62 Ibid.

63 Ibid. 206. Kirby acknowledges the coining of the phrase 'democratic experimentalism' in C. Sabel, *Ireland: Local Partnerships and Social Innovation* (Paris: OECD, 1996).

64 Arts Community Education Committee (Ireland), *Art and the Ordinary:the report of the Arts Community Education Committee* (Dublin: Arts Community Education Committee, 1989)

65 Lee (1990): 645.

66 Ibid. xiv.

67 David Lloyd, (2003): 47.

68 Senia Pašeta, *Before the Revolution: Nationalism, Social Change and Ireland's Catholic Elite, 1879-1922* (Cork: Cork University Press, 1999): 150.

69 Renato Constantino, ed. István Mészáros, Renato Constantino: *Neo-colonial Identity and Counter-consciousness: Essays on Cultural Decolonization* (Merlin, 1978): 23.

70 Pilkington (2001): 5.

71 Ibid., 'Irish theatre history offers a fascinating understanding of the country's complex political and cultural life.'

72 Awam Amkpa, 'Drama and the Languages of Postcolonial Desire', *Irish University Review*, 29.2, (Autumn/Winter 1999): 294-304. See also his monograph, *Drama and Postcolonial Desires* (Routledge, 2004).

73 ' ... the consensus held in such high esteem is the non-thinking politics of no alternative [*la non-pensée comme pensée unique*] ...' Alain Badiou, *Metapolitics* (Verso, 2005): 8.

2 | Independent Ireland: A Successor State

When the Free State came in we were afraid of our life they were going to change the mattresses for feather beds ... the Free State didn't change anything more than the badges on the [prison] warders' caps.[1]

Colonialism, Resistance and Liberation

Wherever colonialism has been and is resisted, anti-colonial activists proclaim decolonization as their historical goal. The teleology implicit in their assertion might be represented as follows:

Colonization—anti-colonial struggle—decolonization.

Experience teaches that their struggles tend to result in the replacement of one elite by another, as the departing colonizers give way to a nascent indigenous bourgeois class.[2] This outcome thwarts the achievement of a decolonized social order, and typically results in disillusion, voluntary exile or even persecution for some of the most radical persons and groups in the successor state. The evolving society itself, deprived of the insouciant energies of such persons, marginalizes radical questioning of the state's programmes and practices. In this way, the triumph of bourgeois social organization is hastened and the movement toward actual decolonization – the establishment and development of open indigenous democracy – curbed.

Awam Amkpa's account of the dynamics of social change in former colonies proposes an iterative historical process of struggle between orders of domination and movements for liberation as follows:

Colonization—anti-colonialism—neo-colonialism—
postcolonialism—decolonization[3]

His phased model of social, cultural and political development suggests a complex dynamic of social change, and enables us to read the process by which those involved in anti-colonial struggle experience frustration and fatigue under conditions of independence. I find it helpful to reconfigure Amkpa as follows, rendering more explicit his understanding of decolonization as less a destination than a journey:

colonization ←→ anti-colonialism
limited decolonization installed as vindication of anti-colonial struggle
neo-colonialism ←→ postcolonialism
ongoing decolonization as utopian project

The struggle to decolonize is as much a part of neo-colonial experience as it is of anti-colonial effort, and the crisis in colonialism which produces anti-colonial consciousness is effectively reiterated when postcolonial critique emerges in response to crises in the neo-colonial social order.

Recalling Ngugi,[4] Amkpa directs inquiry toward issues around democracy, citizenship, subjectivity and agency as constituents of an ongoing moral imperative to decolonize. From an Irish perspective, Amkpa's discussion exposes the slackness with which the concepts *neo-colonial, postcolonial* and *decolonized* are routinely confused. And this confusion has important consequences for analysis. For example, Breen et al. advise, 'Classifying contemporary Ireland requires that we weigh equally Ireland's past as a post-colonial society that achieved independence only within this century, and its present status as a member of the European Community.'[5] There is a strong implication of closure of past struggles in Ireland's 'present status as a member of the European Community'. This arises from the assertion of 'Ireland's *past* as a post-colonial society that achieved independence only in this century' (my emphasis). Thus, a state of being at two historical removes from colonialism is effortlessly posited. Breen et al.'s use of periodization to structure their analysis blunts its critical edge, specifically, from my perspective, by eliding the term 'neo-colonial'. This conceptual choice obscures the actual dynamic of the social order, and disables the kind of critique which might centre decolonization as an ongoing project of critical democracy. By contrast, Amkpa's developmental model proposes that anti-colonial and postcolonial oppositions are constituted in distinct phases of consciousness and struggle: the one contesting colonialism, the other, neo-colonialism. While these phases are in some respects synchronic, their dialectical dynamics, in which action resulting from analysis is subjected to, and informs, further analysis toward more refined action, are fundamental to their utility as agents of social change.[6]

Colonization, Subjectivity and Agency

As an existential phenomenon, colonization is experienced as a state of being, a process of separation, of alienation from oneself, in which the minds, bodies, spirits and languages of the colonized are abused. Colonial education is a process of co-option into contradiction[7] which corrupts one's notion of belonging and suppresses possibilities of becoming. Groups and individuals are presented as other to themselves, and are thus dominated. Self-naming, self-description, and the search for one's own place in which to realize subjectivity are rendered impossible: to be is to be like; to be like is to be like the colonizer. Amkpa reads the colonization of Eliza's mind in Shaw's *Pygmalion*,[8] as a metaphor for bourgeois culture's colonization of the bodies, minds and geographical spaces that constitute society itself. In order to present herself as a bourgeois, Eliza must define herself in terms set by others. She must come to know her desired self as other to her actual self. Her submission to reconstruction by Higgins is a manifestation of the desire of the self-despising colonized subject for abnegation. The autonomous human subject, by contrast, is capable of personal agency and social action.

Declan Kiberd locates the initiation of postcolonial writing at 'that very moment when a native writer formulates a text committed to cultural resistance.'[9] Similarly, Amkpa proposes anti-colonial consciousness as the moment of being able to critique, of realizing that there are options for articulating one's humanity, other than those prescribed and imposed by a narrative of domination. This becomes the organizing stance of emergent countercultural narratives. Amkpa's fortuitous[10] exposure to *Pygmalion* constituted a first step toward realizing his own power to appropriate dramatic narrative to his subjective needs. His oppositional reading of the film amounted to a cultural and political awakening: he identified wholly with Eliza's 'savage tongue', with the contradiction between the oppositional potential of her socially unacceptable forms of speech, and her learned anxiety to domesticate them to civilized bourgeois norms. In this, his position maps on to the work of Paulo Freire and Augusto Boal:[11] awareness of the historical contingency of the actually existing situation enables the realization that there is an option to act for change. A further step is to choose that option, and to develop material practices which enable its enactment, through personal agency for social transformation. Amkpa understands art as public meaning-making, with theatre a material cultural practice, having a potentially key role in critiquing and transforming democratic participation in the state. This 'high ambition'[12] for theatre recalls and renews the expressed purpose of Irish drama since the early twentieth-century, and offers an ethic against which to discuss and evaluate Ireland's dramas during the long 1990s.

Neo-colonialism and postcolonial consciousness

Neo-colonialism is a bourgeois social project, effectively nameless as a state of being, and almost never acknowledged in public discourse[13] in the neo-colonial state.[14] Under colonialism, relations of domination produce anger at systemic state injustice in those dominated. The felt contradictions of neo-colonialism may be even more acute than those of colonialism itself, as the anger of the excluded is compounded by a sense of betrayal by 'our own' which adds bewilderment and pain to their experiences. However, the ability of the neo-colonial order to manipulate the symbols and rhetoric of resistance, makes it highly complex and difficult to engage on anything other than its own terms, which never countenance shortcomings in the common project. As Jacobsen found, in the case of Independent Ireland, it is by means of such rhetorical strategies that emergent elites posit, legitimize and enforce a selective definition of identity, culture and citizenship. Echoing Frantz Fanon,[15] Amkpa is clear on the internal weakness of newly independent states: 'Those who lead the anti-colonial revolution frequently take the place of the colonizers and in fact repeat the processes of colonization.'[16] Such is the power of the national state to demand loyalty that naming its failures – not to speak of denouncing them as a negation of liberationist aspirations – becomes somehow a greater betrayal than acquiescence in a new paradigm of domination. This phenomenon notwithstanding, Amkpa's model suggests that even as the successor state repeats the tropes, dynamics and administrative practices of colonialism, so it will produce a countervailing public consciousness – postcolonial critique.

One of the strengths of Amkpa's theoretical model is the distinction it enables between 'anti-colonial' and 'liberationist'. The 'post' in postcolonial is a strategic epistemological stance, not a periodization of consciousness, or characterization of experience. For Amkpa, the postcolonial moment is the point of emergence of sustained critique of the material circumstances of the social order that has been settled for in the successor state. It marks the emergence of consciousness of, and desires for other options in articulating humanity, beyond limits set by elites in whose interests that state is organized. Neo-colonialism posits and institutionalizes bourgeois liberalism as identical with the aspirations of the mass of the people in the former colony. This involves subordinating the aspiration to social equality to a right to economic liberty under capitalism. Represented as a natural outcome, rooted in a quasi-mythic account of the struggle of an ancient people for self-determination, and supported by the rhetoric of homogeneous community, this is always actually a choice. The fact that the public is not offered such a choice does not diminish the possibility of imagining a world transformed, an achievable utopia. A postcolonial consciousness refuses the seduction of the 'obvious', and asserts the primacy of processes of becoming over the condition of having arrived. As David Lloyd puts it, 'the history of the integration of Ireland and the Irish into Western modernity is not only not the only story but also not the only possibility.'[17]

Towards decolonization – postcolonial desires

Renato Constantino offers compelling reflections on the potential of a progressive nationalist consciousness which is always, in a radical sense, also a form of counter-consciousness.[18] He envisages a dynamic, generative, set of relationships, with the post-independence national state operating as a community capable of formulating new aspirations in response to reflection on the action taken to achieve statehood. The dynamic would operate as a point of critical reference in the new state, and would provide a source of critical, creative energy for evaluating its developmental projects. In other words, Constantino's aspiration/response/action relationship locates decolonization in critical cultural practices. This provokes another radical reading of 'post', one that suggests application, a distribution, by way of an invigorated citizenship project, of the material fruits of modernity: their elaboration across society as a whole:[19]

A philosophy of liberation is not a body of thought given once and for all time. It is itself a growing thing depending on accretions of consciousness ... more of a programme than a philosophy. It is not contemplative; it is active and dynamic and encompasses the objective situation as well as the subjective reaction of the people involved. It cannot be the work of a select group, even if this group regards itself as motivated by the best interests of the people. It needs the participation of the backbone of the nation.[20]

Decolonization is not an event, but a language of inquiry, a progressive 'practice of culture and politics ... a language of perpetual "becoming", challenging structures of domination and subordination.'[21] Marked by practices which valorize difference and hybridity in the constitution of the social order, decolonization announces the potential for, and underpins the practice of democratic citizenship. The alienation of persons and groups in the neo-colonial social order does not, of itself, necessarily create conditions for change. It is more likely to result initially in a barely acknowledged stalemate, experienced as a debased, but 'obviously natural' order of things. For West, human agency is 'always enacted under circumstances not of one's choosing',[22] and identity and citizenship are formed and experienced in negotiating the problematic relations between the interests of individual subjects and those of the national state and its neo-colonial projects. Such projects are usually articulated by, and presented as synonymous with, the concerns of the indigenous elite which emerges in the successor state. While elite concerns are projected as the concerns of all, they are rarely at one with what might be called 'the common good', the historical basis for the legitimacy of the state's claim on citizen allegiance. As inscriptions of the new hegemony, however, they are projected as powerful symbolic manifestations of communal identity: to reject such projects is not simply to oppose a point of view, it is to repudiate a national consensus. Excluding oneself from that consensus amounts to an effective renunciation of one's rights to social participation. With such powerful cultural consequences in prospect, it is hardly a surprise that 'there was little use for idealism and little scope for utopianism in the Irish Free State.'[23]

A Successor State

In 1900, Ireland was still an integral – if uneasy – province of Imperial Britain. By 1922 Independent Ireland had emerged from a sequence of revolt, repression and guerrilla war of independence. Whether persuaded by postcolonial analysis or not, commentators on social, cultural and economic conditions in Independent Ireland are in general agreement on the lack of fit between pre-independence visions of a nationalist Ireland and the independent state that emerged from the Civil War (1922-1924).[24] The very term Independent Ireland refers to a place that has no formal existence, but it has had to come into being as a way of simultaneously evoking and avoiding the meaning of contested constitutional formulations: *Saorstát Éireann* [The Irish Free State] (1922-1949) and *Éire* [The Republic of Ireland] (1949-date).[25] Neither entity can breathe its name untroubled. The Irish Free State bears the weight of its origins in the partition of the country, Civil War, economic conservatism, and imagination perceived as inadequate to the task of nation-building.[26] The Republic of Ireland is primarily a territorial entity, decoupled from the foundational nationalist aspiration to an independent state contiguous with the island.[27]

The term Independent Ireland acknowledges a lack of fit, a set of unquiet spaces, between the EU member-state and the nation unfulfilled, between the appearance of post-coloniality[28] and the realities of neo-colonialism, born of a failure to decolonize. Conceptually, Independent Ireland brackets off *Éire* [The Republic of Ireland] from itself, and the deployment of this critical term acknowledges a felt need, in discussing Ireland post-1922, for a framework which can accommodate the contradictions arising in the Irish Free State and enduring in the Republic of Ireland: structural continuity with the colonial province, in tension with popular aspiration in an autonomous, albeit partitioned state. In this sense, 'Independent Ireland' gives conceptual shape to the achievements, betrayals and evasions of a neo-colonial successor state, a Republic of Elsewhere,[29] always deferred. That Ireland is one for which, according to Peadar Kirby, some 80 years after independence, 'deeper challenges [than self-government and wealth creation] remain.'[30]

Nationalism, Culture and the Successor State

The resilience and appeal of Irish nationalism is grounded in its ability to recognize and exploit the fertility of cultural politics.[31] Recent history notwithstanding, Irish nationalism is less a military movement, governed by appeals to blood sacrifice, than a cultural project, a feat of 'thinking otherwise', of utopian imagining. The radical restlessness of this critical project is the first target of a neo-colonial successor state: 'the counter-consciousness that animated the struggle for independence had hardly developed into a new consciousness before that consciousness was again being modified to suit the needs of a new colonial system.'[32] Breen et al expose this operation in Irish circumstances: 'Irish nationalism ... was untypically an agent of stability rather than upheaval.'[33] In contradiction of its radical foundational rhetoric, 'continuity[34] rather than change (was) the defining characteristic of independent Ireland in its early decades.'[35] Indeed, the primary purpose of the rhetorical invocation of nationalist destiny in the Irish Free State seems to have been simultaneously to underwrite reactionary government policies while removing them and their consequences – notably chronic emigration – from the heat of critical analysis.

The moment of anti-colonial struggle, as replete with contradiction and brutality as the domination which makes it inevitable, forges a powerful sense of solidarity around the idealized homogeneity of the national group. Appealing to the fallacy of independence-as-deliverance, the successor state legitimizes itself as the embodiment of that projected homogeneity, and institutionalizes a denial of difference as a condition of inclusion in its orthodoxy. Acknowledging and valorizing difference, however, is essential to the practice of egalitarianism, and in the active exclusion of this ethic from state structures and practices, the democratic imperative, encoded in signatures of 'belonging' is fatally compromised, and an ultimately conflictual social order is engendered. In tandem with this, the mobilization of an ideal 'native subject locked in a prehistoric and hence apolitical past'[36] as the organizing motif of citizenship, sets the stage for a neo-colonial body politic. In this social order, all discourses of resistance, apart from the (now-vacant) anti-colonial position, are rigorously delegitimized. This operation is visible in the ways in which culture is interpreted, as well as produced. Joe Cleary's reading of a range of artefacts from the 1990s, in which the past figures prominently, articulates a key area of concern:

> As the distance between the present and that past widens, the social ills that obsess these works – clerical dogmatism, domestic tyranny and oppression, sexual repression, poverty of opportunity or whatever – will themselves increasingly come to be identified with the past, with a particular time and not with a social system that subtends both past and present.[37]

With analyses based on the consequences of economic, race and gender inequalities marginalized, or rendered mute, the possibility of confronting the contradictions they would expose – the *sine qua non* of a process of decolonization – is all but negated.

A key objective of official nationalism in the emergent Independent Ireland (1922 –1959) was to play down the primary anti-colonial aspiration to collective liberation and personal redemption in a nation achieved.[38] Such ideals came over time to reside only in platitudinous formulae, empty rhetorical derivations from higher ambitions.[39] Lived experience drifted increasingly far from any prospect of a better life, and became saturated by the limitations, venalities and hypocrisies of the ruling elite and its sustaining myths. Unilaterally constituted as a republic in 1948, Independent Ireland had to wait another ten years for the post-Civil War hierarchy[40] and its administrative expression – what Breen et al refer to as 'the auxiliary state'[41] – to begin to yield ground as a model for Irish society. It was 'the revolution of 1958'[42] that ushered in 'the strongly interventionist State that afterwards aggressively pursued outward-looking economic policies and established a fully-fledged Welfare State.'[43] The conceptual break thus occasioned had an extraordinary impact on the account of Irish nationalism which had developed in, and underpinned 'the auxiliary state': 'Henceforth, the official, state version of Irish nationalism proceeded from an assumption that the primary objective was to reap the benefits from full economic participation in the world economy.'[44] This amounted to a bold reversal of the characteristic position of the auxiliary state: 'The central element of Free State economic policy was the promotion of agricultural exports, anticipating that the resulting profits would in time stimulate more general economic growth. The State's role in that process was to do as little as possible.'[45] Such an extraordinary *volte face* was accomplished by means of an elastic official discourse that 'enabled Irish nation-statehood to appear unremittingly fundamental in a perpetually altering context.'[46]

The autarkic state had been challenged by the actions of the new Fianna Fáil government under Eamon De Valera, during the so-called 'Economic War' of 1932-1935. Kirby records its attempt to 'develop native industry and to decisively re-orient the economy away from dependence on the export of live cattle to Britain.'[47] While there was opposition to such a move from pro-metropolitan interests within the state,

> it was the very structure of the dependency relationship to the British market that led to [its] defeat, as there was no success

in finding alternative markets for Irish agricultural products. The 1938 Anglo-Irish Agreements therefore restored Ireland's position as an agricultural supplier to the British market.[48]

Thus, the continuity of an economic relationship imposed during the colonial period was assured in the face of an administration swept to power on a wave of the most vehement populist rhetoric of self-determination and national reconstruction.[49] This is a precise foreshadowing of the neo-colonial relations inscribed in African contexts, and critiqued by Ngugi wa Thiong'o[50] and others. The Poor Man's Government, the bogeyman of existing elites, including the Catholic Church, never materialized.[51]

It is perhaps also significant that De Valera's *Bunreacht na h-Éireann* [The Irish Constitution], adopted by referendum in 1937, represents, not an attempt to structure a state in keeping with the radical nationalist platform to which its sponsors appealed, but rather the conclusion of a hegemonic compact between the governmental elite, custodians and beneficiaries of official nationalist discourse,[52] and the Catholic Church. It was not until the early 1970s that the disappointments, betrayals and small comforts of the ensuing neo-colonial project were finally confronted, even if only in the field of personal morality. Struggles over access to artificial contraception marked both the emergence of an organized women's movement and the first fatal stumble in the confident stride of a Church/state nexus gradually to be exposed as an amalgam of the evasions, cruelties and exclusions of capitalism, sexism and racism.[53] That nexus paid a heavy price for its initial victories in a series of bitter cultural wars over attempts to amend the constitution to enable legislation on divorce and abortion services, during the 1980s and 1990s. However, even in the wake of a series of quite appalling revelations on church/state complicity in the organized abuse of children,[54] it continues to mediate and compromise the relationship between state and civil society in the twenty-first century.

The economic policies[55] of the 1930s, followed by the isolationism of the 40s and 50s resulted in the most severe consequences for many people, exemplified in the torpid coupling of emigration and late marriage. Breen et al point out that 'The extent of the failure was evident by the early 1950s as the nation's young emigrated to Britain in massive numbers, searching for the jobs that could not be obtained at home. Those who remained experienced a declining standard of living.'[56] Social blight was compounded for the few who managed to obtain a foothold in economic security by cronyism and placement in employment practices, with ardent performances of fealty to official Catholic nationalist sentiments amounting to a new oath of allegiance for those who would aspire even to a minor clerical position in civil, local or semi-state services.[57] Emptied of its radical promise, joint ownership of, and editing rights over official Irish nationalism was extended to a renovated indigenous elite,[58] who pursued an ideological project of national underdevelopment while claiming to be busy with socio-economic reconstruction.[59] Jacobsen identifies a choice by Irish elites of 'a highly dependent model of development,'[60] and attempts to describe and understand 'the ways in which they have legitimized this option.'[61] He concludes that 'Irish elites have chosen to rely on multinational capital, not because this path has been shown to be inherently better, nor because of the lack of alternatives (these have been proposed in Ireland by the left, by trade unions...)' but, he contends, 'because of their power to dominate discourse and allow little space for the consideration of alternatives.'[62]

Limited state activism from the late 1950s led to an era of relative prosperity, popularly associated with the governments of Seán Lemass, De Valera's successor as leader of the Fianna Fáil party. By mid-century the Irish experience was widely interpreted as a kind of paradigm for decolonization across the world, post-World War II.[63] So much so, that Clancy et al. note that 'the Irish experience may be viewed as a microcosm of that found within a number of post-colonial and peripheral economies in the capitalist world order.'[64] By the 1960s, a modernizing, more outward-looking independent state was a place of study for civil and public servants of decolonizing countries like Zambia, seeking a working model of indigenous administration toward which to aim. Breen et al. identify another period of apparently increasing prosperity, in the mid-1970s, and comment: 'Despite a still considerable autonomy and vastly increased capacity, the state did not emerge as the prime mover in Irish society. The consequences of state intervention were largely unintended. The main role was left to market mechanisms.'[65] It would seem that while state interventionism worked through its emergent phase, the habits of the auxiliary state,[66] passive in the face of the free market, remained influential as an active residual culture.[67] Where Breen et al. advance reduced state capacity as an explanation for the persistence of an inegalitarian status quo, Kirby finds that 'the problem lay principally not in the capacity of the Irish state per se but rather in the developmental direction it took, a direction directly responsive to conservative forces in Irish society.'[68]

For most of the twentieth-century, short-termism in economics and politics exercised a formative influence on state policy and social practices. Though, for many, the effects were ruinous, this dereliction met with little organized resistance. Progressive change was consistently thwarted by a corrosive alliance of populist politics,[69] elite promulgation of an official narrative of a mythic nation heroically embodied in the successor state, and chronic emigration:

> Large scale emigration has been a constant of Irish culture since at least the time of the Famine... [and] has had a disproportionate effect on the rural labouring classes, their decimation having become a matter of policy in British administrative circles and among the landlords from the Famine on. But it has also held back the growth of an Irish working class and the formation of specifically Irish forms of class political struggle; it has contributed to the official conservatism of Irish culture and religion by permitting the continuing hegemony of large farmers and petty capitalists through to the late 1960s; it acts as a kind of numbed-out cultural trauma and emblem of economic hopelessness. At the same time, it has performed great service to the state as a social safety valve and as a means to mask the otherwise potentially devastating consequences of our neo-colonial status within the international and transnational movements of the capitalist world system.[70]

The way in which this trauma has, in Lloyd's view, 'been passed over and disconnected from other aspects of Ireland's internal history' alerts us to the dividends accruing from successful manipulation of public narratives.

Fianna Fáil's 'new pragmatism', post-De Valera, was embodied in *The First Programme For Economic Expansion* (1958) and promised a present economic utopia. By 1990, the verdict on progress toward that promise was uncompromising:

> An expanding economy, rising public expenditure, the end of emigration and massive shifts in the occupational structure all promised that the 1960s would bring Ireland's long-postponed social revolution ... that the egalitarian objectives of Irish nationalism could be realised and realised fairly painlessly ... It is our contention that they were not realised, even in part.[71]

One of the costs of the new pragmatism was a buttressing of the hegemony of economic indicators alone in determining prosperity, recovery or slump.[72] Kirby attempts to enable a more complex and critical understanding of the meaning of terms such as 'success', 'expansion', etc.:

> underdevelopment... can be defined as a process that is generating social exclusion of which some of the key elements are poverty, unemployment and inequality in income distribution. This then allows us to define development as a process characterised primarily by growing social inclusion through rising living standards, meaningful employment, active political and social participation and a satisfying cultural life extending to all sectors of society and thus widening the life choices and possibilities for the great majority.[73]

On these terms, by the 1990s, Independent Ireland's record testifies to a negation, in the successor state, of Irish nationalism's historical aspiration to decolonization.

'A betrayed republic'

The direction of state policy away from achieving a balance between the economy and civil society in Independent Ireland is reflected in the absence of strong ideological positions in party politics. Until the 1990s, government office oscillated between two blocs committed to the twin – and essentially incompatible – models of the state identified by Breen et al. Kirby discusses this problem in relation to the hegemony of Fianna Fáil, and illuminates Irish political populism by drawing on studies of similar political practices in Latin America. Such studies help to explain both the success of an essentially egalitarian nationalist appeal in electoral contests and the refusal of the party to use electoral success as the platform from which to restructure society by taking on vested interests while in office. Ngugi draws attention to the capacity of neo-colonialism's cultural control to blunt 'perceptions, and more so the feelings about those perceptions.'[74], and Kirby notes the weakening of political understanding which populism produces in the population over time.[75] He offers an important insight into the development of political hegemony – as opposed to party political ascendancy – in newly independent states when he concludes that the

> use of state resources for the short-term satisfaction of different constituencies ... has characterised not only Fianna Fáil's governance of the Irish state, but also that of its

opponents who have sought to emulate Fianna Fáil's electoral appeal.'[76]

The 1970s saw a gradual hardening of enmities within Fianna Fáil, initially around support for nationalist communities in Northern Ireland, as 'the Troubles' began. The party split in the early 1980s, with the foundation of the Progressive Democrats, an ideologically-driven party of the right. Its emergence catalysed two principal changes in parliamentary and electoral politics: Fianna Fáil began to find it impossible to form single-party administrations, and the Irish liberal/left began to articulate its position more clearly. The former development produced a Fianna Fáil/Progressive Democrat coalition in 1989, which made perfect ideological sense, but was widely viewed as a fine irony, given the dominance of personality-driven narratives in Irish political commentary. The latter process delivered a historic set of gains for the liberal/left in Mary Robinson's narrow victory in the 1990 Presidential campaign, and a strong performance by the Labour Party in the general election of 1992. That achievement led to a real historical irony – a Fianna Fáil/Labour coalition. While history will tell an interesting story of the period, it is fair to say that an overwhelming sense that all political moulds were trembling under Labour's hammer contributed to the party's post-election strategy. Those on the left had waited so long for a breakthrough in electoral terms that they moved to secure a large Dáil majority for a government programme developed to redress the many ills of what one of its ministers called 'a betrayed republic.'[77] Whatever the evaluations which remain to be articulated, it can be argued that the 1990s saw an ideological contest in Irish electoral politics, as significant numbers of people articulated their rejection of Independent Ireland's evolved 'disjuncture between economic growth and social development.'[78]

Postcolonial thoughts on globalization, Ireland and the Celtic Tiger Economy

The Irish Republic was admitted to full membership of the EU in 1973, a move which has had many beneficial results. By the 1990s, the successor state had become used to including in its pieties the recitation of its achievements, both diplomatic and economic, within the EU. The narrative – which has more than a little validity[79] – ran that a small nation had successfully modernized to the point of participating fully in international affairs, as a member of a most affluent group of independent national states. The development paradigm which twentieth-century Ireland was widely agreed to illustrate maps closely onto the utopian promise of anti-colonial nationalism: a glorious progression from servitude to nationhood, or nationhood deferred. While Independent Ireland is by constitution an autonomous political entity, it can be shown that, with the exception of the early work of the Land Commission,[80] and a range of 'de-anglicizing' manoeuvres in the cultural arena,[81] the state itself has never undertaken a project directed explicitly toward decolonization. In short, Independent Ireland is a neo-colonial successor state, 'an entity – it can hardly be called a society – based on exclusion ... It is an economy, not a society.'[82]

The cultural tone of late 1990s Ireland vindicates Ngugi's insight that, as neo-colonial elites move to consolidate and legitimate power, space in which to advocate egalitarian projects of decolonization shrinks.[83] As the twenty-first century begins, attempts to name and move beyond local standoffs on limits to social participation are complicated by challenges to the national state itself. The triumph of corporate capitalism, its control of global communications and its ability to manipulate currency values and flows, and market conditions, for instance, pose problems that elected politicians dare not confront. The development of globalized capital and its wonderful efficiencies does offer some comfort to national elites, however. Relentless corporate persuasion has enabled practices of consumption first to challenge and then to replace politically articulated citizenship as the language of social participation. As Lee protests,[84] inclusion in the social order is predicated not on civic rights and obligations to the common good, but on economic capital, disposable income and personal lifestyle.[85] These processes are greatly enabled by the currency of virtual identifications as stabilizers of human identities.[86]

Because all systems proclaim a vision of the good life, and because capitalist corporations have the resources[87] to communicate their formulations extensively and with remarkable effectiveness, 1990s Ireland sees the proliferation of tropes, discourses and rhetorical figures which serve to align the achievement of a global capitalist system with the goals of liberal democracy in the national state. The weight of the contradictions attending the reconciliation of this paradox may be evident, but its emergence is of great value to a failing neo-colonial social order. While consumers derive satisfaction from dispersed loyalties easily gratified in acts of consumption, with one bound the state can shed its contradictions, evade its day of reckoning and embrace a New World Order which emerges as the national destination transmogrified and writ large: The Land of the Spree. Independence is retrospectively revealed not as a destination in itself, still less as the inauguration of an ethical project of decolonization, but as the ante-room of a global economic order. The revised neo-colonial teleology – enthusiastically rehearsed in mainstream explanations of the period of the Celtic Tiger Economy[88] – may be figured as follows:

> Colonization – post-coloniality – unlimited consumption in a global economic order.

This account of national development enables anxieties about social liberation to be laid aside in the self-evident triumph of full incorporation in global circuits of consumption. Hence the reservations expressed earlier about the use of a chronologically-inflected idea of the 'post-colonial' by Breen et al.:

> Colonization – post-coloniality – fully-fledged EU member-state.

The weakness of this model is that it institutionalizes the neo-colonial teleology whose effects it sets out to critique. Paradoxically, Breen et al. actually conclude that Independent Ireland is a radically unsettled country, scarred by the persistence in the successor state of class divisions which structured relations in the colonial province. What appears to be at work in this summarizing statement is a slippage from the complexity of field data into a narrative discourse drawn from a domain long colonized by the legitimizing rhetoric of the national state. I make this point in order to re-emphasize the need to take account of the paradigmatic quality of the ideology of the national state. Its foundational mythologies of homogeneity, progression and radical change are so pervasive as to retain the capacity to enter and confuse even those projects which critique its very bases.

Understanding modernity in Independent Ireland: broadening the debate

In service to the ascendancy of such mythologies, a significant body of recent descriptive and analytical work approaches the viability of Independent Ireland by engaging with indicators such as GDP and GNP, approximation to Anglo-American or European norms regarding standards of living, education etc., and figures recording levels of social welfare dependency, poverty etc., as measures of national performance. Other work has looked at the nature and role of the state, its tendencies to centralization, the comparative poverty of political life, and the stability or otherwise of the largest political party, Fianna Fáil. Such studies draw conclusions regarding the contingency of Independent Ireland's relationship to the core of the late capitalist world order. The dominance of the neo-liberal account of modernization, not only in public policy-making, but in the critical vocabularies of many studies of its nature and effects begins, during the 1990s, to be acknowledged.[89] Few commentators, however, of whom Peadar Kirby is among the most consistent, are prepared to engage rigorously with the consequences of such a partial, limited paradigm for a country whose claim to developed status is at least contestable.[90]

A sense of the contingency of the very terminology of Irish development, either along the modernist or dependency paradigms, animates Kirby's critical practice. Convinced of the inadequacy of dominant accounts of the nation's performance, he sets out in 1997 to apply development theory 'in a systematic way to the case of Ireland.'[91] The work is motivated by a conviction that

> uncritical acceptance of a form of development that benefits many but marginalizes in a semi-permanent way a significant minority of our population is only shoring up the most serious problems for the future.[92]

Kirby subjects Ireland to an analysis informed by the view that 'social exclusion has become perhaps the most worrying feature of social change throughout today's world.'[93] In examining the development of indigenous industry in Ireland by comparison to the experiences of the so-called East Asian Tigers, he draws on Mary O'Sullivan's *Manufacturing and Global Competition* as follows:

> Enormous effort and cost have been put into job creation in the two decades from 1973-1994; this created a massive 393,885 jobs in that period but 404,376 jobs were lost in the same period.[94]

Kirby concludes:

> Irish industrial policy therefore is running simply to keep up with itself. In this crucial aspect [of support for sustainable indigenous industry] Ireland is far from being a 'Celtic Tiger' and is, in fact, closer to the profile of a [better-off] Third World Country.[95]

This is precisely the sort of contradiction which the linear progression model detected in the statement by Breen et al. above operates to conceal. Kirby cites Girvin's study of economic policy-making in Independent Ireland, as an account of how the state opted for a seemingly painless strategy that 'could be *introduced with few changes to the traditional political structure, to society or its culture.'*[96] Girvin concludes that 'Ireland remains a developing rather than a developed society.'[97] This analysis suggests a real conflict between a dominant narrative of modernization through dynamic and radical state intervention and the fact of perfunctory adjustment to the economic order, which sharpens existing inequalities.[98] The successor state's pursuit of socio-economic continuity, indicates a parallel with 'the weakness of Latin American nationalism *in which the rhetoric of national community has been used to exclude most of the people from the benefits of nationhood.'*[99]

In light of this, it may come as no surprise that nationalist utopianism,[100] the driver of anti-colonial struggle, and the rhetorical touchstone of political elites since the foundation of the state,[101] is conspicuously under-represented as a critical discourse in Independent Ireland during the long 1990s. Tracking this phenomenon reveals some interesting historical negotiations. One of the organizing neo-colonial contradictions of Independent Ireland is that indigenous elites continue to appeal for their legitimacy to the radical content of the nationalist front's original oppositional movement, even as they mobilize the structures of the state bureaucracy itself[102] to negate its objectives.[103] Jacobsen's work illuminates the discursive operations deployed to produce – in spite of this – widespread acceptance of the state's claim to embody the essentially cultural project of Irish nationalism.[104] Once radical and oppositional, when co-opted to official nationalism – 'the ideology of the nation-state, defined by the political elite'[105] – nationalist utopianism wielded mainly rhetorical and negative power in Independent Ireland – a card that once played trumped all others.[106] My readings of Yeats, Beckett, Molloy and Murphy will show that such power had been in decline for some time, well before the emergence internationally of a broadly 'dismissive stance toward nationalism in the postmodernism of the 1980s and 1990s.'[107]

Clare Carroll reads that dismissiveness as a reflection of a general reaction to more celebratory discourses around national movements for decolonization, post-World War II. In Independent Ireland, a revisionist movement among historians, economists and commentators arrived somewhat earlier, given impetus by the emergence of the armed campaign waged by the Provisional IRA in Northern Ireland from the early 1970s to the mid 1990s. A public consensus chose not to essay the frequently deadly distinction between wanton violence and political campaign, and nationalism and its value-base all but disappeared as a form of critique and frame of reference in Independent Ireland from the 1970s on. The virtual banishment of nationalist sentiment from public discourse in Ireland is in the main the result of its collapsing under the weight of unsustainable contradiction. It also reflects the success of a revisionist strategy which collapses all nationalisms into one atavistic, outlaw category in which 'the material historical differences between progressive and retrograde forms of nationalism'[108] are ignored. Unfortunately, in driving the utopian ethic of nationalism underground, as if willing closure on an embarrassing historical episode, the fact of its formative contribution to the dynamics of Irish society, both concrete and psychic, is suppressed. This, I suggest, is greatly to the detriment of attempts to understand the achievements and shortcomings of the neo-colonial social order since 1922. The loss of consciousness of the nation as a community of aspiration/response/action is felt in a crisis in communal aspiration, as the extinction of progressive models of the nation deprived the body politic of powerful, available, and widely-supported bases for social and cultural critique. The loss of cultural nationalism – 'a highly potent force which originates not from elites but from civil society and appeals primarily to the excluded masses'[109] – as a public reference point is highly significant. Allied to this, the gradual discrediting of an official nationalist discourse which had reduced utopian consciousness to a series of empty gestures had the effect of bringing all utopian discourses into disrepute.

Lloyd is clear on the costs arising from this: 'The insistent disavowal of critical questions as to the alternative possibilities has forced the occlusion not only of a vast historical repertoire of social imaginaries but also of critical analysis of the present.'[110] His postcolonial reading of the narrative of Independent Ireland reveals the slippage of the animating anti-colonial vision to the margins of the state's concerns, and 'fulfils Fanon's angry prognosis in *The Wretched of the Earth* that the future of the bourgeois post-colony was to become the conduit of neo-colonial capital.'[111] Lloyd lists a range of other options for consideration, including refusing 'to commit Ireland's future to continuing capitalist colonialism', and opting 'not to disdain but to take seriously the still-persistent recalcitrance of Irish cultural practices to the rhythms and social practices of capitalist modernity.' The strength of resistance to alternatives opened up by such questions suggests acute elite awareness that the achievement of a national state neither satisfies nor finally exhausts the urge for liberation. The high stakes involved, and the terms of revisionist dismissal are revealed in Clare Carroll's rhetoric:

> A nationalist politics that defines people's needs and interests, like a nationalist historiography that defines what those needs and interests have been in the past, is not a matter of mere resentment or a sense of victimization or a fantasy of racial spirit but a struggle against and within institutions.[112]

From my perspective, Independent Ireland's local elites have systematically thwarted decolonization, and have developed a neo-colonial state which has failed both nationalist and republican aspiration, and the majority of the people. The lack of space in which to make such a case, testifies to the pervasive influence of official narratives which deny or dilute the impact of the historical fact of colonialism, and subscribe to a simplistic narrative of moderni-sation.[113] Revisionist narratives support elite positions by attributing to the nationalist project itself the failures of the independent state. This is potentially very serious, as it reflects on the people's collective wisdom, and activates at the core of the national psyche a doubt harboured by all colonized people about the viability of self-government. By contrast, my analysis of the state's performance since 1922 suggests that, in Independent Ireland economic prosperity may be generated, but its fruits will not be distributed beyond elites, and those whose support they require in building a consensus which legitimizes their hold on power.[114] The conclusions drawn by Breen et al., which are upheld and developed in Kirby's work, demonstrate that it was, or should have been, clear to policy-makers at the beginning of the 1990s that Independent Ireland bore little resemblance to an egalitarian, decolonized social order. As the Celtic Tiger episode demonstrates, pouring multiple incentives to capital accumulation into such a society could only lead to quite spectacular exacerbations of the plight of those excluded from or marginal to elite projects. The collapse of the Tiger economy reveals the wretched irony that many of those who subscribed to its culture of crass individualism have colluded in the exile of such persons to spaces wherein reviled principles of social solidarity are their only recourse.

I have raised for discussion the consequences of the revision of utopianism – undifferentiated from an Irish nationalism caricatured as irredeemably atavistic and violent – to the margins of popular consciousness. David Lloyd's work provides a well-argued critique of the cultural profligacy of the revisionist turn, as historical examples of alternative futures are misread, denigrated and suppressed to meet the political agendas of contemporary elites. I have noted Kirby's suggestion that there may be considerable progressive potential in mobilizing civil society. Lloyd is less enthusiastic, pointing to contradictions inherent in civil society's historical implication in modernity's – and colonialism's – market/state/society relation: 'Colonialism is an integrated phenomenon that operates across all the fields that in the West would constitute the public and the private, civil society and the state.'[115] My conceptualization of civil society as the location of critical cultural work underpins the analysis of theatre in the 1990s, and I will return to Lloyd's caveats in addressing Kirby's provocative proposal for a second republic, in my conclusion.

As cultural interventions, the critical projects reviewed in this chapter testify to the robustness of ideas emerging in intellectual work in Ireland from the late 1980s on. They amount to a set of instances of the power of critical ideas to enable understanding – and, when harnessed to practicable means[116] – transformation of human social realities experienced under globalization, among interlocking networks of markets, states and versions of civil society. In common with Lloyd, Kirby concludes that those seeking to understand Irish society look, too often, in the wrong places, and through distorting lenses. Because of its resistance to self-justifying official narratives, postcolonial analysis is potentially trans-formative, enabling alternative histories of lived experience to emerge alongside, and in opposition to, institutions and modes of thinking which have historically silenced or denied their untamed testimonies.[117] It is that critical efficacy which generates enabling insights when applied as a way of reading Irish theatre. Postcolonial interpretations of the actions of *dramatis personae* in fictional worlds constitute a cultural resource for a decolonization of actual worlds. That project has been postponed, negated, and has never been more necessary for Irish people. I move now to consider the critical contributions of artists, and specifically makers of theatre, in Independent Ireland during the long 1990s.

---

1 Brendan Behan, *The Quare Fella* (Methuen, 1977): 21.

2 'The ruling section in this country is ... the Catholic bourgeoisie.' Anthony Cronin, 'What Price Glory?', *The Irish Times*, 6 September 1974, cited in Ronan Fanning, *Independent Ireland* (Helicon, 1983): 52.

3 Awam Amkpa, 'Drama and the Languages of Postcolonial Desire', *Irish University Review*, 29. 2, (Autumn/Winter 1999): 294-304.

4 'For as in the days of colonialism, the African people are still struggling for a world ... in which they will control the economy, politics and culture to make their lives accord with where they want to go and who they want to be.' 'The writer in a neo-colonial state', Wa Thiong'o, Ngugi, *Moving the Centre: the struggle for cultural freedoms* (James Currey, 1993): 73.

5 Richard Breen, Damian Hannan, David B. Rottman, Christopher T. Whelan, *Understanding Contemporary Ireland: State, Class and Development in the Republic of Ireland* (Gill & MacMillan, 1990): 8.

6 This is a point well illustrated in the account of transformative pedagogy in Paulo Freire, *Education for Critical Consciousness* (Continuum, 1992).

7 Amkpa (1999) was first presented as a paper to 'The Shaw Arts Festival', convened by the author, Dublin Institute of Technology, 9 April 1999. Responding to questions on that occasion, Amkpa cited personal experience of being required to learn poems in English about winter and snow even though living in sub-tropical conditions during his boyhood in Nigeria.

8 Amkpa refers to the film by Arthur Asquith, *Pygmalion* (b/w 1935) with Leslie Howard and Wendy Hiller.

9 Declan Kiberd, *Inventing Ireland* (Vintage, 1996): 6.

10 'I first encountered a film version of Bernard Shaw's play *Pygmalion* in the summer of 1976 in Kano, Nigeria ...My encounter with Shaw's film was purely accidental, for the film billed by the British Council in its afternoon program was William Shakespeare's *Othello*. The copy was said to be bad and as a substitute, *Pygmalion* was shown!' Amkpa (1999): 294. Interestingly, the British Council in Nigeria presented *Pygmalion* as a film of the work of an important British playwright, Bernard Shaw.

11 Augusto Boal, *Theatre of the Oppressed* (Pluto, 1987).

12 Patrick Mason, *A High Ambition* (Dublin: The National Theatre Society, 1993). The phrase was coined by W.B. Yeats, in outlining a manifesto for the National Theatre Society.

13 'The bourgeoisie has obliterated its name in passing from reality to representation, from economic man to mental man.' Barthes, Roland, *Mythologies* (Paladin, 1980): 138. 'The flight from the name

'bourgeois' ... is the bourgeois ideology itself, the process through which the bourgeoisie transforms the reality of the world into an image of the world, History into Nature.' Ibid.141.

14 Tim O'Halloran refers to 'an entire class of business and professional people who stand accused (of corruption), a class known as the 'bourgeoisie' before it became politically incorrect even to advert to their existence as an entity.' Tim O'Halloran, letter to *The Irish Times*, 12 July 2000, p. 15. My parenthesis.)

15 Frantz Fanon, *The Wretched of the Earth* (Black Cat Books, 1968).

16 Awam Amkpa, in conversation with the author, Massachussetts, 12 August 1999.

17 David Lloyd, *Ireland After History* (Cork University Press, 1999): 105.

18 Renato Constantino, describes 'a counter-consciousness which alone could restore to identity its dynamic content and which would necessarily oppose ... colonialism.' *Renato Constantino: Neo-colonial Identity and Counter-consciousness: Essays on Cultural Decolonization*, ed. István Mészáros (Merlin, 1978): 66.

19 For a discussion on how Ireland measures up as a 'distributive state', see Peadar Kirby, *The Celtic Tiger in Distress: Growth with Inequality in Ireland* (Palgrave, 2002): 132-142.

20 Mészáros ed. (1978): 23.

21 Awam Amkpa (1999): 302.

22 Cornel West, 'The New Cultural Politics of Difference' *Out There: Marginalization and Contemporary Cultures*, Russell Ferguson, Martha Gever, Trinh T. Minh-ha, and Cornel West eds (MIT Press, 1992): 31.

23 Patrick Lynch, 'The Social Revolution that never was', Desmond Williams, ed, *The Irish Struggle 1916-1926* (London, 1966): 35, cited in Fanning (1983): 81.

24 'The collapse of an agreed political ideal in a partitioned, non-republican Ireland scarred by civil war made the government hold all the more fervently to an intact cultural ideal... the cultural movement appeared more genuinely national than the political movement.' Ibid. 81. See also Christopher Morash, '"Something's Missing": Theatre and The Republic of Ireland Act', *Writing in the Irish Republic: Literature, Culture, Politics 1949-1999*, ed. Ray Ryan (Macmillan, 1999): 64-81.

25 This designation is common among historians of culture and society, as evidenced in Fanning (1983).

26 This is a truism asserted for party political advantage against Fine Gael, the largest opposition party, and descendant of Cumann na nGaedhal, the dominant party in the first Dáil Éireann (national parliament). Recent scholarship suggests that, far from being true, it does not even represent the professional opinion of Eamon De

Valera, who nonetheless propounded it enthusiastically in the political arena.

27 This aspiration was given form, if not substance, in Bunreacht na h-Éireann/The Irish Constitution (1937). The constitutional claim to the territory of Northern Ireland was abandoned following a referendum designed to enable the Good Friday Agreement (1998) to be ratified by the state as an international treaty.

28 Throughout this book, the hyphenated spelling of post-colonial refers to usage which suggests that post-coloniality is a clean break with the epoch of colonialism, its practices and its epistemes.

29 This term is used to suggest the imaginary toward which the gaze of a young generation fostered in Ireland's 'emigrant nursery' is directed. O'Toole, Fintan, *Black Hole, Green Card* (New Island, 1994): 13.

30 Peadar Kirby, *Poverty Amid Plenty: World and Irish Development Reconsidered* (Trócaire, 1997): 144. My parentheses.

31 'The appeal of the national movement for me in my youth was, I think, that it seemed to be an image of a social ideal which could give fine life and fine art authority.' Yeats, W.B., 'Journal' (1909), in *Memoirs* (1972), cited in Christopher Murray, *Twentieth-century Irish Drama: Mirror up to Nation* (Manchester University Press, 1997): 1.

32 Mészáros ed. (1978): 65.

33 Breen et al., (1990): 20.

34 Breen et al discuss the role and nature of that continuity, Ibid. 23.

35 Breen at al. identify 'four major structural features that affected the autonomy of the Irish State', including 'a well-entrenched civil service apparatus with a tradition of autonomous action... inherited from the British administration and retained after independence.' Ibid. 20-21.

36 Chris Tiffin and Alan Lawson, (eds.), *De-scribing Empire: Post-colonialism and textuality* (Routledge, 1994):233.

37 Joe Cleary, 'Modernization and Aesthetic Ideology in Contemporary Irish Culture', in Ray Ryan ed. (1999): 115.

38 For a comprehensive history and analysis of official nationalist discourse, see Katy Hayward, *Irish Nationalism and European Integration: the official redefinition of the island of Ireland* (Manchester University Press, 2009).

39 This turn is exemplified in the pietistic insertion of the National Anthem and *cúpla focal as Gaeilge* [literally, a couple of words in Irish] into the opening and closing of everything from an All-Ireland Hurling Final to a music session in a public house. This became *de rigeur* prior to events conducted entirely in English, enabling the disciples of official nationalism to piously nod toward the sacred aspiration to an Irish speaking country, while never actually doing anything to bring it about.

40 The 'mythic power (of issues revolving around the civil war) could never be discounted.' Fanning (1983): 188.

41 'The state in independent Ireland initially played an auxiliary role, supplementary, though not necessarily subordinate to other institutions within the society.' Breen et al., (1990): 22.

42 Ibid. 38.

43 Ibid. 22.

44 Ibid. 38.

45 Ibid. p. 25.

46 Hayward (2009): 7.

47 Kirby, (1997): 195.

48 Ibid.196.

49 'Both the 1932 and 1933 general elections took place in an atmosphere of press hostility against Fianna Fáil (Dwyer 1991: 159-160), rumours of an impending military *coup d'état*, and Cumann na nGaedheal's insistence that de Valera was "the shadow of a gunman" and that Fianna Fáil was a dangerously revolutionary party (see Keogh 1986: 134-159).' Pilkington, Lionel, *Theatre and the State in Twentieth-century Ireland: cultivating the people* (Routledge, 2001): 116.

50 wa Th'iong'o, Ngugi, *Decolonising the Mind* (James Currey/-Heinemann, 1993).

51 'Fianna Fáil's actual assumption of power was most notable for its uneventful conservatism ... the practical effect of (their) policies was to promote the fortunes of the native bourgeoisie (see Foster 1988: 543; Dunphy 1995: 160). Most important of all, Fianna Fáil allowed the civil service to remain intact, thereby indicating the party's willingness to reform and redirect, rather than to alter fundamentally the economic policies of the state. In this respect, Fianna Fáil's treatment of the state as an 'essentially neutral instrument' was a crucial indicator of its attitude to government. (Dunphy 1995: 146).' Pilkington (2001): 116-7.

52 See Hayward (2009).

53 This triple relationship is derived from Ben Agger, *Cultural Studies as Critical Theory* (Falmer, 1992).

54 See Francis Murphy, Helen Buckley and Laraine Joyce, *The Ferns Report* (Dublin: Government Publications, 2005), and *Report of the Commission to Inquire into Child Abuse (The Ryan Report)* (Dublin: Government Publications, 2009).

55 For a discussion of the economic war in terms of de Valera's policy objectives of national reconstruction, see Peadar Kirby, *Poverty Amid Plenty*: 28-29.

56 Breen et al., (1990): 30. They add, 'The true depth of the recession was recorded in the emigration figures, however, not the unemployment statistics. Some 400,000 persons left to seek employment elsewhere, mainly in Great Britain, during the decade.

Approximately one person out of every five born since independence and resident in 1951 had emigrated by the end of the decade; for those in younger age groups, the rate of departure was nearly twice as great. In many years, emigrants almost equalled the number of births.' Ibid. 35.

57 Ibid. 37: 'The Irish civil service had, by the 1950s, developed its own ethos - meritocratic in recruitment, but strongly nationalist in cultural affinities. Attachment to that ethos was reinforced by a policy of recruiting administrators from among secondary school graduates, rather than holders of university degrees, and using that pool as the source for all promotions to senior ranks.'

58 Breen et al. date 'the change in the composition of the élite' to the 'first phase of transformation', begun 'during the Emergency and continued until the late 1950s.' Ibid. 31. Kirby (1997) cites reference in Keating, P., and D. Desmond, *Culture and Capitalism in Contemporary Ireland*, to the 'new class of politically-dependent capitalists which emerged in the 1960s with close links to senior figures in Fianna Fáil.' (133).

59 Breen et al. (1990) argue, 'DeValera's Ireland was dominated by a re-awakened search for economic and cultural sovereignty ... Free trade was abandoned and replaced by a formidable protectionist wall built out of some of the highest tariffs in the world. National self-sufficiency ...was the touchstone that guided de Valera's government.' (3). They continue, '... after four decades of independence, Ireland in 1960 could be characterised economically as one of the peripheral regions of the United Kingdom,' Ibid. 4, and conclude, 'Equality of opportunity, despite being a goal of State policy, was never pursued by the State.' Ibid. 217.

60 Kirby (1997): 160.

61 Ibid. 160.

62 Ibid. Kirby adds, 'Facilitating this, Jacobsen identifies 'a high degree of deference ... a high propensity by non-elites to defer to policy prescriptions.'

63 See, for example, Edward Said, 'Yeats and Decolonization' in Seamus Deane ed, *Nationalism, Colonialism and Literature* (University of Minnesota Press, 1990): 69-95.

64 Patrick Clancy, Shelagh Drudy, Kathleen Lynch, and Liam O'Dowd, eds, *Irish Society: Sociological Perspectives* (Institute of Public Administration, 1997): 1.

65 Pilkington (2001): 49.

66 The innate and enduring conservatism of the apparatus of the state in Independent Ireland is critiqued in Joseph Lee's metaphor of 'the official mind.' Lee, (1990): 108.

67 The categories dominant, residual and emergent are developed as a model designed to explain the relationship between change and continuity in social formations, in Raymond Williams, *Marxism and*

Literature (Oxford University Press, 1977): 121-26. It is important to keep the flexibility of Williams's formulation in view, when engaging with phased models of historical development such as those conceptualised by Fanon, Said and Amkpa, so as to mitigate risks arising, similar to those which accompany a reliance on chronological periodization.

[68] Kirby (1997): 197.

[69] See Kirby (2002): 176-178.

[70] David Lloyd, 'After History: Historicism and Postcolonial Studies', in Carroll and King eds, *Ireland and Postcolonial Theory* (Cork University Press, 2003): 56.

[71] Breen et al., (1990): 6.

[72] 'As the authors of a volume examining social inequality in Ireland concluded, "Irish policymakers have consistently prioritised the needs of the economy over social objectives".' Kirby (2002): 181.

[73] Kirby (1997): 41.

[74] 'Freeing Culture from Eurocentrism' in Ngugi wa Thiong'o (1993): 49.

[75] 'The dominance of populist politics (is) a major element constraining the Irish state.' Kirby (1997): 199.

[76] Ibid. 198.

[77] 'A republic that was defined simply in terms of territorial integrity betrayed the social and inherent rights content of a republic.' 'Michael D. Higgins 1993', in Joe Jackson, *Troubadours and Troublemakers* (Blackwater Press, 1996): 211-212.

[78] Kirby (1997): 16.

[79] See J.J. Lee, 'From Empire to Europe: the Irish state 1922-73', *Contesting the state: Lessons from the Irish case*, Adshead, Maura, Peadar Kirby and Michelle Millar eds (Manchester: Manchester University Press, 2008): 25-49.

[80] See Terence A.M. Dooley, *'The land for the people': the land question in independent Ireland* (Dublin: University College Dublin Press, 2004), and Mary E. Daly, *The Slow Failure: Population Decline and Independent Ireland, 1920-1973* (University of Wisconsin Press, 2006).

[81] Notoriously, the failed policy of Irish language revival by making its study compulsory in primary and secondary schools, and ability to speak the language essential for employment in most areas of the public service.

[82] Joe Lee, 'A Sense of Place in the Celtic Tiger?' in eds Harry Bohan and Gerard Kennedy, *Are We Forgetting Something: Our Society in the New Millennium* (Veritas, 1999): 80, cited in Kirby (2002): 145.

[83] Ngugi (1993): 49.

[84] Lee, in Kirby (2002): 145.

[85] See Toby Miller, 'Culture and the Global Economy', *Performing Hybridity*, May Joseph and Jennifer Natalya Fink eds, (University of Minnesota, 1999): 35-45.

86 Annual coverage of British football clubs on global tours features shots of their local supporters wearing club shirts and consuming related merchandise. The power of virtual imagery in constructing contemporary identities across time and space is clearly illustrated.

87 Henry A. Giroux refers to contemporary cinema and television as 'popular teaching machines', Giroux, Henry A., *Fugitive Cultures: Race, Violence and Youth*, (Routledge, 1996): 23.

88 See Kirby (2002) for a sustained critique of the cheerleading tendency.

89 'The response to globalisation, European Integration and to a revived economic neo-liberalism would appear to encourage Irish sociologists to think more wholistically as they struggle to interpret the lack of fit between economy, state and society on the island.' Clancy et al. (1997): 18.

90 'The economy displays only some of the innovative indigenous capacity that characterises (an enterprise) economy. Instead, it resembles far more a dependent Third-World-type economy, extremely reliant on foreign investment ... For the last two years Ireland has come second last on the UN's poverty index for developed countries.' Katherine E Zappone and Peadar Kirby, 'Harney got it wrong about our "inclusive" society', *The Irish Times*, 13 August 1999: 15

91 Kirby (1997): 13.

92 Ibid. 14.

93 Ibid.

94 Mary O'Sullivan, "Manufacturing and Global Competition" in J.W. O'Hagan, ed., *The Economy of Ireland: Policy and Performance of a Small European Country* (Gill & MacMillan, 1995): 370, cited in Ibid. 132.

95 Ibid. 132-133.

96 Ibid. 167.

97 Ibid. (My emphasis).

98 See Breen et al.

99 Kirby (1997): 185. (My emphasis).

100 Renato Constantino defines national consciousness as 'that sense of oneness which comes from a community of aspiration, response and action,' István Mészáros ed. (1978): 25.

101 Hayward (2009) identifies 'the early and continued dependence of official discourse on the language of nationalism.'(61).

102 De Valera established a Commission of Inquiry into the Civil Service (1932-1935), the reactionary nature of whose conclusions was contested by a Labour member, Luke Duffy. He is cited in Lee (1990: 197): 'It is the duty of someone in this country to design for the state a form of organisation which harmonises with the traditions and responds to the aspirations of the Irish people. I entertained the hope that the present commission ... would sketch the outlines of an

organisation suitable to the needs of this country, and regret that they should have based their conclusions on the existence of an organisation designed to serve other purposes.'

103 '(Department of) Finance officials made their mark upon the Irish Free State less by what they did than by what they prevented others doing.' Fanning (1983): 64.

104 Pilkington (2001), offers a sustained critique of this notion.

105 Hayward (2009): 20.

106 This practice was in use from an early stage. Lee (1990: 207) records that when, in 1937, 'a few educated women did repudiate the kitchen sink role allotted them in (De Valera's) constitution', *The Irish Press*, the newspaper founded by De Valera, 'sneered at "the learned ladies (the National University Women Graduates Association) whose zeal in the national cause had in many cases been conspicuous by its absence".'

107 Clare Carroll, 'Introduction: The nation and Postcolonial Theory', in Carroll and King eds (2003): 9.

108 Ibid.

109 John A. Hall, "Nationalisms, classified and explained" in Sukumar Periwal, *Notions of Nationalism*, (Central European University Press, 1995): 20, cited in Kirby (1997): 179-180.

110 Lloyd (2003): 49. His references to Ireland here include the entire island, and not simply the successor state which is my immediate focus.

111 Ibid.

112 Carroll (2003): 10.

113 Conor McCarthy, 'The Intellectual and the State: Irish Criticism Since 1980', *Beyond Boundaries: Mapping Irish Studies in the Twenty-first Century,* Harte, Liam and Yvonne Whelan eds (London: Pluto, 2007): 90. McCarthy poses 'seven questions that, it seems to this writer, Irish criticism is *not* asking,' and raises the implications for intellectual work of an unacknowledged erosion of state sovereignty, a pervasive culture of quietism, and the consequences of globalization.

114 'This, of course is particularly important in the case of middle-class sectors on which elites depend, at least for ideological deference. It helps explain the careful attention demonstrated by the Irish state to ensure Ireland's middle classes gain the greatest benefits from the state's taxation and welfare systems, and its educational system.' Kirby (2002): 176.

115 David Lloyd (2003): 47.

116 Kirby (2002: 189) draws attention to the need for utopian programmes to meet a criterion of practicality.

117 See, especially, David Lloyd, *Ireland After History* (Cork University Press, 1999), and *Irish Times* (Field Day, 2008).

3 | Theatre, subjectivity, and change

'Silenced voices inevitably emerge.'[1]

'Culture does its hegemonic damage at the level of lived experience.'[2]

Benedict Anderson understands the nation itself as a feat of imagination.[3] Among the material and psychic conditions of colonial abjection, a nationalist movement announces the possibility of a better life: utopia may not exist, but it may be imagined. In mobilizing commitment to an autonomous, decolonized nation, such a movement responds to, and amplifies collective desires for liberation. In its anti-colonial phase, nationalist discourse identifies liberation unambiguously as a specific destination – the national state[4] to be founded after the departure of the colonial power. Although their origins and development are historically distinct – notably in relation to the power position of the indigenous bourgeois classes – both anti-colonial and postcolonial consciousness emerge and are experienced as antagonistic responses to domination. Postcolonial desire reiterates key aspects of anti-colonial nationalism, not least in its mobilization of utopian aspiration. As each process emerges in its historical moment, the representation of utopian conditions, events, and relationships becomes acutely important. In Independent Ireland, postcolonial desiring constitutes, and derives from a felt need for society transformed as a community of aspiration, response and action: a republican praxis whose purpose takes up the unfinished project of the European Enlightenment: *égalité*. The ideal of social equality demands commitment and creativity if representational strategies adequate to engaging with the historical predicament of neo-colonialism are to be developed.

Renato Constantino affirms the constitutive and transformative powers of imaginaries upon which anti-colonialist solidarities draw in constituting themselves. Liberation is experienced in human practices, and Constantino argues that collective yearning for a better way is not sated by attendance at the carnival of the transfer of power. In differentiating the moment of state-founding from the achievement of liberation, he exposes the limits of nationalism's teleological assumptions. A philosophy of liberation is 'a growing thing, depending on accretions of consciousness'5 and popular aspirations to liberation persist, and mutate, as collective postcolonial desires respond both to residual manifestations of colonialism, and to emergent neo-colonial domination in the successor state. Civil society, the location of culture, is negotiated in sites where the meaning of humanity itself, as subjectivity and agency, is contested. It is important, therefore, to attempt to theorize the nature of artistic creation as postcolonial desiring, and to situate cultural work as a borderland between individuals and communities, and the state.

Culture, Nation and Lived Experience

Irish nationalists devoted considerable energies to imagining an Irish nation, from the late-eighteenth century on, but thinking on the practicalities of constituting a state was somewhat underdeveloped, not least because 'there were three core versions of nationalism [which] occupied conflicting positions regarding the ideal notion of Irish nation-statehood.'6 When, in the 1930s, De Valera inherited a partial, but self-consciously national state from the conservative revolutionaries he had sought to supplant, initially by force of arms, he moved to conclude a constitutional agreement not with the people, but with the Catholic Church. Shaw's observation of 1906 testifies to a neo-colonial continuity at work in this arrangement: 'The British Government and the Vatican may differ very vehemently as to whose subject the Irishman is to be; but they are quite agreed as to the propriety of his being a subject.'7 Thus, the failure of imagination of which the state is often accused may be equally or principally a failure of constitution, of structuring a vision into being. Its consequences include a radical weakening, to the point of disappearance of a public sphere, of civil society. This may account for the particular alienation experienced by political radicals, and by artists and intellectuals, in Independent Ireland. Cultural work produced in the decades following independence speaks insistently of decolonization postponed, a nation deferred. Across generations, works by painter Seán Keating, poets Austin Clarke and Patrick Kavanagh, playwright Billy Roche, and songwriter Christy Moore provide images and metaphors of an unquiet country, a place of exclusions and silences, of the disruption of the most intimate moments by the state's coercive insistence on fealty to a pale and fearful version of Irishness.

The passionate coupling of young heterosexual bodies, and Catholic Church control of its transgressive capabilities, is visited frequently as a metaphorical site for the standoff between authoritarianism and desire which defined life for too many, too long. Paul Durcan[8] imagines a telling collision of the ancient *jouissance* of human desire and the regulatory gaze of De Valera, manifestation of Independent Ireland's peculiarly coupled Church and State:

> But even had our names been Diarmaid and Gráinne
> We doubted De Valera's approval
> For a poet's son and a judge's daughter
> Making love outside Áras an Uachtaráin.[9]
> I see him now in the heat-haze of the day
> Blindly stalking us down;
> And, levelling an ancient rifle, he says 'Stop
> Making love outside Áras an Uachtaráin.'[10]

Chapter Two has shown that the relationship of Independent Ireland to Colonized Ireland is characterized by continuity of administrative structures and socio-economic relations. In a parallel way, the relationship of Irish artists to Irish society is characterized by continuity of alienation, in some cases leading to exile – James Joyce and Samuel Beckett from colonized Dublin; Seán O'Casey and Paul Vincent Carroll from the Irish Free State. Life in Independent Ireland was itself frequently figured by artists as a kind of banishment, and the flight into magic realism of Flann O'Brien in the capital of the Ireland of De Valera and John A. Costello (1943-1953) finds an echo, decades later, in the title of Dermot Bolger's *Internal Exiles* (1983).[11] The poems in the section titled, 'A New Primer for Irish Schools'[12] rewrite those of Patrick Pearse, emblematic leader of the 1916 Rebellion. In 'I Am Ireland (After Pearse)',[13] Bolger sets Pearse's prescriptive visions of Ireland, 'free,

Gaelic and Catholic' against stark personal experiences of emigration from Independent Ireland:

> I am Ireland
> Older I am than Birmingham's tower blocks
> From a land disowning me
> To this city not my own
> The first ache of exile[14]

In '1958/1959',[15] De Valera is figured as 'The State's father',

> Suffocating the country
> Like a cobweb in our bloodstream
> Clotting till it burst asunder.[16]

It is at the level of lived experience that the texture of Irish experience as a neo-colonial rather than a post-colonial phenomenon most tellingly emerges. The continuity of alienation communicated in the work of artists, in such agonized figures, amplifies Breen et al's conclusion that 'Irish nationalism... was untypically an agent of stability rather than upheaval.'[17]

Flann O'Brien's prose works, especially *At Swim-Two-Birds* (1939)[18] and *The Third Policeman* (1967),[19] develop fantastical worlds in an effort to negotiate the nightmarish conditions of independence, Irish style. In his wildly inventive critical essay on James Joyce,[20] he envisages the Irish artist:

> Sitting, fully dressed, in the toilet of a locked [train] carriage where he has absolutely no right to be, *resentfully* drinking somebody else's whiskey, being whisked hither and thither by anonymous shunters, but keeping fastidiously the while on the *outer* face of his door the simple word 'Engaged'.[21]

Daily life in Ireland is figured as a set of procedures in which the individual passively complies with the whimsical ordinances of the agents of the national bourgeoisie.[22]

The stalled railway carriage is fully provisioned but going nowhere, abandoned in a tunnel under the Phoenix Park in Dublin, location of Áras an Uachtaráin. The figure of the artist, deadened with alcohol and bitterly withdrawn from social relations, is wholly exposed to the violent, capricious manoeuvrings of the 'shunters'. His existence – a series of radically unpredictable and ultimately purposeless relocations – provides grim witness to a remorseless hollowing-out of critical consciousness which still persists in Independent Ireland.[23]

The position of indigenous bourgeois classes in successor states is a key index of progress toward or away from the utopian projects of anti-colonial nationalism. Frantz Fanon[24] grounds their contradictory relationship to decolonization in their retaining and pursuit of ties with their counterparts in metropolitan societies, ultimately more durable than those they form in the heat of battle with oppressed groups within their own national borders.[25] In consolidating their hegemony in the successor state, neo-colonial elites deploy the civic 'we'[26] as a profoundly cynical and exploitative ideological tool. They invest heavily in disseminating a received wisdom which allocates to their views and their interests a natural quality. This plays out in cultural matters, and their preferred account of 'Art'[27] stresses its 'natural', transcendent 'universality', and delegitimizes artists who corrupt themselves and their allocated social role by engaging with public issues in the actual world to which they belong: 'There's a danger of being written off by people if you call yourself political. In arts circles, the minute the word "political" raises its head, people think you're serious and earnest.'[28] In light of this, it is perhaps an exemplary neo-colonial contradiction that Irish poets and playwrights are read by oppressed peoples around the world as witnesses to liberation and personal redemption in the achievement of nationhood.[29]

O'Brien's artist embodies this paradox – suspended at a point, during the first phase of independence, when Fanon's contradictions are no longer containable by the homogenizing tropes of nationalist rhetoric, and the neo-colonial quality of the successor state emerges in plain sight. Edward Said sees anti-imperial struggle developing in two distinct phases, nationalist and liberationist,[30] and what he calls 'liberationist anti-imperialism' emerges at this point as other to neo-colonialism. In Said's terms, neo-colonialism usurps the promise of decolonization and repeats the social organization and economic models of colonialism, or imperialism. In a parallel argument, Joe Cleary conceptualizes in Independent Ireland a phase of 'autarkic development'[31] coinciding with the emergence of Fianna Fáil as the party of government (1932), and ending with the 'opening' of the economy to a form of modernization dependent on foreign direct investment (1958). The experience of Irish people in the period from the end of World War II to 1958-59 alerts us to the fact that the emergence of Said's 'liberationist' consciousness is intensely contested by the indigenous elite, and does not inevitably attract popular allegiance as the triumph of deferred emancipatory aspiration. Nevertheless, I will argue that as it plays out in Ireland, this phase is marked by signs – in the beginnings of struggle against neo-colonial domination – of a resilience captured in Fanon's phrase, 'overpowered but not tamed.' Human experience is a site of ongoing contestation in which social change, and projects which seek to enable human subjectivity, are always marked by contingency and uncompletability.

Drama and the Limits of National Consciousness

Cultural artefacts, symbols, images and narratives enable access to the human consequences of 'living through'[32] historical struggles. Cultural projects, and individual acts of cultural production have always been important to the relationship between public consciousness and political ideas, as the critical histories of *Cathleen Ní Houlihan* (1902), *The Playboy of the Western World* (1907), *The Plough and the Stars* (1926) and *Mise Éire* (1959) reveal. Something is at stake in the production and reception of such artefacts, and as the stakes change in a society, attention to altered readings of reworkings or rescreenings of such works may reveal something of the nature of those mutations. From a postcolonial perspective, twentieth-century Irish theatre engages in a sustained dynamic relationship between felt desires for the good life, political projects which proclaim themselves the route to and guarantors of that life, and the social contradictions which result from the gap between decolonizing rhetoric and neo-colonial reality experienced by the majority of people. The foundation of the National Theatre Society in 1903 marks a moment at which, as cultural nationalism asserts itself in the service of anti-colonial struggle, a group of dramatic artists, including W.B. Yeats, Lady Augusta Gregory and J.M. Synge, set out the terms of a necessary debate on the nature of national civil society, and the constitution of a national 'we'.

Lionel Pilkington usefully excavates the ultimately reformist, or unionist purpose of the Irish Literary Theatre project, but, as P.J. Mathews intimates, the period 1899 to 1903/1904 was marked by robust debate, and the motivations and understandings of those involved developed in dialogue with broader social arguments on nation, authenticity, entitlement and representation.[33] Robert Welch establishes that the National Theatre Society was not a vehicle, pure and simple, of the small group of privileged writers and directors usually associated with the Irish Literary Theatre. Yeats, Gregory and Synge were joined in the aesthetic and critical projects of the National Theatre Society by an indigenous company of actors, scenic artists and directors, who had other options available to them. Specifically, they could have developed their own already successful commercial theatrical activities, or opted to associate themselves with the radical separatism of Maud Gonne's Cumann na nGaedheal Theatre Company,[34] which she styled in 1903, The Cumann na nGaedheal National Theatre.[35] The Fay brothers and others chose, nonetheless, to align themselves with the 'high ambition' of Yeats and Gregory, and became part of a cultural process which, however characterized by Yeats's own stubborn assertion of the primacy of his artistic judgement, appropriated space in public consciousness for critical representation. I regard that critical purpose as the primary contribution of the Abbey during the nationalist anti-colonial and emergent official nationalist phases of twentieth-century Irish history.

The Abbey, then, sets out specifically to produce a kind of 'prophetic criticism,'[36] in which explicit 'moral and political aims' interact with national consciousness. For instance, the emergence of spiritual and political inertia as aspirations to nationhood confront the realities of statehood is predicted in *Cathleen Ní Houlihan*, by Augusta Gregory and Yeats, and in J.M. Synge's *The Well of the Saints* (Chapter 4). Synge's work specifically critiques the contradictions between the coercive potential of Catholic nationalist constructions of the Irish peasant[37] and transgressive desires among the actually existing peasantry for, in Yeats's phrase, 'a fuller, more opulent life'.[38] The negative energy of *Purgatory* (1938) is an attempt to awaken public horror at the frustration of desire, as a means of renewing communal will to a 'high ambition' for Independent Ireland. The perils of periodization notwithstanding, I suggest that the anger of Yeats's Old Man dramatizes the end of the utility of Independent Ireland's nationalist anti-imperialist consciousness. However, as artefacts of prophetic critique, creative cultural representations anticipate what will not emerge as a dynamic in public affairs for some years to come. Historically, what happens next is not at all a neat adjustment to Said's next phase, but a suspension lasting between ten and twenty years. The period known as 'The Emergency' enables a pause during which the hegemonic forces of neo-colonialism might begin to aspire to their own permanency as a ruling caste, around the enduring figure of De Valera. The Free State's isolationist policy during the 'Emergency', the meticulous censorship of dissenting voices, and the inward-looking reassertion of the trope of peasant life in Eamon De Valera's St Patrick's Day address of 1943 testify to a crisis in official nationalism, and the exhaustion of utopian will. The coalition of such conditions postpones the reckoning demanded by Yeats's Old Man, and inaugurates a period of paralysis, during which, dreams undone and dreamers derided, there is no constituency for utopian imagining. In Cleary's terms, although the autarkic phase of nationalist anti-colonial endeavour was exhausted by 1939, World War II disrupts historical process and underpins a temporary reprieve for the authority of those advocating life's 'frugal comforts' for the mass of people in Ireland.

At the vanishing point of national capacity to dream a better future into being, Samuel Beckett's *Waiting for Godot*, begun in post-war Paris in 1948,[39] dramatizes both the crises of a European continent wasted by war, and an Ireland in which not only is there 'nothing to be done', there is 'no lack of void.'[40] Roche points out that, during the war, Beckett remarked sardonically, 'My friends eat sawdust and turnips while all Ireland safely gorges', and observed that the 'cosy insularity' of Ireland meant it 'was least likely to mark the end of World War II with profound change'. Instead, it sought to maintain the conditions and climate which had prevailed during and before the hostilities.[41]

I will argue in detail (Chapter Five) that *Waiting for Godot* dramatizes a moment of exhaustion, stasis and spiritual emptiness in the wake of the climactic surge of anger and violence which was Yeats's Old Man's response to thwarted desire in *Purgatory*. For Beckett's tramps, abandoned in a ruined landscape, there is only the memory of action, the ghost of desire, and the inevitability of disappointment. Bystanders at history's parade, Vladimir and Estragon mark the moment at which the residual anti-colonial tropes of official nationalist consciousness are exposed as a strategy for concealing the neo-colonial project that Independent Ireland had become. Far from embracing decolonization, the apparatus of the state – grounded in 'the distinction (begun in the first years of statehood) between the defining *ideology* of the nation-state and the *practice* of the state as the representative of the nation'[42] – curbs expectations, thwarts originality and suppresses dissent. In this light, *Waiting for Godot* is a play 'for a culture which no longer trusts the utopian, which in some respects believes itself to have passed beyond utopia'.[43]

The dramatic worlds generated in the early to mid-twentieth century, whether in anticipation of, or among the social realities of Independent Ireland, are marked by a sense of doubleness. In the case of *Cathleen Ní Houlihan* (1902) and *The Well of the Saints* (1905), that doubleness plays out as a marker of a lack of resolution of fundamental questions around identity and human subjectivity. This contest also animates the dramatic world of M.J. Molloy's *The Wood of the Whispering*[44] fifty years later (Chapter 5). As will be shown (Chapters 4 and 5) these dramas stage radical interrogations of an actually existing Ireland by persons prepared to struggle for a more ennobled human state. The dramatic action is a play of authoritarian and utopian forces, in which boundaries to subjectivity inscribed by official nationalism are transgressed by the dreamers of dreams. My detailed analysis of these plays will point to their drawing on forms and devices which exceed the conventions of realism. In so doing, I suggest that, in performance, these plays elaborate what I will call a postcolonial aesthetic of disrupted realism. The political significance of such dramas lies in their enactment of the social necessity to disrupt what Lionel Pilkington refers to as 'national pieties' in the interests of human actualization. Disrupted realism, then, is a postcolonial aesthetic strategy in Irish theatre, observable in dramas contesting both anti-colonial and neo-colonial conditions, from the 1900s to the 1950s. At the level of representation, metaphorical disruptions of the apparently real are signatures of enduring desires for decolonization.

Hayward points out that 'the strength of Fianna Fáil was of great consequence to the development of official nationalist discourse in the 1930s',[45] and so the emergence of cultural and political opposition to Fianna Fáil during the late 1940s and early 1950s, gives form to the first stirrings of what Said calls liberationist consciousness, and Amkpa, postcoloniality. *The Wood of the Whispering* by M.J. Molloy was an enormously significant vernacular drama during the 1950s, forming a central part of the repertoire of rural and small-town amateur drama groups. It is an artefact of emergent postcolonial desire, or liberationist anti-colonial consciousness in Independent Ireland. That play, and its production history during the 1950s, announces and accompanies a decade of relative turmoil in the politics of Independent Ireland. Anti-colonialist tropes underpinning official nationalist rhetoric proved unable to guarantee quietism in the face of national economic crisis and manifest social division. Molloy's 'Preface to

"The Wood of the Whispering",[46] from which this book's title is drawn, is an explicit statement of intent to deploy drama to critique a failed post-revolutionary state. The dramatic action takes the actual crisis of rural depopulation as a starting point, and plays out a solution generated from resources of imagination and performative capacity resident in the *dramatis personae* themselves. In the figure of Sanbatch Daly, ragged as Beckett's tramps, angry as Yeats's Old Man, and cunning as Synge's Martin Doul, Molloy's drama embodies the potential of even the most wretched to enable collective action for social transformation.

As the public identified the figure of De Valera more with privation than plenitude, Fianna Fáil spent some six years out of office in the period 1948-1957, and it was clear that its version of neo-colonial hegemony needed to reinvigorate itself if the future of the elites whose interests it served was to be secured. A political response to the crisis with which Molloy engages emerged before the decade was out, in the form of T. K. Whitaker's *First Programme for Economic Expansion*: a highly significant mutation in the dominant account of what, if not whom, the nation was for. In the name of modernization, Taoiseach Seán Lemass committed the state to embracing opportunities presented by opening the economy to international capital. For Joe Cleary, this was the moment 'when the strategy of autarkic development was jettisoned and the state embarked on an alternative strategy of dependent development.'[47] The paradigm shift from inward-looking nationalism to a 'small open economy' was facilitated by the symbolic continuity provided by the colossal figure of De Valera, guarantor of Fianna Fáil's fidelity to the ideals of the revolutionary period.[48] As fundamental change[49] gets under way, the project of maintaining narrative continuity with the revolutionary movements of the late nineteenth and early twentieth century, is manifested politically in De Valera's occupation of the symbolic office of President of the Republic of Ireland, and culturally, in the film *Mise Éire* (1959).

As Morrison's film is distributed widely throughout the country, Tom Murphy's and Noel O'Donoghue's *On the Outside*[50] (1959) emerges as a critical other to its worldview (Chapter 6). *Mise Éire* propounds a narrative of national progression, originating in the Rebellion of 1916, whose cohesion is guaranteed by the historical durability of Fianna Fáil, and which addresses a homogeneous Ireland, at one with itself and the wider world. Murphy's dramatic voice, urban-centred and unflinching in its refusal of social conditions in Independent Ireland, functions as an emergent challenge to dominant cultural enunciations, both formal and non-formal. This double effect distinguishes Murphy's *Famine*[51] (1968), in which a real historical calamity is decoupled from its pivotal location in the nationalist anti-colonial narrative of historical oppression. Restored as a material effect of economic forces, famine as metaphor draws critical attention to questions of structure and governance in Independent Ireland. The fictionalized historical situation, staged using epic form, grounds a dramatic world which critiques 1960s' Independent Ireland as a site of enduring hunger in the body politic, resulting from the persistence of relations of domination.

Epic dramaturgy is again brought to bear on local thematics in Dermot Bolger's *The Lament for Arthur Cleary* (1989), as Wet Paint Arts use drama to stage and critique the social devastation caused by the heroin economy of 1980s Dublin (Chapter 7). The Wet Paint Arts project seeks to represent the internal 'others' of Independent Ireland's economy, and to enact the dramatic worlds they generate before audiences who live out similar experiences of exclusion and betrayal. Even though *The Lament for Arthur Cleary* 'ends up' on the stage of the Peacock Theatre, wreathed in laurels from the Edinburgh Festival Fringe, it originates on, and makes visible, the margins of Irish theatre and society.[52] In terms of form, expressionist aspects of Molloy's dramaturgy develop toward epic theatre in the works of Murphy and Bolger. In the dramatic action of *Famine*, meta-theatrical strategies reposition the representational strategies of Irish drama itself, as transformative cultural resources. In *The Lament for Arthur Cleary*, Dermot Bolger and his director, David Byrne, infuse epic dramaturgy with epiphanies enabled by magic realism, and turn a canonical text of official nationalist culture, *Caoineadh Airt Uí Laoire*, into a site of contestation of contemporary cultural meanings. In so doing, they extend Murphy's engagement with culture itself, foregrounding and problematizing the means by which cultural workers and their artefacts are positioned in the social order.

The 1980s was a time of sharp cultural conflict in Independent Ireland, with the female body one of its principal sites. From the struggle for contraceptive rights, to divorce, to abortion legislation, conservative and progressive forces enacted a kind of civil war. One of the key figures on the side of the so-called 'liberal agenda' was the distinguished lawyer, Mary Robinson. Her election as President of

Ireland in 1989 was an act of postcolonial will, in which the presidency was reconfigured as a focus of civil society, a locus for imagining alternative realities. The practice of reworking established cultural tropes and signatures in the service of public critique distinguishes Mary Robinson's rhetorical style, especially when contrasted with that of De Valera. In theatrical terms, such a project is developed and extended in Donal O'Kelly's *Asylum! Asylum!* (1994 and 1997) and *Farawayan* (1998). *Farawayan* becomes necessary because the terms of Independent Ireland's encounter with Europe's colonized others exceed the fictions of the dramatic world of *Asylum! Asylum!* in the space of a mere three years (Chapter 7). The mixing of epic and magic realist aesthetics underpins both plays, but it is the genesis of one in the other that marks the commitment of the artist to public conversation.

The topography of mainstream Irish theatrical practice is reorganized by the interventions of Calypso Productions, which take up and develop the public pedagogical project of Wet Paint Arts. Both Wet Paint and Calypso contest the boundaries of social relations, and of theatrical convention, especially the stage/audience dichotomy. They do so in the service of avowedly critical and utopian purposes, and I read them as examples of 'new cultural workers' in Cornel West's usage. The artefacts produced, which include Charlie O'Neill's *Rosie and Starwars*, are intended as critical interventions in a neo-colonial social order, and I include them as exemplary dramas of postcolonial desiring. The journey from Molloy to O'Neill, via Murphy, Bolger and O'Kelly takes us directly into the heart of postcolonial desiring as critical other to a neo-colonial Ireland. Drama enables the playing out of hoped-for better worlds even in times of oppression and despair, and these liberationist projects rehearse and extend the concerns, the ambition and the positionality of Gregory, Yeats and Synge. This is a theatre decentred in the social order, privileging questions over pronouncements, suggestion over prescription, poetic excess over realism's reductions.

In the late-nineteenth century, the consolidation of nationalism as a non-formal counterpoint to the colonial province offered Irish people other possibilities for individual and collective identifications than those narrated by the colonial centre. Even though Irish politics and Irish society changed a very great deal between the 1890s and the 1990s, Independent Ireland is marked, at the turn of the twenty-first century, by a sense of lack. Cleary concludes that contemporary Irish cultural production reveals 'a society with neither the resources nor the strategies required to meet the challenges of the future.'[53] Nonetheless, David Cairns and Shaun Richards argument still holds currency:

> The belief in the efficacy of art in the creation of a national consciousness remains, albeit that the contemporary expression of this belief has abandoned the desire to consolidate sectarian exclusivism and moved to the advocacy of democratic pluralism. The expansion of this political and cultural activity is now the urgent requirement.[54]

I move now to consider the nature and significance of theatrical practices for human subjectivity in a society awaiting decolonization.

Theatre, Subjectivity and Postcolonial Critique

Subjectivity is neither an individual project nor a given attribute, but a function of processes of understanding and negotiating multiple (and perhaps contradictory) points of identification, a reconfiguration which grounds Amkpa's notion of 'third citizenship or non-formal citizenship.'[55] 'Non-formality' acknowledges the constitutive contributions of both global and local allegiances and alliances to personal experiences, both virtual and real. It is in the non-formal sphere that desires for self-actualization, central to one's ability to contribute socially, are brought into being and negotiated. When mobilized across groups of people in solidarity, their communal articulations are powerful motors of postcoloniality:

> What I call *postcolonial desire* – the act of imagining, living and negotiating a social reality based on democracy, cultural pluralism and social justice ... signifies an act of refusal to assume the passive, static, essentialist identity of that 'Other'. Rather, it draws upon the resources of non-formal citizenship to fuel a perpetual act of becoming.[56]

Drama, the art form which is a social process, does not offer actual subjects for contemplation, and dramatic action stages fictional *dramatis personae* engaged in symbolic negotiations between contradictory points of identification. An enabling criticism should seek to reveal in acts of theatre the functions and possibilities of subjectivity and human agency struggled for among the mutating realities of fictional worlds. In setting out to read moments of performance as manifestations of utopian desires, strategies which influence how they are framed in the actual worlds of theatre audiences must be taken into account. Reflecting on the state of theatre criticism in 1990s Independent Ireland, Jocelyn Clarke exposes an unholy alliance between the commercial world of journalism and the blunted interpretive tools of the reviewer of plays, manifest in 'the problem of contemporary critical practice – the difference between writing a review and writing a critique'.[57] Individual critics tend to write as 'representatives of the audience … And as they write their reviews, they report on their experience of that night, what they liked or didn't like, what were the salient stories of the plays and who the characters were.'[58]

Questions of agency, subjectivity and citizenship are rarely acknowledged in reviewers' discourse as a lens through which to gain insight into the meaning of the actions, circumstances and events in which the *dramatis personae* are depicted. Read primarily in psychological terms, subjectivity is treated as more or less the same thing as individuality. In addressing dramatic content, the struggle of the individual for freedom is generally assumed to be the same thing as the struggle for individualism. As a result, plays in performance are seen as encounters with pyschologically-determined characters and their predicaments. Differentiation of subjectivities represented in dramatic worlds – in terms of social or cultural capital, for instance – is elided by substituting for the complex, contradictory negotiations of self-actualization, the individualistic freedom 'to do what you want, without being told what to do or how to think': the goal of bourgeois individualism installed as the destination of all human endeavours and desires. Critical perspectives drawn from conventional readings of prose fiction seek out realism over poetry, 'place' over site of cultural negotiation. The experience of theatre, as a communal, public witnessing is rarely adverted to. During the 1990s, 'theatre-going' came to be framed in discourses shared with shopping and eating out – as an expression of the imperatives of consumption, as opposed to, for example, assertions of citizen engagement. David Nowlan's exhortation at the end of his review of Druid Theatre Company's production of Marina Carr's *On Raftery's Hill*, 'Go see. Go buy',[59] encapsulates this position.

A refusal to read contradictions in *dramatis personae* as anything other than evidence of psychological turmoil, for instance, parallels the resistance in the neo-colonial social order to cultural critique. The body of the actor becomes an analogue for the body politic, and reading strategies which misrecognize or refuse the contradictions engendered by the gap between desire and actuality reiterate the silencing strategies which support the persistence of inequalities in the social order itself. In important ways, the crisis, both for civil society and theatre artists, is one way of seeing otherwise: inadequate reading, reader positions and reading strategies produce a crisis of readership analogous to crises of citizenship. The community of aspiration finds evasion instead of response, inertia in place of action. Said sees this as a situation typical of the historical phase of liberationist anti-imperialism:

> It is in this phase that I would like to suggest that *liberation*, and not nationalist independence, is the new alternative, liberation which by its very nature involves, in Fanon's words, a transformation of social consciousness beyond national consciousness.[60]

In enabling this transformation, which is central to initiating processes toward decolonization, theatre artists and theatre scholars have an important role to play.

The Subject of Drama

Ideas governing public perceptions of the nature of Drama have profound consequences for the transformative potential of the artform in a given social order. In other words, the extent to which rich enabling experiences actually come into being in moments of performance and reception depends greatly on audience stances in relation to reading acts of theatre.[61] In the Anglo-American world in which Irish theatre circulates, Literary Studies – 'a moral technology ... heavily in the service of ideology'[62] – introduces and canonizes Dramatic Literature, and inscribes a fundamental denial of the performance artefact. In determining eligibility for canonization, the valorization of the written text is decisive. Literary Studies accepts the novel, the poem, the story as texts for study, and sees Dramatic Literature as another source of stable, authored texts,[63] which are acknowledged with varying degrees of enthusiasm, as having another life in the theatre.[64] Drama, and its individual acts of theatre, is expected to conform to the bourgeois construction of 'art in general'. Denied particularity, art occupies a non-place, a transcendent elsewhere untroubled by issues of participation, power and silence.[65] Compounding this, the popular conflation of art and culture[66] positions art as yet another commodity for those of comfortable means,[67] and empties culture of its historical role and its radical potential.

Against this, the terms I deploy here, 'cultural production', or 'cultural work', suggest activities positioned in history, dynamic in their own time. They release drama from the bourgeois private sector, repositioning it in an expanded public space. The Romantic myth of art as the self-expression of a discrete and uncompromised individual subject, is challenged by positioning cultural production as a series of acts of communication. As the ultimate significance of acts of cultural production is heavily dependent on the strategies of interpretation into which they play, this strategy enables content/performer/audience to be read as a dynamic relationship. The historical task of dramatic artists is deliberately to place significant material before audiences in ways that invite engagement with its contradictions. Even when artefacts are produced out of socially radical intent, they may not necessarily play out as transformative interventions in the social order. Meaning may be denied – on aesthetic grounds, as in the case of Calypso Theatre Company's *The Business of Blood*[68] – subverted or even inverted, as the reception of Tom Murphy's *Famine* demonstrates. Joe Cleary's account of how, for bourgeois audiences, the human concerns of dramas located in past times 'come to be identified with the past, with a particular time and not with a social system that subtends both past and present'[69] is tellingly illustrated in Garry Hynes's experiences of audience deployment of conservative ways of seeing which reposition *Famine* as a play about 'them then', not 'us now'. She recalled her frustration at audiences' deflection of Murphy's socio-political critique by misreading the dramatic action as a literal narrative of historical injustice, rather than a poetic metaphor for contemporary shortcomings.[70] Some readings went so far as to negate the play's critique, by using its depiction of social injustice under colonialism as a pretext for inferring that the colonizer's departure had swept away all things colonial, including a social order divided on the basis of economics and social class.

Criticism, class and dramatic impact

Critical perspectives matter, as they structure public expectations of theatre, and set out limits for innovative practices in terms of content and form. David Nowlan's review of *The Business of Blood*[71] demonstrates the deployment of a pre-existing meta-narrative for drama, to align popular terms of engagement with the art form with points of view which serve and consolidate a commitment to an aesthetic of illusionism:

A mode of artistic experience that has as its most central characteristic a desire to (psychologically) penetrate individual experience: its primary appeal is to the emotions rather than to the intellect, desiring the audience's empathetic involvement with the events presented before them ... it has a closed form which implies a certain artistic autonomy, a self-validation; it prefers to regard the medium of expression as somehow transparent, neutral, having no 'point of view' of its own; language wants to be overlooked, effaced.[72]

Illusionist dramas may stage instances of individual dilemma or familial disturbance, generally within the confines of comfortable family homes and gardens, but they rarely take a presumed homogenous audience any closer to a critique of the underlying social meaning of what is presented.[73]

In Independent Ireland, depoliticized readings and 'versions' of Chekhov, which haunt the stage like a structuring *geist*, enable the local bourgeoisie to be erased, even as it is staged. Brian Friel's version of *Uncle Vanya* (1999), staged at the Gate Theatre in Dublin, demonstrates this, but not as well as his own Chekhovian *Aristocrats*, performed in the same theatre during the Friel Festival that same year. In these plays, Friel frames bourgeois characters by means of a type of eccentricity, shorthanded as Britishness in both production choices and audience reception. In *Aristocrats* the unfortunate Casimir is written and played as British – down to the hinted-at impairment of his masculinity as a result of experiences at boarding school. His sister's husband, Eamon, is the bearer of reciprocal signs of Irishness, opposing Casimir's eccentricity and suspect masculinity with drunken bonhomie and sexual attractiveness. Johnny Hanrahan[74] reads this as a way of refusing the existence of an indigenous bourgeoisie by setting out a stereotypical Britishness as their defining characteristic, and leaving the rest to residual anti-colonial sentiment. If it cannot be figured as Irish, then it follows that the bourgeoisie, in important ways, does not actually exist in Ireland, and cannot be held accountable for its own social impact in the sites opened up by drama. In Barthes's phrase, the 'exnominating operation'[75] is completed in the act of representation itself.

Suppression of class differences by such means was a deliberate cultural strategy in De Valera's neo-colonial project, whose official 'nationalism proclaimed the unity of the classes in the common name of Irishman.'[76] Its effects were such that Gibbons, Lee and Pilkington all argue that, until the mid-1980s it was scarcely possible, outside the academy or the concrete experiences of excluded persons, even to discuss the dynamics of class-based power relations in Ireland. Class belonged to the colonial past, and could be represented there, as evidence of an ancient inequity, banished at last. In the face of this received wisdom, Tom Murphy's *Famine* (1968) applies epic, anti-illusionist dramaturgy to represent and critique neo-colonial class relations as a reiteration of colonial relations of domination. Anti-illusionist practices[77] begin from the proposition that the world is knowable, but that events and experiences are represented in forms which are always already distorted by their positioning in dominant ideological constructions. In anti-illusionism, content is offered for demystification, in aesthetic forms which seek to enable critique. Anti-illusionist artefacts provoke dialogical relationships in which spectators are re-imagined as readers, making and interpreting connections between dramatic worlds, their own lived experiences and future aspirations as participants in dynamic social and cultural processes.

Accordingly, the historical famine functions throughout *Famine* as a metaphor for the depredations of 1960s neo-colonialism.[78] In 'The Relief Committee' episode, members of the native *gombeen* class are depicted in conference with the familiar villains of the 1840s, the landlord and his agent. The Roman Catholic clergy, passionate advocates of famine relief, are agents of popular quietism. By means of ironic juxtaposition – a powerful tool of Brechtian anti-illusionism – 'The Relief Committee' produces insights into the relations between dominant colonialism and emergent neo-colonialism, by exposing the contradictions which emerge when all present are lined up side by side to consider 'the people'. Garry Hynes's 1993 production further confronted illusionism by staging the members of the committee, not seated at a conference table, but standing face-on to the audience. Hynes's 'persistent search for the meaning of tragedy' drove her to push further the epic nature of *Famine*'s aesthetic, presenting a stage world in which visual signifiers produce semiotic collisions between the present, history and pre-history. [79] This approach to *mise en scène* draws attention to the fact that 'representational strategies are creative responses to novel circumstances and conditions,'[80] in this case, the need to counter reactionary ways of seeing, so as to enable questions posed in the fictional world to trouble the audiences' actual worlds. Specifically, and in sharp contrast to Friel's domestic concerns in *Aristocrats*, her staging of 'The Relief Committee' episode exposes not only the existence of a native bourgeoisie, but the locus of their relationship to the continuity of oppression: property.

Misreadings – readings closed to the metaphorical, which remain at a level of the literal, or the crudely symbolic – are culturally very costly indeed. Rather than positioning content for significance, misreadings cause its location to be circumvented, avoided, or ignored, as theatre-as-spectacle is assumed to be all there is to see, and its forms are avidly consumed. West's notion of representation as strategy foregrounds both the role of human choice in shaping artefacts and the positionality of representations in sites of contestation of meaning. Interpretive strategies speak to, and arise from, similar circumstances. Awam Amkpa asserts that 'there is no act of representation which is not also an act of interpretation,'[81] and it is equally true that there is no act of interpretation which is not also an act of representation. The work of theatre practitioners is to load meaning into performance events so that readers may experience disturbance and contradiction when confronted by them. Drama offers multiple layers of signification, literal, symbolic and metaphorical. The richest dramatic experiences enable simultaneous access to all three, in complex, concentrated image-metaphors. This is an important theoretical point, and it is worth exploring by means of an example from a play central to my concerns, *The Wood of the Whispering*.[82]

Appearance, Irony, Substance

Fintan O'Toole credits Hynes and Druid Theatre Company with 'a long demythologization of the West ... through such great productions as *The Playboy of the Western World* (and) M.J. Molloy's *The Wood of the Whispering*'.[83] Molloy's play is set in 1950 outside the crumbling gates of a west of Ireland 'Big House'. The fictional world of the play parallels the actual circumstances of peasant communities in that part of Ireland at that time. Many small communities were in terminal crisis due to the disastrous commingling of economically-driven emigration, enforced celibacy and late marriage. The dynamics of depopulation are staged all the more starkly in the light of the protagonist's all-consuming desire to bring about marriages and social regeneration. The penultimate scene sees Sanbatch Daly having his friends and neighbours tie him to a tree as a madman. His performance of madness is a desperate personal intervention staged in order to force all around him to join a collective project to keep their community alive, and the eligible couples opt to marry rather than emigrate. Their decision to do so enables Sanbatch to escape incarceration in the local mental hospital. At a literal level, this episode appears as the resolution of a naïve dramatic narrative: a device by which a playwright who had essayed an unwieldy theme gets himself off the hook. It is instructive that influential critical discussion of the scene leaves it at that.

From my perspective, in what has been dismissed as a 'structural flaw' in the work of a minor playwright, *The Wood of the Whispering* anticipates by nearly forty years the deployment of a postcolonial aesthetic of disrupted realism in such plays as Dermot Bolger's *The Lament For Arthur Cleary* (1989) and Donal O'Kelly's *Asylum! Asylum!* (1993). It resembles the formal signature of a common postcolonial form, magic realism, a hybrid cultural discourse which exemplifies in its artefacts Edward Said's contention that 'in the cultural forms of decolonization, a great many languages, histories, forms, circulate'.[84] In a social order with a colonial past and a neo-colonial present, the crisis in realism emerges in its inadequacy to the task of staging popular desire. If the persistence of realism is an analogue for attempts to posit a stable social reality as imagined by a comfortable elite, disrupted realism manifests the urgency of postcolonial desires. Tellingly, this aesthetic emerges in a place and at a time which make it specifically readable as a manifestation of a consciousness Amkpa calls postcolonial, Said, liberationist.

The penultimate scene of *The Wood of the Whispering* is rich in metaphorical material, with Sanbatch as a pagan 'folk-Christ' volunteering to assume the role of one who has 'lost himself'[85] for the greater good of 'saving the village'. The final episode, a calm coda on the frenzy before it, also yields an example of the complexity of image-metaphor. Sanbatch, resurrected after his voluntary 'crucifixion', offers a quasi-theological meditation on the state of things past and the hope of things to come:

> **Sanbatch.** In the English Army, as soon as wan man is killed they enlist another. And that's God's plan, too: for each person that dies, a child to be sent into the world. But around here we reckoned we were men of brains, as good as God, and we reckoned we could do without ye, and God never said wan word only let us go ahead and ruin ourselves: and then Himself scattered all women and girls away from us to the ends of the world ... But maybe now He thinks we have enough good sense

got again, and maybe soon He'll bestow children on the village again. If He does, we'll have nothing more to want or to do, only wait for the death, and then die happy because we will be leaving room for more.[86]

Sanbatch is talking to Sadie – rescued from self-imposed withdrawal from the world by her impending, long-delayed, marriage to Hotha. In the final image, she and Sanbatch sit on a log among the ruins of Sanbatch's improvised camp. Outside the redundant gates to the estate of the departed aristocracy, they envisage a frugal future, both of and beyond this world. The speech, a complex and heady mix of utopian discourses delivered by a ragged peasant man to a ragged woman, amplifies the power of the metaphorical pairing of physical wretchedness and doomed, melancholic Irishness in the visual composition of the scene. In this moment of closure, then, the fictional world of *The Wood of the Whispering* appears to content itself with a fatalistic attribution of economic failure to the blind hubris of peasant manhood. At the level of spoken language, this culmination appears to evade the play's profound and multiplying accretion of ironies around desires it stages for subjectivity, community and national liberation. All these desires are human, and can be brought into being by human acts, yet they are consigned to ineffable fate in Sanbatch's discourse – the recognizable rhetoric of clerical quietism ironically issuing from a pagan Christ. Such ironies are manifest at a metaphorical level, in the pairing, and the persons, of Sanbatch and Sadie, redeemer and redeemed – saved too late, but safe at last.

Apart from his appearance, language, and his longings, which identify him with the pristine peasant of national myth, in whose presence difference is foreclosed,[87] Sanbatch's cultural co-ordinates are English. In a brief expository comment in Act One – making this an irony easily overlooked – Stephen reveals that his unusual name derives not from his father, but from a local landowner: 'Sanbatch is his nickname ever since he used to be training dogs for oul' Captain Sanbatch.'[88] Sanbatch's degraded state contrasts unfavourably with his quasi-filial security in the social structure of the colonial province: at least under paternalistic colonialism he had employment, and shelter. Compounding this, this defender of official nationalism's talismans of home, family and community aspires to a social order run according to the harmonious precepts of the divine, and made flesh in the macabre efficiencies of 'the English Army'. The evocation of the hated colonizer's military enforcer as a social ideal, as Sanbatch sits amid the debris of his apocalyptic performance, is no idle gesture in this metaphorical collage. The ghastly irony is that anti-colonial struggle has produced only a neo-colonial reality which must now be resisted in the very habitations and bodies of the people if their unaddressed desires for liberation – however circumscribed – are to have any hope of fulfilment.

The play's final scene is a complex reflection on the regenerative power of fellowship in an organic community: a practical enactment of the communal values invoked and betrayed by neo-colonial elites. When read literally, this scene plays directly into, and appears to illustrate the formidable political consequences of the Catholic doctrine of salvation through personal suffering, in rural Ireland. And yet there is no priest in this play, an absence of extraordinary eloquence, only thirteen years after the adoption of De Valera's constitution, in a time of unrestrained clerical power in the state and in rural Ireland.[89] Half a century earlier, Synge makes use of absence as structuration in his staging of Shaun Keogh's total conformity to the wishes of the never-seen Father Reilly, in *The Playboy of the Western World*. It is an aesthetic strategy that further complicates ways of seeing drama grounded in a metaphysics of presence, and marks the work as an artefact of postcolonial consciousness. With neither priest nor official depicted – the Guards who were to remove Sanbatch to the asylum are 'turned back', and never appear – the state and the church, regulators of civil society's transgressive desires, repositories and enforcers of homogenizing narratives of identity, community and national liberation, are absent. The decision not to represent them or their agents is consistent with Molloy's ringing indictment of neo-colonial elites in his preface to the play:

> For forty years Ireland has been free, and for forty years it has wandered in the desert under the leadership of men who freed their nation, but who could never free their souls from the ill-effects of having been in slavery. To that slave-born generation it has always seemed inevitable and right that Anglo-American plutocracies, because they are rich, should be allowed to destroy us because we are poor – destroy us root and branch through mass emigration.[90]

In contesting these circumstances, Sanbatch's strategy of 'losing himself' provides a precise instance of a resistant postcolonial consciousness, enacting Eagleton's insight that 'where human subjects politically begin, in all their sensuous specificity, is with certain needs and desires, yet needs and desires are also what render us non-identical with ourselves, opening us up to some broader social dimension ...'[91]

Enabling Audiences/Enabling Change

The pervasive effects of neo-colonial elitism in Ireland, its relationship to bourgeois culture across the Anglo-American world, and the dominance of conservative ways of seeing produce effects which neutralize producers and publics in their engagement with the content and meanings of artworks and cultural practices. As my remarks on misreadings suggest, audiences may produce conflicting – even oppositional – readings of the most hegemonic texts. Similarly, popular resistance to reading culturally critical meanings may reduce or disempower the transformative potential of plays that stage postcolonial desires for decolonization. If in this case, Sanbatch and Sadie are configured by conservative audiences as the benighted embodiment of peasants 'satisfied with frugal comfort,' the radical social critique in *The Wood of the Whispering*, which I set out here, may not emerge in the theatre. The high cultural stakes laid down in a moment of theatre require some consideration of issues arising on the interpretation side of the representation-interpretation relation.

Outside of reputable examples of applied theatre,[92] there is little evidence of engagement with the quality of audience experience or the impact of reader perspectives on the formal choices which frame the art form for its publics.[93] This is not the same as suggesting that audience perspectives are ignored in processes of production. All theatre practitioners assume an audience typology, and create and frame their works to challenge, undermine or enlarge existing publics for theatre, perceived constituencies for ideas. Mainstream theatre practice attempts, for the most part, to increase the numbers of people attending performances. Even when the audience is positioned simply as a lumpen mass of 'theatre-goers', some working concept of who 'they' are informs the phases of writing, rehearsal, publicity, performance and criticism. In Ireland, I have shown that canonical critical accounts of stage/audience relationships during the 1990s emerge from and endorse a paradigm of authoritarian narration and passive reception: the 'fictional stage world' narrates an account of reality which is consumed, and whose encoded meanings are faithfully decoded by a homogenous mass audience.

Susan Bennett's dialectical negotiations, her 'testimony to the contemporary emancipation of the spectator'[94] refuse this construct, and open up the gulf between representation and interpretation as a site for critical attention. Virginia Nightingale amplifies this perspective on audience, in order to

> promote an understanding of *audience activity* as cultural production not limited to reception or to intellectual activity (like thinking, evaluating, etc.) but as reaching beyond into a performative dimension where the discourses of everyday life are enacted in a landscape scattered with monuments from the past.[95]

As Hynes's experiences testify, the critical potential of emancipated audience responses will not emerge spontaneously from persons or groups schooled in the ways of seeing that I have reviewed. They must be enabled by critical, scholarly, pedagogical and creative practices, as Wet Paint Arts so notably set out to do (Chapter 7). I advocate a reflexive representation-interpretation-representation relation that further refines both Bennett and Nightingale: images produced onstage are the outcomes of hermeneutic struggle on the part of the cultural workers involved in the play; in their hermeneutic acts, audiences produce potentially powerful ideal representations of human worlds.

Drama, and the acts of theatre in which it is embodied, occupies liminal spaces of flux, uncertainty and indeterminacy. Haunted by multiple futures striving to emerge, it stages contests between versions of the past, and exhibits them in an uneasy present. Fully engaged, it offers critical lenses to the social order, through which to regard the play of its own images of itself and others. In the acts of fictionalized near-selves, it others the stablized subject to itself and exposes the contingency and incompleteness of lived experience. Wole Soyinka reads theatre's liminal 'Fourth Stage', not as a site, but as a precarious crossing, suspended over a chasm: 'to dare transition is the ultimate test of the human spirit, and Ogun – god of theatre – is the first protagonist of the abyss.'[96] Thus conceptualized, the location of critical cultural work is a perilous border territory, an idea that speaks urgently to Kirby's concern to reinvigorate civil society, in the interests of a vigorous, plural cultural democracy. It speaks in a voice which, I suggest, is inflected by Lloyd's concern not to project onto a creature of modernity the power to undo modernity's projects,[97] by the imperative to 'live through'[98] historical contradiction, and by the acknowledgement that human agency is 'always enacted under circumstances not of one's choosing.'[99] However powerful the caveats, one of the principal advantages of civil society is that it is an available construct. Radicalized as the location of culture – a creative interchange of counter-consciousness and progressive critical purpose – it may well emerge as the transformative site for which Kirby argues.

Conclusion

This chapter reviews the marginalized position of critical cultural production in Independent Ireland, locating it in structural failures at the moment of 'founding and forging' the successor state. Lloyd's play on the pejorative meaning of 'forging'[100] seems suggestive here, as many creative persons experienced daily life in the successor state as an extended fraud. Just as the successor state sought to confine cultural work within acceptable limits, it set about deploying impediments to critical interpretation of cultural work. These included the sponsorship of narrow academic and popular critical models, which served a generalized resistance to critique among the national bourgeoisie. I have reviewed those tropes which tend to define theatre in popular public discourse, and recommend a more sophisticated postcolonial relation of representation-interpretation-representation, as a reading strategy responsive to West's notion of 'prophetic criticism.' I assert the primacy of the performance event over the written script, and a dissenting, democratic preference for cultural work over privatized artistic creation. I suggest that ways of understanding audience deserve critical attention, in enabling theatre's potential as a cultural site in which urgent political projects identified in Chapter Two may be initiated. I conclude by bringing the sociological construct of civil society into dialogue with Wole Soyinka's account of the transformative, utopian potential of liminal spaces. I suggest that that dialogue has the potential to radicalize Kirby's advocacy of, and mitigate Lloyd's reservations on, the transformative capacity of civil society. Chapter Four offers close readings of plays from the early twentieth century, all of which had revivals in Dublin in the 1990s, relating them to the cultural projects of anti-colonial nationalism from which they emerged, and to the neo-colonial society in which they are re-presented.

1 Edward Said, 'Afterword: Reflections on Ireland and Postcolonialism', in Clare Carroll and Patricia King eds, *Ireland and Postcolonial Theory* (Cork University Press, 2003): 182.

2 Ben Agger, *Cultural Studies as Critical Theory* (Falmer, 1992): 193.

3 Benedict Anderson, *Imagined Communities* (Verso, 1993).

4 'The actual substance and meaning of a "national view" or "national life" were integrally related to the official conceptualization of the Irish nation, territory and state.' Hayward, Katy, *Irish Nationalism and European Integration: the official redefinition of the island of Ireland* (Manchester University Press, 2009): 93

5 Renato Constantino, cited in Istvan Mészáros, 'Introduction' to *Renato Constantino: Neo-colonial Identity and Counter-consciousness*, ed. Istvan Mészáros (Merlin Press, 1978): 23.

6 Hayward, (2009): 64.

7 Bernard Shaw, "Preface for Politicians", *John Bull's Other Island*, (Penguin, 1984): 19.

8 Paul Durcan, 'Making love outside Áras an Uachtaráin', *The Selected Paul Durcan*, ed. Edna Longley (Blackstaff Press, 1982): 85.

9 Áras an Uachtaráin is the official residence of the President of Ireland.

10 Durcan (1982).

11 Dermot Bolger, *Internal Exiles* (Dolmen, 1986).

12 Ibid. 31-55.

13 Ibid. 38.

14 Ibid.

15 Ibid. 41

16 Ibid. 41.

17 Richard Breen, Damian Hannan, David B. Rottman, and Christopher T. Whelan, eds, *Understanding Contemporary Ireland: State, Class and Development in the Republic of Ireland* (Gill & MacMillan, 1990): 20.

18 Flann O'Brien, *At Swim-two-birds* (Penguin, 1968).

19 Flann O'Brien, *The Third Policeman* (Picador, 1974).

20 Flann O'Brien, 'A Bash in the Tunnel', *Stories and Plays* (Paladin, 1991).

21 Ibid. 173.

22 O'Nolan was a civil servant in the Department of Transport and Power, with intimate knowledge of *Córas Iompair Éireann* [The National Transport Company].

23 Kirby records that, on returning to Ireland in 1999, the poet Michael O'Loughlin 'found that artists were valued not for their artistic achievements but for their financial ones and he wondered at the dismissal of the critical voice in public discourse.' Kirby, Peadar, *The Celtic Tiger in Distress: Growth with Inequality in Ireland* (Palgrave, 2002): 158.

24 Frantz Fanon, *The Wretched of the Earth* (New York: Black Cat Books, 1968).

25 'What is emerging is a global social structure cutting across national boundaries which is conceived of as a three-tier arrangement of concentric circles representing the elites, the contented and the marginalised.' Kirby (2002): 198.

26 It was notable, as economic crisis followed the collapse of the Celtic Tiger economy, that phrases such as 'we all have a part to play' began to proliferate in official and popular discourse. Michael Cronin comments, 'Such individualization of problems has the dual advantage of concealing the real power differentials between different players in society ("you have just as much responsibility as Tony O'Reilly") and making politics a continuation of market forces where what matters most is consumer preference and the sustainability of Brand Ireland.' Cronin, Michael, 'Active Citizenship and Its Discontents', *Power, Dissent and Democracy: civil society and the state in Ireland*, Ó Broin, Deiric, and Peadar Kirby eds (Dublin: A&A Farmer, 2008): 66-67.

27 'The term 'Art' as we now understand it began to take on its modern meaning in the Eighteenth century: an original creation, produced by an individual gifted with genius. This creation is primarily an object of aesthetic beauty, separate from everyday life.' Mary A. Staniszewski, *Believing is Seeing: Creating the Culture of Art* (Penguin, 1995): 111.

28 Playwright, Donal O'Kelly, quoted in Victoria White, 'Desperately Seeking Asylum', *The Irish Times*, 26 August 1994: 15.

29 See, for example, Edward Said, 'Yeats and Decolonization', *Nationalism, Colonialism and Literature*, ed. Seamus Deane (University of Minnesota, 1990): 69-95.

30 Ibid.76.

31 Joseph Cleary, '"Misplaced Ideas"?: Colonialism, Location and Dislocation in Irish Studies', in Carroll and King eds (2003): 18.

32 Eagleton, Terry, 'Nationalism: irony and commitment' in Deane ed. (1990): 38.

33 See his discussion of debates over the relationship between culture and nationalist politics in P.J. Mathews, 'A Battle of Two Civilizations?: D.P. Moran and William Rooney', *The Irish Review* 29.3 (Autumn 2002): 22-37. Hayward (2009) identifies three strands of pro-independence nationalism – "unionist", "constitutional" and "republican" in late nineteenth-century Ireland (64-79).

34 In 1903, 'as the (Irish National Theatre) Society went into rehearsals for the autumn season, Dudley Digges and Máire Quinn, supported by Maud Gonne, set up a rival company, calling itself the Cumann na nGaedheal Theatre Company.' Welch, Robert, *The Abbey Theatre 1899-1999: Form & Pressure* (Oxford University Press, 2003): 24.

35 Ibid. 25.

36 Cornel West, 'The New Cultural Politics of Difference' *Out There: Marginalization and Contemporary Cultures*, Ferguson, Russell, Martha Gever, Trinh T. Minh-ha, and Cornel West, eds (MIT Press, 1992): 31.

37 An example of what Lawson and Tiffin characterise as 'a spurious claim (or capitulation) to "native" authenticity, [which] has the effect of itself foreclosing on difference.' Tiffin, Chris, and Alan Lawson eds, *De-scribing Empire: Post-colonialism and textuality* (Routledge, 1994): 232-233.

38 Morash acknowledges a body of plays in which a utopian future 'is mourned before it arrived', in Morash, Christopher, '"Something's Missing": Theatre and The Republic of Ireland Act', *Writing in the Irish Republic: Literature, Culture, Politics 1949-1999*, ed. Ray Ryan (Macmillan, 1999): 71.

39 '*En Attendant Godot* ... was written between 9 October 1948 and 28 January 1949.' Roche, Anthony, *Contemporary Irish Drama: from Beckett to McGuinness* (Gill & Macmillan, 1994): 41.

40 Beckett, Samuel, *Waiting for Godot* (Faber and Faber, 1975): 9.

41 Anthony Roche, (1994): 37.

42 Hayward (2009): 98.

43 Morash (1999): 71.

44 M.J. Molloy, *The Wood of the Whispering, Selected Plays of M.J. Molloy*, ed. Robert O'Driscoll (Colin Smythe, 1998): 113-177.

45 Hayward (2009): 97.

46 Molloy, 'Preface', O'Driscoll ed. (1998): 111-112.

47 Cleary, Joseph, 'Modernization and Aesthetic Ideology in Contemporary Irish Culture', in Ryan ed. (1999): 106.

48 De Valera regularly reminded the public, and his political opponents, of his revolutionary credentials: 'I, therefore, am holding to this policy, first of all, because if I was the only man in Ireland left of those in 1916 – as I was senior officer left – I will go down in that creed to my grave.' Cited in Fanning, Ronan, *Independent Ireland* (Helicon, 1983): 7.

49 See the discussion of 'The Revolution of 1958' in Breen et al (1990): 38-40.

50 Tom Murphy and Noel O'Donoghue, *On the Outside*, Tom Murphy, *Plays 4* (Methuen, 1989): 165-192. The play was written in 1959, but not professionally produced until 1974. See Fintan O'Toole, *Tom Murphy: The Politics Of Magic* (Dublin: New Island, 1994): 47.

51 Tom Murphy, *Famine* (Gallery Press, 1984).

52 'No matter where (the play) opens, when the lights go down for the opening blackout I still see those makeshift venues in the Dublin suburbs on winter's evenings.' Bolger, Dermot, 'Author's Note' *A Dublin Quartet* (Penguin, 1992): x.

53 Cleary (1999): 126-7.

[54] David Cairns, and Shaun Richards, *Writing Ireland: Colonialism, Nationalism and Culture* (Manchester University Press, 1988): 153-4.

[55] See Awam Amkpa, *Drama and Postcolonial Desires* (Routledge, 2004): 12-13.

[56] Ibid. 13.

[57] Jocelyn Clarke, '(Un)critical conditions', *Theatre Stuff: Critical Essays on Contemporary Irish theatre*, ed., Eamonn Jordan (Carysfort Press, 2000): 98.

[58] Ibid. 99.

[59] David Nowlan, *The Irish Times*, 10 May 2000.

[60] Edward Said, , 'Yeats and Decolonisation' Deane ed. (1990): 83.

[61] Contributing to a public discussion on *The Arts Plan 1995-1997,* attended by the author, Luke Gibbons pointed out that it is one thing to develop new forms, or to refigure existing works of art, and another thing entirely to consider how they may be read by popular audiences. (Gate Theatre, Dublin, October 1995).

[62] Bill Ashcroft, 'Postcoloniality and the future of English',*Understanding Post-Colonial Identities: Ireland, Africa and the Pacific*, ed. Dele Layiwola (Ibadan: Sefer Books, 2001): 8.

[63] Niall McMonagle, writing on the new Leaving Certificate English syllabus, lists a series of literary texts, including novels, non-fiction 'and Frank McGuinness's play *Someone Who'll Watch Over Me*', McMonagle, Niall, 'Shiny new texts and new ideas ...' *The Irish Times Weekend*, 26 June 1999.

[64] Christopher Murray asserts the primacy of Dramatic Literature, in differentiating between drama as 'the creation of texts for performance' and theatre, 'the formation of the means of production and conditions of reception of drama', Murray, Christopher, *Twentieth-century Irish Drama: mirror up to nation* (Manchester University Press, 1997): 3.

[65] A report entitled 'Wexford film director has major win in Galway' exemplifies the flight from particularity - and from meaning - which this institutionalises: *Buskers* tells the story of the battle between an Irish boy and a young Romanian immigrant to secure a begging space at a Dublin train station ... it raises the issue of immigrants *the world over and the marked lack of charity often shown to refugees in society. Wexford People*, 26 July 2000 (my emphasis).

[66] 'The most widespread use (of the word culture is as an) independent and abstract noun which describes the works of intellectual and especially artistic activity.' Raymond Williams, *Keywords: A Vocabulary of Culture and Society* (Fontana, 1989): 90.

[67] '(Art) remains a leisure-time activity for a relatively circumscribed population.' Staniszewski (1995): 288.

[68] See David Nowlan, 'Polemic driven to a foregone conclusion', *The Irish Times*, 15 September 1995.

[69] Cleary (1999): 115.

[70] Garry Hynes, in conversation with the author, 24 August, 1994.

[71] David Nowlan, 'Polemic driven to a foregone conclusion', *The Irish Times*, 15 September 1995. This review, and Fintan O'Toole's response to it, is discussed in Chapter 7.

[72] Martin Walsh, *The Brechtian Aspect of Radical Cinema* (London: BFI, 1981): 11-12.

[73] 'The bourgeoisie has obliterated its name in passing from reality to representation.' Roland Barthes, *Mythologies* (Paladin, 1980): 137-8.

[74] Johnny Hanrahan is artistic director of Meridian Theatre Company, Cork. He made this point in conversation about the difference between Friel's representations and his and John Browne's staging of the Cork bourgeoisie in their critique of Celtic Tiger morality, *Craving* (1998).

[75] Barthes (1980): 138.

[76] O'Toole, (1994b): 37-38.

[77] 'The aesthetic position which Eisenstein, Brecht and Godard hold in common is a hostility to illusionism'. Walsh (1981): 11.

[78] Garry Hynes, in conversation with the author, 24 August, 1994, cited the costume and set design of her Abbey production (1993) as an example of meeting audience aversion to meaning head on.

[79] Wole Soyinka, *Myth, Literature and the African World* (Canto, 1995): 140.

[80] West (1991): 31.

[81] Amkpa, in conversation with the author, Massachussetts, 12 August 1999.

[82] Molloy (1998b): 109-177.

[83] Fintan O'Toole, 'The Leenane Trilogy' *Critical Moments: Fintan O'Toole on Modern Irish Theatre*, eds, Furay, Julia and Redmond O'Hanlon (Carysfort Press, 2003): 181.

[84] Said (1990): 86.

[85] This is the suggestive vernacular phrase used to denote madness used throughout the play. It has some resonance with ideas of subjectivity as self-actualisation under neo-colonial conditions.

[86] Molloy (1998b): 176-7.

[87] See Chris Tiffin and Alan Lawson, eds, *De-scribing Empire: Post-colonialism and textuality* (Routledge, 1994): 232-233.

[88] Molloy (1998): 121.

[89] For a play which thematises the lives, persons and power of the Catholic clergy in late 1930s Ireland, see Carroll, Paul Vincent, *Shadow and Substance* (Whitefish, Montana: Kessinger Publishing, 2005).

[90] Molloy (1998a): 111.

[91] Terry Eagleton, 'Nationalism: Irony and Commitment', ed. Deane (1990): 37-38.

92 This category includes theatre for development, youth theatre, theatre in education and community theatre projects. Outreach programmes tend to concentrate on deeper engagement with what the producing house would do in any case.

93 See my discussion of Wet Paint Arts for an example of how formal innovation around audience/content relations and intention to social praxis forms a fault-line in Irish theatre practices since the mid-1980s. Merriman, Vic, 'Centring the Wanderer: Europe as Active Imaginary in Contemporary Irish Theatre' *Irish University Review* 27. 1 (1997): 166-181.

94 Susan Bennett, *Theatre Audiences: Toward a Theory of Production and Reception* (Routledge, 1990): 186.

95 Virginia Nightingale, *Studying Audiences: The Shock of the Real* (Routledge, 1996): xi. My emphasis.

96 Soyinka (1995): 158.

97 A cautionary stance summarised by Lorde: 'For the master's tools will never dismantle the master's house. They may allow us temporarily to beat him at his own game, but they will never enable us to bring about genuine change.' Lorde, Audre, *Sister Outsider,* (Berkeley: University of Berkeley Press, 1984): 100.

98 According to Terry Eagleton, Marx's work is characterised by the 'belief that to undo ... alienation, you had to go, not around class, but somehow all the way through it and out the other side.' Eagleton, Deane ed. (1990): 23.

99 West (1991): 31.

100 David Lloyd, *Anomalous States: Irish Writing in the Post-colonial Moment* (Dublin: Lilliput Press , 1993).

4 | Intranational Problematics: staging the anti-colonial moment

Irish drama's claim to social significance rests on the pledge that in acts of theatre something more than box office, or the reputation of an individual artist, is at stake. Theatre is part of a broader cultural conversation about who 'we' are, how 'we' are in the world and who and how 'we' would like to be. Theatre is a powerful means of constituting and invigorating community. The questioning stance of dramatic artists is essential to the development of critical citizenship, without which no social order can remain healthy. Such views informed the discussions of those active in the foundation of the cultural movements of the late nineteenth and early twentieth centuries, which created the cultural conditions for the establishment of the Abbey Theatre as a national theatre. From the point of view of the nationalist movement, a National Theatre made sense insofar as it consolidated the anti-colonial feeling which was approaching critical mass in the country, and among Irish groups in Britain, the USA and Australia. Many plays current in the early-twentieth century clearly drew on and embodied anti-colonial desires crystallizing in the collective consciousness of an emergent independent citizenry.

The Abbey, however, set out to exceed its particularity as an organ of national consciousness, specifically when such a role was circumscribed by pressure to evangelize on behalf of a nation 'free, Gaelic and Catholic'. The early Abbey – pre-independence – is best understood as a theatre of the nation, claiming the right to continue to dream dreams, rather than a building-based monolith, dedicated to promulgating the pieties of a new order, for which Pilkington criticizes it, post-independence. W.B. Yeats's assertion of the primacy of artistic judgement over financial governance or political control of a state-funded national theatre is sometimes taken simply as evidence that Yeats remained an aesthete of sorts, a man seeking to transcend 'the greasy till' and 'the filthy modern tide'. In view of his commitment to the new state, continuing not only to live and work in a social order which had swept his own people away, but contributing robustly as a senator in its upper house of parliament, this explanation is plainly inadequate; hence my use of the idea of 'excess' rather than 'transcendence' at the beginning of this paragraph. Drama is the art form with people in it, and Yeats, Gregory and Synge created stage worlds populated by *dramatis personae* drawn from people actually existing in Ireland at the time. One of nationalism's principal cultural goals is to communicate to its own people their homogeneity. In the plays written for the early Abbey, that goal is critiqued. Synge notably staged people who exceeded in their lived experiences the limitations of anti-colonial myth-making – especially in respect of the idealized peasantry of the western world.

Edward Said and David Lloyd situate W.B. Yeats as an artist of Irish decolonization, in ways suggestive to my own analytical project. Said situates Yeats's work in the first phase of his sequential model of the trajectory of decolonizing movements, the moment of nationalist anti-imperialism.[1] Lloyd identifies a parallel phasing of concerns: 'Where the earlier writings are devoted to the project of founding and forging a nation, the later writings, in the wake of the Irish Free State's foundation, subject all acts of foundation to the most rigorous examination.'[2] This thematic development is reflected in formal choices. Finding in Yeats's earlier writings, that 'a symbolist aesthetic is inseparable from the politics of cultural nationalism',[3] Lloyd argues that the later writing, the locus of the critique of foundational moments, deploys 'a set of aesthetic terms which are profoundly antithetical to any tradition of symbolism.'[4] Lloyd's interdisciplinary analysis of Yeats's poetry accords considerable significance to performative issues in exposing a rich vein of indeterminacy in the work. His observation that 'performative presentation reduces what could be taken as purely mimetically represented ... to equivalence with the purely emblematical'[5] recalls Said's insistence that 'in the cultural discourses of decolonization, a great many languages, histories, forms circulate.'[6] I suggest that this hybridity marks individual works of art as well, and needs to be taken into account when attempting to understand the significance of works from what Amkpa calls anti-colonial, Said, nationalist anti-imperialist, and Lloyd the 'founding and forging' phase of decolonizing cultural production. I accord to artefacts a critical relationship to content, rather than a mimetic or propagandist one. Acts of theatre are especially unstable in their representations – which is one of the reasons I have sought to tease out the unsuitability of dominant ways of seeing as interpretive tools for theatre. I will now apply an elaborated sense of representational instability and an engagement with the indeterminacy of performance to what appears as Yeats's most thoroughly nationalist play, *Cathleen Ní Houlihan*. I suggest that, in performance, this play has the potential radically to problematize the relationship of the emergent petit-bourgeois class to the project of cultural nationalism itself. In short, in its dramatic action the play anticipates the emergence of a neo-colonial bourgeois elite and the frustration of the Yeats's hopes for the project of national autonomy which drove the movement for cultural nationalism.

Cathleen Ní Houlihan is set 'in the interior of a cottage close to Killala, in 1798'.[7] The play was first performed in Dublin in 1902, a time of intense nationalist activity in the wake of the Second Home Rule Bill, and with Wyndham's Land Act in preparation. The following year would see the establishment of the Irish Literary Theatre, and two years later, the foundation of Sinn Féin. The choice of Killala, landing site of a French expeditionary force in the year of revolution, 1798, establishes the play as a contribution to the consciousness necessary to 'founding and forging' a nation. In this, and in many other important ways, the play intervenes in and supports the nationalist anti-colonial project. The opening dialogue makes reference to the 'native' game of hurling, and to a rural community of neighbours, both powerful signatures of nationalist discourse. It is the eve of Michael Gillane's marriage to Delia Cahel, and his parents are discovered making preparations for the wedding. His young brother, Patrick, is also present. All three await Michael's return with Delia's dowry or 'fortune'. Michael's entry is followed soon after by a strange old woman. She enthralls Michael with her tale of unjust treatment in her own home, of strangers in her house, and of her need for young men to fight for the restoration of her lands. Said points out that these are powerful themes of nationalist desires for decolonization: 'For the native, the history of his or her colonial servitude is inaugurated by the loss to an outsider of the local place, whose concrete geographical identity must thereafter be searched for and somehow restored'.[8] Michael's decision to join the search has the mystique and finality of a religious epiphany. Delia arrives only to witness his leaving, in thrall to the Old Woman's seduction, to join the crowds rallying to the French forces.

It is tempting to read this play as it presents itself, as an explicit endorsement of militant nationalist insurrection. Many commentators, including Yeats himself, emphasized its status as a provocation to Irish nationalists to drive the British out of Ireland by force.[9] In the circumstances of its first performance, it is difficult to see its being read in any other way. What I want to suggest here is that such a reading depends on eliding the indeterminacy of the art form in performance, and subordinating Yeats's intervention here to Fintan O'Toole's proposition that 'the mind set of ... Yeats is that of a single world'.[10] That single world would play out in *Cathleen Ní Houlihan* as a unified organic peasant community transformed toward a decolonized utopia by the intervention of the symbolic figure of the Old Woman, the embodiment of Ireland herself. This reading is unsustainable when the dramatic meaning of the relationships between marriage, money and woman as developed in the action of the play is analysed. The dramaturgy also signals the radical disjunction of Michael/Old Woman/The Past from Michael's home, family and impending wedding/Delia/The Future. There is no complementarity here, and to point this out is not simply to note the human catastrophe of the bridegroom who will not survive his wedding day. The people we meet in *Cathleen Ní Houlihan* are not revolutionaries, because they have no material need for revolution. They are open only to the projects of the petit-bourgeoisie, all of which centre round land and the acquisition of personal wealth, frequently at the expense of near neighbours. Already, in the most heated moment of 'founding and forging', the dramatic action is pointing not toward the triumphant teleology of a nationalist project of liberation, but toward a fracturing of the national community around issues of property and inheritance.

Michael's entry is framed by two comments from Peter, his father. When Patrick sees his brother returning, Peter remarks:

> **Peter.** I hope he has brought Delia's fortune with him safe, for fear her people might go back on the bargain, and I after making it. Trouble enough I had in making it.[11]

This comment positions grudging acquisitiveness as a dominant force in communal life. This is clearly a recipe for division and hierarchy rather than unity and community. It also points to the father's explicit concern that the marriage produce, not primarily happiness and communion between two families – let alone two young people – but a hard competitive advantage for his own position. The amount in question, one hundred pounds, suggests at once that these people are more readable as persons of the early-twentieth century than of the late-eighteenth century, and inaugurates a kind of naturalistic aesthetic around them which proposes a close identity with original audiences for the play. The discussion of Patrick's disenfranchisement from property, as second son, and the possibility of 'making Patrick himself a priest some day, and he so good at his books'[12] draws attention to 'an Irish solution to an Irish problem' grounded in the accumulating power of the bureaucratic church triumphant since the 1880s, rather than the subaltern church of the 1790s.

After Michael's opening explanation of his late return, which takes the form of question and answer with his mother, his father speaks again:

Peter. Have you got the fortune, Michael?
Michael. 'Here it is.'[13]

This is followed by an action sequence of great significance, described as follows in the stage directions:

He puts the bag on the table and goes over and leans against the chimney jamb. Bridget, *who has been all this time examining the (wedding) clothes, pulling the seams and trying the lining of the pockets, etc., puts the clothes on the dresser.*[14]

Michael's response does not simply confirm that he has brought the money into the house. It accompanies and amplifies his performance of bringing the money home. His words direct the onstage gazes toward the money bag, thus centring it as an object of desire for himself and the family, and enthroning it centre stage for the audience's focused attention. Crucially, all except the father withdraw to a distance. These movements enable contemplation of the money bag, and draw attention to Peter's infatuation with it.

The stage direction reminds us that Bridget's table-clearing signifies the displacement of the young man's wedding clothes, the adornments of the passionate body, by the money. Marriage, in this community, is a matter of contracting possessions through the union of people. Peter's next action develops this meaning: 'Getting up and taking the bag in his hand and turning out the money'.[15] There are three distinct actions enumerated in sequence here. There is a sacerdotal quality to the rising from the table, the taking of the bag, and the turning out of the coins. The resonance of Christ's betrayal for thirty pieces of silver accompanies such action, and qualifies Peter's reverential actions with a disturbing ambiguity. While Peter's remarks over the money are framed as an address to Michael, they have a trance-like sense to them, which suggest the possibility of playing them as a disconnected monologue, a form of talking to oneself in the mesmeric presence of the gleaming coins. This performance choice would be supported by Bridget's next comment:

> **Bridget.** You seem to be well pleased to be handling the money, Peter.[16]

The sequence directly following the arrival of the money, and its symbolic displacement of the corporeal pleasures of the impending marriage, extends the domain of the money to the female body itself. Bridget was not accompanied by such a dowry, but:

> (*She is vexed, and bangs a jug on the dresser.*)
> **Bridget.** If I brought no fortune, I worked it out in my bones ...[17]

This completes the invasive dominion of the cash settlement at the heart of the marriage pact, and inaugurates the conditions for a radical destabilizing of the symbolism of the nationalist project itself. As the play develops we will be invited to accept woman as the locus of anti-colonial desire: the motor and symbol of nationalist narratives of decolonization. It is worth noting that Peter's relationship with the money overpowers his relationship with his family. The action which takes place, from Michael's entry to Bridget's comment on his absorption in the coins on the table, sees him dislocate from the human context in which he is represented, and enter a liminal space of pure desire. In this, the dramaturgy inaugurates a qualitatively different sense of doubleness than that signalled by the awareness of events outside the room, at once remote and other, and intimately connected to the family group. This exploitation of the simultaneity of the actual and the liminal is a hallmark of the presence of anti-colonial and postcolonial desires in dramatic action. It is even more significant in the action sequences from the Old Woman's entry to Michael's departure.

Following the episode described, in which the father's desires are mapped on to, and privilege, possession of money and its promise of property acquisition over love for a woman, Michael states 'The fortune only lasts for a while, but the woman will be there always.'[18] His desires oppose those of his father, and position the younger man as a passionate, romantic lover. It brings to a close the episodes staging opposing male views around the anticipated wedding, and confirms Michael as one who looks to the future for personal fulfilment. The closure of the exposition of this thematic is immediately signalled by Patrick's news of more sounds of cheering outside. This leads into the approach of the Old Woman to the house. Bridget makes ready to share some of the bounty of the wedding with her, while Peter moves to conceal the money. Michael's response occurs at two levels: the gaze and language. There is the mingling of his gaze with that of the Old Woman as she passes outside and '*looks at Michael as she passes*',[19] his deferential movement '*to make way for her*',[20] which has him take in her entry to the house as an observer, and, as his parents begin to speak to her, '*Michael watches her curiously from the door*'.[21] After meeting her eye, Michael states, 'I'd sooner a stranger not come to the house the night before the wedding'.[22] He does not speak again, nor does he move, until the Old Woman 'begins singing half to herself'.[23] Her song of a dead patriot draws him toward her and – literally – moves him to speak:

> **Michael.** *(Coming from the door)* What is that you are singing, ma'am?
> (*She goes on singing, much louder.*)

The Old Woman's song, and Michael's responses to it mark the emergence of a liminal space within the naturalistic setting of the cottage. It is a space of desire for the nation the Old Woman represents, and its language is that of the Old Woman, formal, closed, ritualized. Michael begins to inhabit this space, drawn to it by the power of the folk ballad, and the quality of the singer's voice.[24]

As the Old Woman withdraws into the suspended time of the national dreaming, Peter and Bridget continue to pursue the immediate concerns of daily life. They offer her food, shelter and money, all of which she declines. There follows a sequence in which the Old Woman eschews what is offered, while enunciating a powerful, all-consuming desire yet to be requited:

(Peter *goes to the box and takes out a shilling.*)
Bridget. (*To the old woman*) Will you have a drink of milk?
Old Woman. It is not food or drink that I want.
Peter. (*Offering the shilling*) Here is something for you.
Old Woman. That is not what I want. It is not silver I want.
Peter. What is it you would be asking for?
Old Woman. If anyone would give me help he must give me himself, he must give me all.
(Peter *goes over to the table staring at the shilling in his hand in a bewildered way and stands whispering to* Bridget.)
Michael. Have you no man of your own, ma'am?
Old Woman. I have not. With all the lovers that brought me their love, I never set out the bed for any.[25]

Michael's question inaugurates an almost incantatory sequence of question and response between him and the Old Woman, which leads to her saying her name, to her departure and to Michael's eventual rejection of Bridget's and Delia's appeals, and his leaving. As to the playing of the sequence above, the gaze of the actor playing the Old Woman is crucial to Michael's question and her answer, in which her desire is mapped on to sexual longing, and she displaces Delia as the object of his passion. In performance, she must hold Michael's eyes in hers as she intones her responses to Peter's offers of sustenance and silver. This develops the performative quality of her power over him, established before she enters, and enables the sexually charged response to Michael's question. As to Michael's attraction to such an old woman over Delia, Patrick's final statement, the closing line of the play, offers an insight to the actors:

(*Michael and the Neighbours go out.*)
Peter. (*Laying his hand on* Patrick's *arm*) Did you see an old woman going down the path?
Patrick. I did not; but I saw a young girl, and she had the walk of a queen.[26]

In the naturalistic world of the kitchen, the Old Woman appears to the parents as she must appear to the audience in the theatre, old and poorly dressed. In the liminal space opened up by her song, and into which Michael enters, she is already that idealized woman, carrying the full charge of sexualized attraction. In this way, the play's action suggests that, in the colonized social order, no degree of material comfort can displace the aching longing for decolonization. As soon as it is manifest, the liminal realm of desire exercises a more urgent domain over personal action than actual human relationships or the needs of the everyday.

Cathleen Ní Houlihan stages the desire for a nation in an allegorical female figure who turns out to be not the nation but desire itself. This figure is not recognized, or even seen as such by the majority of the people we meet in the play. She is manifest only to young men and boys. The older people are fully occupied with the struggles and joys of living in a remarkably stable bourgeois state with regular correspondences with Ireland in 1902, for all that the play is set in 1798.[27] The illusionist project of audience identification with realistic minutiae is carried through even as the visitor to the house exposes the lack which haunts Michael's apparently comfortable existence. Yeats offers two worlds in conflict – an Ireland of people who, within their own political economy are 'doing well', and a future vision, unrealizable unless radical dissatisfaction sets in. The abstraction of nationalist desire from the lived concerns of the mass of the people is suggested here. Far from naturalizing nationalist aspiration, *Cathleen Ní Houlihan* mystifies it, and maps it onto an elitism which inaugurates and anticipates the failures of Independent Ireland. Significantly, Bridget's taking second place to her husband's avarice is reiterated in Delia's displacement as the object of Michael's desire. Yeats was to observe, of Independent Ireland, 'That is no country for old men'.[28] This play suggests, also, that it was to become no country for any woman, regardless of age or material circumstances.

The dramatization of desire and corporeal passion in this play, and in other works of the period, as that which must be abandoned in the pursuit of the nation marks a significant detour in cultural nationalism away from human self-actualization. As Seamus Deane has it, nationalism pursued and ordained

> a liberation into a specifically Irish, not a specifically human identity ... In other words, Irish freedom declined into the freedom to become Irish in predestined ways. In that deep sense, the revolutionary impulse of the early part of the century was aborted.[29]

Among the proliferating paradoxes of the Irish nationalist project, the play's end draws attention to the deployment of images of monarchy as figures of its utopian, republican vision. The rhetorical playing out of this contradiction sees nineteenth-century nationalism retrospectively locate a longing for the Catholic Stuart monarchy in the republican spirit of the revolutionaries of 1798. This travesty is one of the markers of what Norman Porter calls 'Catholicism's attempted hijacking of all things Irish',[30] the colonization of Irishness by Catholic nationalism which produced the narrow, coercive tone of De Valera's Ireland. Its political manifestations endure in the fabric of the neo-colonial state which has developed since independence.

Yeats's penultimate play moves focus from *Cathleen Ní Houlihan*, the idealized female figure of nationalist desire to a location, *Purgatory* (1938),[31] where souls are said to languish, tormented for a time before achieving paradise. The commentary on the emergent neo-colonial state is damning before the play even begins. *Purgatory* is a drama of return to Lloyd's 'founding and forging' moment. It is a drama which finds an echo in Hamm's epithet 'Accursed progenitor!'[32] and offers a bitter reflection on a neo-colonial state cemented by De Valera's constitution, enacted the previous year. Suggestively, those objects and symbolic figures which resonate in the dramaturgy of *Cathleen Ní Houlihan* create the material of this dramatic dystopia. There is nothing now but the memory of a house, 'a ruined house with a bare tree in the background.'[33] There is a bag of money, for possession of which other considerations will be set aside. The certainties of marriage, land and money have been replaced by questions which answer themselves, and speak of social and moral collapse:

> **Boy.** What's right and wrong?
> My grand-dad got the girl and the money.[34]

The idealized figure of woman endures only in memory, finally mated with a lover who did not have to choose between passion and property. The central action, in which the Old Man kills his son, the Boy, with the same knife he had used to kill his father, occupies the same stage space as another liminal zone, the past present to the Old Man and the theatre audience, but, except for one terrifying moment, not to the Boy. In that zone, the father – recognized by the Boy as 'A dead, living, murdered man!'[35] – and his bride appear to re-enact the sexual act by means of which the Old Man was conceived. The Old Man's second sight produces no heroic vision of the future, although the woman he sees is just as compelling as Michael's vision. He can return only to a past, endlessly attempting to find meaning therein, even as he damns the choices made at that foundational moment. The fatalism of the closing lines of the play appears to confirm Said's view that while Yeats's artworks anticipate in certain ways the postcolonial moment, they cannot fully engage it, being focused completely upon anti-colonial desirings for decolonization, and the trauma of their frustration in the Irish Free State:

> **Old Man.** Her mind cannot hold up that dream.
> Twice a murderer and all for nothing,
> And she must animate that dead night
> Not once but many times!
> O God,
> Release my mother's soul from its dream!
> Mankind can do no more. Appease
> The misery of the living and the remorse of the dead.[36]

Purgatory stages an embodied retort to neo-colonialism's growing need for what Alice Maher would call, in 1999, 'an ornamental form of Irishness (as) the preferred image of ourselves.'[37] I argue that such a critical stance imbues the dramaturgy of *Cathleen Ní Houlihan* also, providing an exemplary instance of the historical role of the artist in anti-colonial and postcolonial circumstances: the duty to represent futures in critical relationship to the conflictual forces involved in bringing them into being. Yeats's penultimate drama plays into a new Ireland, which is figured as an impossible home. The persons of the play are exiles from the world itself, not to mention from Corkery's prescriptive markers of Irish identity: land, nationality and religion. Memory, the motor of liminality in *Purgatory*, is no longer the clear sequential narrative of the Old Woman of *Cathleen Ní Houlihan*. It is a site of painful, contested meanings, endlessly yielding, both in Yeats's vision and in the fabric of people's lives, the pain of thwarted hopes. As the fatal father/son relationship depicted stages the future as reiteration of past events and circumstances, it functions as an allegory of the sterility of energy diverted into neo-colonial reiterations of colonial relations of domination. A gloomy denial of the myth of constant progression – fundamental to the nation-state's modernizing rhetoric – substitutes for historical development the playing out of mutations of crises from an unresolved past. This is drama from the abyss, and even still, at the nadir of disaffection, the tortured occupant of Purgatory continues to cry out, demanding a better way. The desire for something better, which animates all anti-colonial movements, has been replaced by a cry to end historical time, frozen in the frustration of the aspiration to decolonize.

J. M. Synge's prophetic drama, *The Well of the Saints* (1905)[38] offers a carefully phased vision of relations between history and desire, between the coercive community and its recalcitrant near-selves. Far from staging the 'single world' suggested by O'Toole, this play depicts the incompatibility of the bourgeois fantasy of emergent 'national community' and the realities of its social project organized around property and the division of labour on class and gender lines. In the problematic mysticism of the Saint, the role of the Catholic Church as social engineer of a new national order, and its development as a bourgeois cultural project from which all but the appearances of spirituality have been expunged, is subjected to unrelenting exposure and critique. As Luke Gibbons observes, in his essay on Synge's *The Playboy of the Western World*:

> It would be wrong to characterize the clash between Anglo-Irish and orthodox nationalist versions of the west (in terms which suggest that) mere representations of Ireland alone were at stake. For these were, in Yeats' phrase, 'masterful images', and what we find in the confrontation between Synge and his Catholic nationalist opponents is a struggle over access to dominant ideology, to a controlling vision of Irish life.[39]

Gibbons identifies Synge's thematic concern in *The Playboy of the Western World* as 'the power of "the big lie", of images and representations, in transforming society,'[40] and this is a crucial concern, also, of *The Well of the Saints*. As has been pointed out earlier, Gibbons has lamented the lack of critical, interpretive discourses to complement creative, representative acts in Irish culture. *The Well of the Saints* is as close as you can come to a work which performs both functions.

The Well of the Saints[41] is structured in three acts – Autumn, Winter, Spring – which enable and demonstrate transformations in time and space. The structure corresponds to, anticipates and critiques the anti-colonial moment, independence and neo-colonial appropriations, and postcolonial critique of neo-colonialism and desires for decolonization. Act I (the autumn of empire) stages Martin's and Mary's longing for full participation in an idealized elsewhere, achieved through the central metaphor of the play, the restoration of their sight. Brokered by Timmy, the smith, the Saint admits them as members of a homogenous social group by restoring sight to them. Act II (the winter of neo-colonialism) stages an allegory of the fate of those dispossessed under empire in a unitary state, conceived and organized as an organic national community. It is set in hell – a hell of hard labour for Martin. He is estranged from Mary, who has failed in reality to live up to the attractiveness he imagined for her, while blind. He is bound to the devilish figure of the smith, Timmy, and distracted by hopeless desire for Molly Byrne, Timmy's bourgeois fiancée. The association of living female figures with longing and disappointment ironizes the seductiveness of Yeats's anti-colonial Cathleen in the light of Synge's wager as to how far a national entity achieved by the emergent nationalist bourgeoisie would depart from the decolonized social order posited in the iconicity of the idealized female.

Act III (the spring of postcolonial desire) returns to the site of longing of Act I, and stages the couple's banishment as the self-regarding homogenous community is consummated by the Saint, in the marriage of Timmy and Molly. Martin and Mary, blind again, refuse the Saint's healing powers, despite the aggressive demand of Saint and 'people' that they 'Kneel down!'[42] and accept the faculty of sight. The setting for Act III is '*Same as in first Act, but gap in centre has been filled with briars, or branches of some sort*'.[43] This gap is an escape route for the blind couple, no longer available to them as the neo-colonial successor state achieves triumphalist affirmation in the joining of the bourgeois couple. It is a closed society, guaranteed by the Saint's social power to include and exclude. He has become both totem and functionary of the will of the choric 'people', whose sentiments echo those of the smith that 'If you're a foolish man itself, I do be pitying you, for I've a kind heart, when I think of you sitting dark again, and you after seeing a while and working for your bread.'[44] Inclusion in the community of the smith's 'kind heart' means accepting the hierarchies he inscribes in the world he has, literally, forged, and taking your place within them.

The Well of the Saints is, as W.B. Yeats made clear in his preface to the 1905 edition of the play, a drama of desire: 'Mr Synge sets before us ugly, deformed or sinful people, but his people, moved by no practical ambition, are driven by a dream of that impossible life.'[45] This remark can only be read as a gloss on the representations of Martin and Mary, as the other persons depicted are driven by no such impossible dream. The audience for this preface would most probably have been drawn from the audiences for the original production of the play, and Yeats's mollifying tone suggests a level of discontent among them with Synge's representational choices. Indeed, Ann Saddlemyer refers to a conflict between Synge and the original cast of the play as a tension 'between the narrow nationalist fervour of some of the actors and his own determination to present the play as he saw it'.[46] While the uproar surrounding *The Playboy of the Western World* drew attention to Synge's affront to a nationalist project heavily reliant on the figure of the pristine peasant – and especially the peasant woman – the enormity of this affront is best grasped by pondering the fact that *The Well of the Saints* was staged only intermittently in Dublin in succeeding decades. In sharp contrast, *The Playboy of the Western World* was recast as a national classic, translated into many languages, performed internationally, and adapted by Bertolt Brecht for performance in Berlin directly before his death in 1956. It took the advent of nationalist Independent Ireland, the consolidation of De Valera's cultural project as the authoritative source of images of Irishness, and the achievement of such unquestioned hegemony by the church/state collusion to create circumstances in which this work might be framed for innocuousness.

The Well of the Saints actually anticipates the entire set of arrangements by which an elite imposes a fantasy of homogeneity on lived experience, in order to repudiate difference and silence dissenting voices. This play is distinctly at odds with nationalist propaganda, as its critical focus exposes the tenuousness of social solidarities extant in the country, and plays this out in a narrative of exclusion and banishment precisely of those who would 'dream of that impossible life'. The fact that the well of the title is located at *Teampall an Cheathrair Álainn* [the church of the four beautiful saints] on *Inis Mór*, the largest of the Aran Islands, is important in understanding the directness of Synge's challenge to nationalist myth-making, and the perceptiveness of the critique as a prophecy of social mutation under independence. The people depicted in this play are from Wicklow, in the Pale, or area of most profound and obvious colonial hegemony. Their acknowledgement of the Saint's powers, deriving from a well in Ireland's Western World, rehearses the nationalist myth of the western peasant, and his/her traditions, as repositories of Irishness. It is the home of Lawson and Tiffin's 'native subject locked in a prehistoric and hence apolitical past.'[47] As Gibbons points out, the idealized west of bourgeois nationalism is replete with 'sites of cultural survival, the sole remaining enclaves of traditional values in a world corrupted by progress and industrialization.'[48] Act III's representation of the well-water as a terrifying, coercive libation is an extraordinarily fierce commentary on the destructive potential of ideological tropes to limit longed-for liberty to Deane's formulation of 'the freedom to become Irish in predestined ways.' The desire for social transformation in human solidarity is a founding principle of Irish nationalism, and the animator of anti-colonial struggle. *The Well of the Saints* stages tensions within that desire itself, and, in the contest between actuality and aspiration, holds up to question the ability of Irish society, as constituted in the early-twentieth century, to deliver the human solidarities necessary to a democratic, decolonized social order.

The dramatic world of *The Well of the Saints* is a poetic meditation on possible events through its questioning of a popular metaphor – blindness as loss/seeing as restoration. The play's significance is not necessarily revealed at the level of the thematic, in that its most powerful effects are achieved performatively. The cloaking of Martin in the Saint's garb in Act I[49] prefigures his transformation into a full member of the community of sighted people. It also performs playful familiarity with the things of the spiritual world, and rehearses the myth of a peasantry whose nature is close to divine, so at home are the young girls with the trappings of piety and healing power. By Act III, those trappings have become coercive and fearsome. 'The Lord protect us from the saints of God!' prays Mary,[50] before Martin compares the threat of the approaching Saint and people to that posed by 'a hundred yeomen.'[51] This echo of the fugitives of 1798 hiding out in the Wicklow mountains can easily be played for a laugh, but, like many laughs in the theatre, it is far from funny. The mapping of the terrified blind couple fleeing their 'cure' on to rebel fugitives from what nationalist narrative posits as a high point of anti-colonial struggle is profoundly ironic. It demands that Saint and people be read as an oppressive force, repeating the depredations of the hated yeomanry. The fact that the historical yeomanry was composed of Irish people under colonial military direction amplifies the destabilizing implications of this connection. It is directly after this that Martin finds the landscape itself to be closing in around them in the new dispensation:

> **Martin Doul.** [*taking her hand*] Come a bit this way, it's here it begins. [*They grope about gap*] There's a tree pulled into the gap, or a strange thing happened since I was passing it before.[52]

The geographical recovery identified by Said as a principal animator of nationalist anti-imperial desires is realized in the completion of the closed circle around the precincts of the ruined church, and those who continue to dream are themselves ensnared by the very landscape itself. After they have been discovered by the wedding party on its way to church, Martin 'covered with dust, and grass seeds'[53] is addressed by the people. Content, tone and action are authoritarian, closed and brutal. The effect is clearly inscribed in the bodies of the old, transgressive couple:

> **People.** You're going wrong. It's this way Martin Doul.
> [They push him over in front of Saint near centre. Martin Doul and Mary Doul stand with piteous hang-dog dejection][54]

Martin pleads with the Saint to leave them alone, and not to attempt to 'cure' them again:

> **Martin Doul.** [*with distress*] Let you go on your own way, holy father. We're not calling you at all.[55]

As the Saint indicates a loss of patience with Martin's obtuse refusal to abandon transgression, and to take the steps necessary to enable himself to perceive the world as all others do, the blind man realizes he must give an unambiguous account of the sources of his objection.

> **Saint.** [*severely*] I never heard tell of any person wouldn't have great joy to be looking on the earth, and the image of the Lord is thrown upon men.

> **Martin Doul.** [*raising his voice, by degrees*] That's great sights, holy father ... What was it I seen my first day, but your own bleeding feet and they cut with the stones, and my last day, but the villainy of herself that you're wedding, God forgive you, with Timmy the smith. That was great sights maybe ... And wasn't it great sights seeing the roads when north winds would be driving and the skies would be harsh, and you'd see the horses and the asses and the dogs itself maybe with their heads hanging and they closing their eyes?[56]

The direction to the actor playing Martin, calls for a gradual building of emotional energy and performative power. This produces a crescendo on the image of hang-dog dejection, which the actors playing Martin and Mary have already been directed to communicate to the audience. In this moment, the physicality of the wretched pair is tied to beasts of burden and lowly curs traversing the road in permanent winter. After the Saint proposes a vision of 'the summer and the fine spring in the places where the holy men of Ireland have built up churches to the Lord',[57] Martin compounds his apostasy from God and nation:

> **Martin Doul.** [*fiercely*] Isn't it finer sights ourselves had a while back and we sitting dark smelling the sweet beautiful smells do be

rising in the warm nights and hearing the swift flying things racing
in the air [*Saint draws back from him*], till we'd be looking up in
our own minds into a grand sky, and seeing lakes, and broadening
rivers, and hills are waiting for the spade and plough.[58]

This is both a contest between ways of seeing, and a struggle for
the right to perceive the world in ways other than those offered by
the alliance of priest and mass of people. The heresy here is in
persisting to dream after those who have taken the ascendancy in
the community decree the dreamtime to have come to an end. In
asserting the primacy of desires worked through in idealized
imaginings, Martin's example draws recognizably on the elements of
what Said refers to as 'the primacy of the geographical (in) the
imagination of anti-imperialism.'[59] Martin's preferred option is to
return to the project of dreaming the nation – to erase the attempt
at nation-founding and to create a springtime of pure desire in
preference to a winter of thwarted hopes and hard labour. The
elements of his vision are unmistakably those of pre-independence
anti-colonial narratives, and they are responded to in unambiguous
terms in the new social order:

> **Mat Simon.**[*roaring laughing*] It's songs he's making now, holy
> father.
> **Patch.** It's mad he is.
> **Molly Byrne.** It's not, but it's lazy he is, holy father, and not
> wishing to work, for a while since he was screeching and longing
> for the light of day.[60]

This sequence plays neo-colonialism as the return of colonialism
itself. The dismissals of Martin repeat three enduring characteristics
of colonial discourse with regard to indigenous, colonized peoples:
they are subject to childlike fantasies, mentally incapable, and
sinfully reluctant to work. Mat Simon's contempt for song-making
draws attention also to the close parallel that exists between colonial
discourses and strategies used to marginalize artists and
intellectuals in bourgeois society. The staging of neo-colonial
domination as the repetition of the oppressive tropes of colonialism
is precise. The cauldron of passions fomented around the priest-
figure will return in very close parallel in Tom Murphy's great play
of 1960s Ireland, *Famine*.[61] Indeed, the Saint's banishment of
Martin could be inserted in its entirety into Murphy's play:

> **Saint.** [*imperiously to People*] Let you take that man and drive
> him down upon the road.[62]

The Saint, egged on by the increasingly frantic people, turns to 'cure' Mary Doul. At this, Martin begins to perform an outlandish obsequiousness, which causes the Saint to command his release. The critical action of the play takes place after Martin kneels beside Mary, before the Saint, in a performance of willingness to receive the blessing of the well-water, and have their sight restored:

> **Saint.** [*speaking half to the people*] Men who are dark a long while and thinking over queer thoughts in their heads aren't the like of simple men, who do be working every day, and praying, and living like ourselves, and with that it's my part to be showing a love to you would take pity on the worst that live. So if you've found a right mind at the last minute itself, I'll cure you, if the Lord will, and not be thinking of the hard, foolish words you're after saying this day to us all.
>
> **Martin Doul.** [*listening eagerly*] I'm waiting now, holy father.
> **Saint.** [*with can in his hand, close to* Martin Doul] With the power of the water from the grave of the four beauties of God, with the power I'm saying, that I put upon your eyes –
> [*He raises can.* Martin Doul *with a sudden movement strikes the can from the* Saint*'s hand and sends it rocketing across stage*]
> **People.** [*with a terrified murmur*] Will you look at what he's done. Oh, glory be to God. There's a villain surely.[63]

The Saint's self-serving statement of his own forbearance in the face of Martin's transgressions offers an early example of how the rhetoric of Christian charity will be deployed, not to set people free, but more fully to confine them in neo-colonial circumstances. Its tone confirms Martin's intuition that the Saint is, above all, performing an authoritative piety which depends on the ostentatious demonstration of his own acquiescence to complete its effect, not on Martin, but upon the witnessing public. This is emphasized in the direction to the actor playing Martin that he communicate an attitude of eager listening in his demeanour. As the people draw back in horror from his blasphemous assault on the can of well-water:

> **Martin Doul.** [*stands up triumphantly, and pulls* Mary Doul *up*] If I'm a poor dark sinner I've sharp ears, God help me, and it's well I heard the little splash of water you had there in the can.[64]

The double quality of the performance of listening is exposed: it completes the illusion of saintly authority and enables the act which will overthrow it. This places the dramatic action among Fanon's notions of the resistant quality of bivalent self-representations,

Bhabha's account of the transformative potential of engaging with
stereotype as strategy, and Brecht's identification of cunning as a
weapon in the struggle for revolutionary change. Martin's scattering
of the water is a profoundly revolutionary act, by means of which he
and Mary can continue to pursue their desires for the good life on
terms that enable them to pursue self-actualization.

The Saint's hollowing out by Martin's action is quickly erased by
the people. They have a compact with him, and what he represents,
which stabilizes their fantasies of homogeneity. His sanctity and
their force having been repudiated in Martin's revolutionary
gesture, Mat Simon mobilizes folk superstition as a justification for
expelling the blind pair. When the Saint deploys a carefully nuanced
response, the People act as one:

> **Mat Simon.** It'd be an unlucky fearful thing, I'm thinking, to
> have the like of that man living near us at all. Wouldn't he bring
> down a curse upon us, holy father, from the heavens of God?
> **Saint.** [*tying his girdle*] God has great mercy, but great wrath for
> them that sin.
> **People.** [*all together*] Go on now, Martin Doul. Go on from this
> place. Let you not be bringing great storms or droughts on us
> maybe from the power of the Lord. [*Some of them throw things at
> him*][65]

Each of the social interest groups onstage – the banished couple,
the bourgeois couple, and the Saint – is accorded a final statement:

> **Martin Doul.** Keep off I'm saying. [*He takes Mary Doul's hand
> again*] Come along now and we'll be walking to the south, for
> we've seen too much of everyone in this place, and it's small joy
> we'd have living near them, or hearing the lies they do be telling
> from the grey of dawn till the night. [*They go*]
> **Timmy.** There's a power of deep rivers with floods in them where
> you do have to be lepping the stones and you going to the south, so
> I'm thinking the two of them will be drowned together in a short
> while, surely.
> **Saint.** They have chosen their lot, and the Lord have mercy on
> their souls. [*He rings his bell*] And let the two of you come up now
> into the church, Molly Byrne and Timmy the smith, till I make
> your marriage and put my blessing on you all.[66]

The blind couple embrace banishment as a principled refusal to
deal with deceit and the betrayal of a dream of a better world
desired. Having lived through the hellish experience of sightedness,
they are more than prepared to live through the vicissitudes of the
road and rough countryside. In this commitment, they recall

Eagleton's insistence that liberation is achieved, not by announcing the end of struggle, but by recognizing and living through the enduring contestations which mark the commitment to libertarianism.[67] It is worth pointing out that Martin's and Mary's turning back on the community is not an individualistic gesture, opposed to solidarity. It is an act of solidarity between them and against a coercive homogeneity, deriving from a fantasy of society as analogue to a single, undifferentiated body. Brecht's observation that the smallest social unit is not one person, but two people, is movingly inscribed on their departing bodies.

For the circumscribed community which remains onstage, the chapter of dealing with difference is closed. The Saint, a hollow figure, deploys the ceremonial trappings of bell and blessing at the behest of a people wilfully blind to all but their own 'ornamental image of Irishness'. The people have neither dreams nor reason, but draw on coercion and superstition to bolster the authority of their chosen totemic figures: bourgeois social values and religious forms devoid of spirituality. Significantly, the Saint turns to the ruined church building as a truly secular figure, who will make and bless the marriage, not in God's name, but in his own. This shift is barely perceptible, but it marks the culminating acknowledgement of the fraudulence of invoking an early Christian mixture of nature and spirituality as a cloak for a remorseless project of neo-colonial modernization. In this light, the closing action of the play amounts to a chilling image of conformity and repudiation of otherness: The Saint *'turns to the church, procession forms, and the curtain comes down, as they go slowly into the church'*.[68]

I have read Yeats's work in the light of Said's account of his art as an engagement with anti-imperialism and the frustration of its ideals in the achieved realities of Independent Ireland. Synge's project emerges, in this reading, as one of prophetic witness, grounded in engagement with his own time and the contradictory forces at work within the decolonizing consensus. The issues raised in the trajectories of *The Well of the Saints* anticipate, not only actual historical events, but tensions between change and consolidation in emergent social relations. In extraordinarily clear ways, the play performs the appropriation of an idealized past as the motor of an inegalitarian project of modernization. Timmy's forge is a site of technology produced by the labours of those coerced by economic need, but capable of finer things. Timmy is both devil and damned, in Martin's Blakean vision of his future: 'Into his forge and be sitting there by himself, sneezing, and sweating, and he beating pot-hooks till the judgement day'.[69] The triangular relationships posited by Synge – between elite and hangers-on, producers and performers of legitimating narratives for those elites, and those outside or who refuse the dominant vision – have continued to animate dramatic representations since the first performance of *The Well of the Saints*. In that sense, the play stands as an exemplary work, and an example of postcolonial theatre. There is another sense in which the postcoloniality of the work is signalled: where *Purgatory* envisages history as endless cyclical repetition, *The Well of the Saints* enacts a contested linearity. History is staged both as choices made, and as choices which remain or reappear. In this sense, the processual quality of decolonization is enacted.

This reading situates Yeats and Synge as critical interlocutors of the utopian credentials of the nationalist project, and not the canonical founding fathers of Irish cultural nationalism in the theatre. As others[70] have pointed out, the identification of the Abbey and Peacock project as the foundational moment of Irish theatre is in itself problematic, as it erases both popular performance forms and the nineteenth-century dramas of Boucicault, at one stroke. That objection notwithstanding, the plays discussed in this survey rehearse thematic concerns and formal questions which still trouble Irish theatre in the 1990s, and all who participate in the public images and conversations which it seeks to represent and interpret. Key questions around equations of economic bankruptcy with moral squalor return again and again as a citizenry struggles to understand how the poor and the marginalized – including the dreamers – may be understood in the light of socio-economic forms owing more to bourgeois capitalism than anti-imperialist desires impose themselves, and are embraced in the developing political economy of Independent Ireland. The poor perform the historical role of the other, simultaneously desired as idealized peasants and despised as economic outcasts. Among the pietistic tropes of liberal dramas of 'man's inhumanity to man', they return time and again as themselves, as metaphors of state failure, as exemplars of persistent humanity in a world gone mad, and as figures of fear and contempt. The bodies of the poor are persistently inscribed with their own hardships and with the repressed desires of the neo-colonial elites. And the poor is a category of endless capaciousness. It can accommodate urban types such as Joxer Daly, travellers such as Rosie Joyce and monsters such as inhabit the dramatic worlds of

McDonagh's Connemara or Carr's midlands. Frequently participating in related discourses of exile and exclusion, the poor can also return as *nouveaux riches*, as in Tom Murphy's *The Wake* (1998). The continuing elaboration of allegorical relations between sexual desire for woman and money draws attention to the problems created when inexhaustible appetite is mapped on to economic power, and associated with the veneration of a feminized nation.

The cultural projects of anti-colonial nationalism set out to produce representations of Irishness conceived in opposition to Arnoldian stereotyping of the Celt as barbaric other of the Anglo-Saxon. Such representations have proved durable in Independent Ireland, and Alice Maher's castigation in 1999 of 'an ornamental form of Irishness (as) the preferred image of ourselves'[71] highlights their relationships to ways of seeing, and the constitutive power of debased cultural imagery in setting the terms of public engagement with imagery itself. There is a real and persistent problem with ways of seeing that has a highly significant impact on the efficacy of cultural production as transformative social intervention. Lee suggests that there is a need 'to think very seriously about the implications of the way in which visual images can be used to exert such powerful influence on our perspectives,'[72] and he links this question to the viability of democracy itself. Postcolonial cultural projects provide lenses with which to perceive such discursive formations, the ways in which they play out, and the significances of choices around representation and interpretation in engaging with contemporary Irish theatre. There are other lenses, some of which have value in discerning the artefact itself, but accounts of performance which privilege categories such as sense of place, ear for dialogue, fine observation, quality of star acting/ensemble performances, appropriateness of design and technical precision go no further than documenting the quality of theatrical spectacle. Such (un)critical perspectives – to borrow Jocelyn Clarke's formulation[73] – are wholly inadequate to critique what plays amount to as cultural interventions. What is at issue here is the meaning of these representations as constitutory events in the evolution of civil society. What is being played – about whom, to whom and in whose interests? What are its meanings, and their consequences?

Postcolonial critique acknowledges and seeks out diversity in meaning-making, a range of possible meanings rather than a single definitive encoding. Postcolonial perspectives seek and produce meaning in ways which provoke a radical complementarity with other ways of seeing. They may also oblige the reader to reformulate his/her stance toward not only the artefact, but toward his/her allegiance to received ways of seeing theatre. As to making theatre, one of the questions raised by the discussion of Yeats, in particular, and central to my critical project, is the ways in which postcolonial desire plays out on the Irish stage. It may be signalled, as will be suggested in relation to plays by M.J. Molloy, Dermot Bolger and Tom Murphy, by the disruption of the space of concrete representation by the image of the lack which is the locus of desire. It may also be signalled by the disruptive magic-realist image of what Said calls 'the birth of violence, or the violent birth of change ... that juncture where the violence of change is unarguable, but where the results of violence beseech necessary, if not always sufficient, reason.'[74] Such images are played out in murder and conception in *Purgatory*, and in Martin Doul's desperate scattering of the well-water in *The Well of the Saints*.

People and places in acts of performance are not fictions, pure and simple. They are fictionalized versions of real people and real places: sites for the poetic articulation and contestation of ideas, conflicts and events from or with resonance for the real world settled for by their audiences. They are not so much other as near-self, and this is reflected in audiences' tendency to demand of – and attribute to – theatrical events documentary accuracy and verisimilitude. It also accounts for the extraordinary vigour with which unfavourable dramatic representations will be denounced. In reading the relationship between Irish theatre and its publics, the enduring significance of early Abbey plays is underpinned by their uneasy relationships with propagandist narratives. Even a play like *Cathleen Ní Houlihan*, which appeared to Shaw[75] to contain a powerful distillation of fervour for the (Catholic) nationalist cause, contains within its first scene a critical stance which places it otherwise in relation to the emergent hegemonic 'we' of Irish nationalism. Gregory and Yeats here enact the role of dramatic artist as critical cultural interlocutor. In this way, and for this reason, the play earns its right to public attention. When Synge produced his 'Playboy' to inhabit civic space opened up by the national theatre, he demonstrated the critical vigour of performative images themselves. Far from demanding space to express or enunciate a rarefied 'aesthetic' position, the theatre of Yeats, Gregory and Synge inaugurates a conversation with 'Ireland'. These early twentieth-century works critique triumphant nationalism with oppositional, or more tellingly, ambivalent narratives and images of community. In so doing, they establish an ethical practice of staging autocritical social worlds and experiences which exemplifies the interrogative power of artists in society.

---

[1] Edward Said, 'Yeats and decolonization', *Nationalism, Colonialism and Literature*, ed. Seamus Deane (University of Minnesota Press, 1990):76.

[2] David Lloyd, Anomalous States: Irish writing and the post-colonial moment (Dublin: Lilliput, 1993): 60.

[3] Ibid.

[4] Ibid.

[5] Ibid.75.

[6] Said (1990): 86.

[7] W.B. Yeats, *Cathleen Ní Houlihan, W.B. Yeats Selected Plays* ed. A.Norman Jeffares (Gill & McMillan, 1991):3. It is accepted that the play was a collaboration with Lady Gregory, and that Act One, at least, was substantially written by her.

[8] Said (1990): 76.

[9] W.B. Yeats, 'The Man and the Echo', 'Did that play of mine send out/Certain men the English shot?' *W.B. Yeats: Selected Poetry*, ed. A. Norman Jeffares (Macmillan, 1972).

[10] Fintan O'Toole, 'Irish Theatre: The State of the Art', *Theatre Stuff: Critical Essays on Contemporary Irish Theatre*, ed. Eamonn Jordan (Carysfort Press, 2000): 50.

[11] Yeats (1991a): 4.

[12] Ibid. 6.

[13] Ibid. 4.

[14] Ibid.

[15] Ibid.

[16] Ibid.

[17] Ibid. 5.

[18] Ibid.

[19] Ibid.7.

[20] Ibid.

[21] Ibid.

[22] Ibid.

[23] Ibid.8.

[24] See discussion on Yeats and his sense of the power of sean-nós singing in Welch, Robert, *The Abbey Theatre 1899-1999: Form & Pressure* (Oxford University Press, 2003): 16-17.

[25] Yeats (1991a): 9-10.

[26] Ibid. 13.

[27] Lionel Pilkington locates the past/present ambiguity as effects both of the casting of Maud Gonne in the title role, and of her performance choices: For the spectator it was ... impossible to separate the role of the Poor Old Woman from the political activism of Maud Gonne.'

Pilkington, *Theatre and State in Twentieth-century Ireland: cultivating the people* (Routledge, 2001):34. In James W. Flannery's production (Peacock Theatre, The Second Annual Yeats International Theatre Festival, 1990), Olwen Fouéré's stylized movement, pale make-up, and searching gaze produced a simultaneous sense of agedness and allure which produced the effects described in this reading.

[28] W.B. Yeats, 'Sailing to Byzantium' Jeffares ed. (1972): 104.

[29] Seamus Deane, 'Introduction' to Deane ed. (1990): 13.

[30] Norman Porter, 'The Ideas of 1798: Do they have any meaning for contemporary unionism?', *1798: 200 Years of Resonance*, ed. Mary Cullen (Irish Reporter Publications, 1998): 109.

[31] W.B. Yeats, *Purgatory*, Jeffares, ed. (1991): 209-218. James W. Flannery presented *Purgatory* with *Cathleen Ní Houlihan* and *The Dreaming of the Bones* (Peacock Theatre, The Second Annual Yeats International Theatre Festival, 1990).

[32] Samuel Beckett, *Endgame* (Faber and Faber, 1976): 15.

[33] Yeats (1991b): 211.

[34] Ibid.212.

[35] Ibid.216.

[36] Ibid.218.

[37] Alice Maher, 'The Celtic Tiger has no Eyes', *The Irish Times*, 28 December 1999.

[38] John M. Synge, *The Well of the Saints, The Playboy of the Western World and Other Plays*, ed. Ann Saddlemyer (Oxford University Press, 1995): 51-94.

[39] Luke Gibbons, 'The Myth of the West in Irish and American Culture', *Transformations in Irish Culture* (Cork University Press, 1996): 35.

[40] Ibid.

[41] *The Well of the Saints* was directed by Patrick Mason at the Abbey Theatre (1996). The dramatic actions described in this reading derive from Mason's interpretation of published stage directions cited.

[42] Synge (1995b): 91.

[43] Ibid. 83.

[44] Ibid.88.

[45] W.B. Yeats, 'Preface to *The Well of the Saints*' in Saddlemyer ed. (1995): 55.

[46] 'Introduction', Ibid. xv.

[47] Chris Tiffin and Alan Lawson, eds, *De-scribing Empire: Post-colonialism and textuality* (Routledge, 1994): 233.

[48] Gibbons (1996): 23.

[49] Synge (1995b): 65.

[50] Ibid. 86.

[51] Ibid. 87.

[52] Ibid. 87.

53 Ibid. 88.
54 Ibid.
55 Ibid. 89.
56 Ibid.
57 Ibid.90.
58 Ibid.
59 Said (1990): 77.
60 Synge (1995b): 90.
61 Tom Murphy, *Famine* (Gallery, 1984).
62 Synge (1995b): 91.
63 Ibid. 92.
64 Ibid. 92-3.
65 Ibid. 93.
66 Ibid. 93-4.
67 Eagleton (1990): 23.
68 Synge (1995b): 94.
69 Ibid. 81.
70 See, for example, Lionel Pilkington, 'Theatre History and the Beginnings of the Irish National Theatre Project', *Theatre Stuff: Critical Essays on Contemporary Irish Theatre*, ed. Eamonn Jordan (Carysfort Press, 2000): 27-33.
71 Maher (1999).
72 Joe Lee, 'Commentary', *Nationalisms: visions and revisions*, ed. Luke Dodd (Film Institute of Ireland, 1999): 80.
73 Jocelyn Clarke, '(Un)critical conditions', *Theatre Stuff: Critical Essays on Contemporary Irish Theatre*, ed. Eamonn Jordan, (Carysfort Press, 2000): 95.
74 Said (1990): 90.
75 'Gregory recorded the reaction of Shaw watching a London performance in 1909: "When I see that play I feel it might lead a man to do something foolish."' Nicholas Grene, *The Politics of Irish Drama: Plays in Context from Boucicault to Friel* (Cambridge University Press, 1999):70.

5 | Hope deferred: Neo-colonial relations on Ireland's stages

The postcolonial readings of *The Well of the Saints* and *Purgatory* (Chapter Four) divine a movement in Irish drama during the first fifty years of the twentieth century, from prophetic witness in the early plays of Synge, to a heartsickness of hopes deferred in Yeats's *Purgatory*. This movement is readable as the teleology of what Amkpa calls anti-colonial, Said, nationalist anti-imperialist, and Lloyd the 'founding and forging' phase of nationalist consciousness. *Purgatory* stands on the edge of an abyss which opens in front of the Old Man. It is a theatre of broken dreams, a meditation on the moment of despair itself. In an important sense, *Purgatory* marks the crisis of a generation tantalized by the possibility of decolonization, and tortured by the coercive reality emerging in Independent Ireland. It is an exhausted lamentation for a battle won, and a war lost. Its force as a public event exceeds the particularity of authorial personality, and the problematics of what Pilkington has identified as a socially regressive tendency in Yeats's involvement with theatre.[1]

Edward Said's account of historical process under colonial conditions suggests the necessity, and ultimate inadequacy of the nationalist anti-imperialist phase, at the end of which stands the Old Man of Yeats's *Purgatory*. Said posits a development toward a more refined utopian project of human liberation, in a phase he calls 'liberationist anti-imperialist'. Similarly, as Chapter Two sets out in detail, Awam Amkpa sketches the aspirational teleology of anti-colonial movements as follows:

colonization—anticolonialism—decolonization.

Anti-colonialism is explicitly constructed as a decolonizing project. In practice, historical change provoked by resistance to colonization works out as follows:

> colonization–anticolonialism–neo-colonialism–postcolonialism-- decolonization.

Amkpa sees the intrusion of the neo-colonial moment in the aspirational teleology of nationalist movements as a development that reproduces relations of domination in the social order. In response, postcoloniality emerges as the characteristic psychic environment among the dominated, and the location of desire for the better life. My elaboration of Amkpa's historical trajectory

> colonization ←→ anticolonialism
> limited decolonization as anticolonial raison d'être
> neo-colonialism ←→ postcolonialism
> ongoing decolonization as utopian project

draws attention to a moment which corresponds to that which is reached in *Purgatory*: the point, not only of frustration, but of exhaustion. The Old Man will wander alone, not least because those who might have supported his protest are worn out by struggle. The majority of people will settle for respite from long sacrifice, which Yeats observed 'can make a stone of the heart.'[2] At such a moment, an emergent neo-colonial hegemony may find circumstances favourable to its consolidation. This is the moment of limited decolonization, where the exhausted enjoy a brief sense of historical progression in the wake of the colonizer, and what may well pass for peace in the absence of war. I suggest that this is the moment staged, but rarely acknowledged as such, in Samuel Beckett's *Waiting for Godot*:[3]

> Despite the fact that the effect of his work is to unsettle the very grounds of political subjectivity, Beckett has rarely been addressed in terms of the political implications of his work or even in relation to his historical moment.[4]

In concluding their survey of 'post-colonial theatre',[5] Brian Crow and Chris Banfield formulate an important question: 'Friel ... has emerged from and writes about a ... colonial and neo-colonial context ... Is it fanciful, then, to read ... the undisputed masterpiece of postwar Western drama (*Waiting for Godot*) in the light thus generated?'[6] I take up the challenge implicit here and in John Harrington's writings (547), contest the prevailing view of Samuel Beckett as a conjuror of avant garde 'no-places',[7] and read his work as a series of explorations of what, for Frantz Fanon, are the psychic wounds of colonialism.[8] In the spirit of David Lloyd's repositioning of Beckett's prose,[9] I suggest that Beckett's dramas are those of an Irish playwright engaging with the problem of being, and may be read productively as stagings of the frustration of desire in a neo-colonial state. That the specifically Irish stage world of *Waiting for Godot* was first created in French and presented in Paris is, in one sense, an exemplary neo-colonial contradiction.[10] Beckett's decision to live, like Joyce, in exile, has the quality of a lesson learned from Synge's experiences of the hostility which awaits the oppositional dramas of postcolonial critique in the home place.

For Anthony Roche, recovering the Irishness of Beckett's work has implications for reading the broader field of contemporary Irish drama itself:

> The critical act of placing Beckett in the context of contemporary Irish drama reveals preoccupations that he shares in common with other more clearly 'rooted' Irish playwrights: a rejection of naturalism and the linear plot of the well-made play as inappropriate to a post-colonial society like Ireland.[11]

This approach can be further developed by reading Paris, and places European, as they appear in the play, not merely as markers of an elsewhere defined as a kind of 'not-Ireland'. France also functions as a figure, a state of being in modernity, and evocations of France exceed the specificity of physical locations. References to France in *Waiting for Godot* function as metaphors for a modernity on which, in the 1940s, Independent Ireland appeared to have turned its back.

Beckett's tramps take up the structure and thematics of Yeats' *Purgatory* in significant ways. They are found by a bleak roadside, where a leafless tree embodies 'all the dead voices'[12] of past struggles, hopes and defeats. Act II will find them there again, with the tree improbably in leaf. They will be visited by the domineering, self-regarding Pozzo, and his incongruously named slave, Lucky. Two small social units endlessly enacting the dynamics of hopelessness,[13] with the barbarous binary relationship of master and slave the only available model of social organization. Only the tree and a wandering boy exist as apparently alternative, but actually complementary sources of life and lived experiences. The Boy is a servant of Godot, and testifies to his capacity for brutal and capricious practices, as oppressive as anything enacted by Pozzo.

The tree has potential only as an improvised gallows. The play's languages speak through the lyrics of permanent loss the endlessly postponed drama of the tramps' return to a better place:[14]

> **Vladimir**. We've nothing more to do here.
> **Estragon**. Nor anywhere else.
> **Vladimir**. Ah Gogo, don't go on like that. Tomorrow everything will be better.[15]

These *dramatis personae* agree that the abyss exists, but will busy themselves fashioning a version of existence along its edges. At such times, and in such places, better futures are taken always to be in prospect, even if the material conditions for their development are in short supply. There is no shortage of time to fill, 'no lack of void',[16] and there are formal strategies for filling it, such as repetition of stories, mimicry of those capable of acting on the world, and preoccupation with the minutiae of narratives and mundane actions. Didi and Gogo subsist in the afterglow of great events, in an extended present, trying things out. They are conscious of past heroism, even if its memory now seems inappropriate to their circumstances:

> **Estragon**. Do you remember the day I threw myself into the Rhône?
> **Vladimir**. We were grape harvesting.
> **Estragon**. You fished me out.
> **Vladimir**. That's all dead and buried.[17]

Even when, in Act II, with Pozzo and Lucky impotent before them, they are called upon to act, no action is possible:

> **Vladimir**. Let us not waste our time in idle discourse! (*Pause. Vehemently.*) Let us do something, while we have the chance! ... Let us represent worthily for once the foul brood to which a cruel fate consigned us! What do you say? (Estragon *says nothing.*) It is true that when with folded arms we weigh the pros and cons we are no less a credit to our species.[18]

In this sequence, the content of the rhetorical flow is counterpointed by the performance instructions given in the stage directions. Vladimir's call for urgent action is followed immediately by a pause. This gives way to a torrent of exhortation to do something, in the name of humanity itself, the net effect of which – Estragon's silence – exposes it as an example of the idle discourse which Vladimir decries. Estragon's silence is met by a lengthy temporizing on the part of Vladimir, culminating in a justification of inaction. The echo of Yeats's Old Man's rage in 'the foul brood to which a cruel fate consigned us' is neutralized immediately in the image of the human being as bystander,[19] arms permanently folded. With sights set so low, it is entirely possible to linger on the edges of places where battles were engaged, and find oneself 'a credit to our species'. These men are waiting for Godot, after all.

> **Vladimir**. We are not saints, but we have kept our appointment. How many people can boast as much?
> **Estragon**. Billions.[20]

The call to action shrivels into inertia and preoccupation with the banal. The high point of personal morality and courage is realized in the petty bourgeois comfort that one's timekeeping may be relied upon. In this moment of exhaustion, the time for questioning an emergent *status quo* may be recalled, but it has long since passed:

> **Vladimir**. We should have thought of it a million years ago, in the nineties.[21]

The occasion of the option to consider an existence kinder than one in which Estragon receives nightly visitations from faceless thugs as he tries to sleep in a ditch, is precise. The 1890s in Paris was a time and place where George Moore, Synge and others encountered modernity and began to fashion the tools with which to imagine a humanist future, installing social progress as a destination of greater moral weight than any other available option, including the achievement of a nation. It was in Paris that one encountered a breadth of vision which could comprehend, exceed and critique both the iniquities of imperialism, and emerging programmes of popular nationalism. The capital of modernity offered an unparalleled vantage point from which to regard future options:

> **Vladimir**. Hand in hand from the top of the Eiffel tower, among the first. We were presentable in those days. Now it's too late. They wouldn't even let us up.[22]

In the play's moment, 'fifty years perhaps'[23] later, the scale of the missed opportunity is evident. As things have turned out, Beckett's *dramatis personae* are not presentable in the locations of modernity. Neither does nationalist Ireland's glorification of an innocent, idealized pre-modernity nurture resources necessary to human existence in the twentieth century. This double exclusion is signalled in a chronic failure to deal with the measurement of time, and the impact that failure has on a sense of location. Time management is a key signature of modernity, but the tramps, who dramatize a society which has elected to attempt to thwart modernity by withdrawing from it, lack even the locational sense and interpretive facility of primitive humanity:

> (*Silence.* Vladimir *and* Estragon *scrutinize the sunset.*)
> **Estragon.** It's rising.
> **Vladimir.** Impossible.
> **Estragon.** Perhaps it's the dawn.
> **Vladimir.** Don't be a fool. It's the west over there.
> **Estragon.** How do you know?[24]

Unable to tell whether the sun is rising or falling, Vladimir and Estragon are stranded without physical co-ordinates. Their inability to distinguish east from west produces, in passing, a bitter comment on official nationalism's appropriations of the west to its ideological programmes. Only a fool would turn west and expect to find a future.

The Pozzo/Lucky pairing is everything the tramps are not. Vladimir and Estragon are different enough to be complementary, but in most particulars are roughly equal. The tramps are poor, Pozzo is a man of property, and Lucky a function of that status. It is worth noting that, in the written script, and in performance, Pozzo participates in the signs of Englishness, and is specifically aligned with the role of colonizer.[25] When he pronounces his servant's name, 'My Lucky!'[26] it sounds to Irish ears like lack-eh, or 'lackey'.[27] In performance then, the name exceeds the ironic idea that this abject creature might be fortunate in his station. It amplifies Pozzo's status as a source of authority, suggested by his name, which is Italian for 'well', source of water and sustainer of life itself. Vladimir learns, to his horror, that, while waiting for Godot, they have encroached on Pozzo's domain. There is a chilling reminder of the reach of his authority in the exchange that follows, in which Pozzo's offhand remarks suggest the controlling menace of the colonial master:

> **Pozzo:** The road is free to all.
> **Vladimir.** That's how we looked at it.
> **Pozzo:** It's a disgrace. But there you are.[28]

Act I presents the colonial relationship of Pozzo and Lucky as the intrusion of a residual social model into the permanent present of the tramps. Past its power to direct events, it continues to exercise an influence on perceptions of what is possible. In the dramatic world of the play, the colonial binary thus exemplifies Williams' formulation of a residual social structure. The tramps are defeated by time, Pozzo is a master of time, and Lucky its plaything. Pozzo possesses a watch, and embodies progress in his pursuit of schedules and forward trajectory and his 'professional worries!'[29] The contrast between his fidelity to a timetable and the aimlessness of the tramps underscores the nature of imperialism as a project of modernity. Vladimir's position is that of one for whom, with official nationalism detouring into the veneration of anti-modernity, further development is impossible:

> **Pozzo.** (*He consults his watch.*) But I must really be getting along, if I am to observe my schedule.
> **Vladimir.** Time has stopped.[30]

With coercive but efficient past structures no longer effective, and a bitter parody of what might have emerged from colonial resistance embedding as a new dominant, Vladimir's and Estragon's journey toward subjectivity is suspended. Pozzo's progress, even when he appears in Act II, blind, and with Lucky now dumb, is relentless. Though gravely impaired, the old binary retains the capacity to act in the world:

> **Vladimir.** What do you do when you fall far from help?
> **Pozzo.** We wait till we can get up. Then we go on.[31]

At the end of Act I, the colonial past embodied in the relationship between Pozzo and Lucky moves on, and the tramps are left to their own devices. The search resumes for strategies to fill the void of time and space, and Vladimir gradually begins to adopt Pozzo's vocabulary.[32] His already more loquacious and assertive personality mimics the forms of Pozzo's domination of Lucky, in his relationship with Estragon. This is a concrete example of Amkpa's account of the mindset induced in the colonized by colonial systems of education: 'to be is to be like; to be like is to be like the colonizer.'[33] The reiteration of an oppressive social model from the past is a key feature of neo-colonialism. Indigenous elites have many self-serving motives for ensuring continuity in social relations, and the oppressed are schooled in playing their parts in them. This cultural reality is elaborated into dramatic action when Vladimir locates Lucky's hat, discarded during a fracas in Act I:

> **Vladimir.** We could play at Pozzo and Lucky.
> **Estragon.** Never heard of it.
> **Vladimir.** I'll do Lucky, you do Pozzo. *(He imitates Lucky*

sagging under the weight of his baggage. Estragon looks at him in stupefaction.) Go on.
Estragon. What am I to do?
Vladimir. Curse me.[34]

In this sequence, Vladimir impersonates Lucky, and plays out the role of Pozzo. Estragon has erased all memory of colonial relations, and cannot now recognize them when they re-emerge. Vladimir continues prompting Estragon to command and humiliate him, and, when Estragon fails to participate, speaks in imitation of the master's voice, while moving in the servant's body:

Estragon. I'm going.
Vladimir. Dance, hog! (*He writhes.*)[35]

The combination of the voice of the master and the body of the slave, in a performance of simultaneous command and compliance, stages Vladimir's seduction by a key trope of imperialism: a world in which everyone has a clearly defined place, and there is someone to give orders. Where Lucky has no choice but to perform to Pozzo's dictates, Estragon can refuse Vladimir:

(*Exit Estragon left, precipitately.*)
Vladimir. I can't (*He looks up, misses* Estragon.)
Gogo! (*He moves wildly about the stage.*)[36]

Without an audience, the performance of bully and victim collapses, in an image suggestive of Said's and Fanon's account of colonial domination as a psychic phenomenon, bound up in the elaboration of cultural forms. The presence of audience sustains the oppressor in his coercive power. Its absence causes order to collapse into chaos. The fact of audience, as surveillant or voyeur, is elsewhere invoked specifically in the play's dramaturgy. The image of the bystander, arms folded, waiting, is ever present, and on two occasions the presence of persons watching the tramps is incorporated into the dramatic action:

Estragon. Charming spot. (*He turns, advances to front, halts facing auditorium.*) Inspiring prospects. (*He turns to* Vladimir.)
Let's go.[37]

Early in the play, this moment confirms the ironic tone of the action, and typically elicits a knowing chuckle. By Act II, the watchers in the real world of the auditorium have mutated into a terrifying prospect. Estragon imagines that hostile forces – perhaps

the faceless thugs who beat him every night – are closing in. He
rushes to Vladimir in panic:

> **Estragon.** I'm in hell! ...
> **Vladimir.** (*He takes* Estragon *by the arm and drags him toward
> front. Gesture towards front.*) There! Not a soul in sight! Off you
> go. Quick! (*He pushes* Estragon *towards auditorium.* Estragon
> *recoils in horror.*) You won't? (*He contemplates auditorium.*)
> Well, I can understand that.[38]

Not even the threat of joining the damned would make Vladimir
or Estragon join an audience in which there isn't a soul in sight. As
pointless and contradictory as their existence may be, when
contrasted with moral emptiness it is comparatively fulfilling.

Waiting for Godot rewards the reading suggested by Crow and
Banfield, and yields up a series of postcolonial parables from among
the flux of its ambiguities. All Estragon's dreams turn out to be
nightmares, all Vladimir's hopes are dashed. All that remains is the
possibility of oblivion:

> **Vladimir.** We'll hang ourselves tomorrow. (*Pause.*) Unless Godot
> comes.
> **Estragon.** And if he comes?
> **Vladimir.** We'll be saved.[39]

Even that would entail action, however, and that has ceased to be
a possibility, as the exhaustion of accumulated struggle to exist
produces only solipsistic activity. In a moment of reflection, at the
end of Act II, Vladimir considers what he knows that might
approximate to truth:

> **Vladimir.** Astride of the grave and a difficult birth. Down in the
> hole, lingeringly, the grave-digger puts on the forceps. We have
> time to grow old. The air is full of our cries. (*He listens.*) But habit
> is a great deadener.

In *Waiting for Godot*, as in *Endgame*, *Krapp's Last Tape* and
Happy Days, ritual performances of actual selves are not
explanatory gestures, but the only possible way of creating
realities.[40] Vladimir and Estragon are suspended in a repetitive,
tedious cycle, forced each day to make some sense of an existence
with no enduring purpose. Vladimir's first daily duty is to prove that
he is in the same place he was in yesterday. While he and Estragon
search constantly for meaning in their existence, the only possible
meanings are those they construct themselves, among their own acts
and words. Meaning, such as it is, is performative, and a function of

the present. Neither past knowledge – radically ambiguous – nor future aspirations – bound to be disappointed – are worthy of investment.

Beckett's dramaturgy in *Waiting for Godot* produces stage poetry of a highly developed kind. Almost every utterance and every action speaks of more than its immediate purposes in the evolution of the dramatic moment. Pozzo carries with him specifics which at once suggest his Britishness, his generality as a European bourgeois, and his Irishness. The location of the play is marked by references to the Rhône, the Pyrenees, Paris, Dublin and Connemara. The play is enacted when, for the tramps, 'time has stopped', and it is located also some fifty years on from the 1890s. The ambiguities multiply in the patterns of dialogue which perform instability and the interpenetration of narrative, situation, time, place, memory, recognition and misrecognition. In arguing that the play speaks out of and into realities specifically Irish, and alerting the reader to its significance as a parable of postcoloniality, the postcolonial challenge to the critical trope of aesthetic universality is laid down.[41]

It is equally important to acknowledge that the play's world does not illustrate an 'Irish condition' so much as resonate with it. It is also always readable as a parable of modernity and as a drama of post-war continental Europe. In its elaboration of existence scratched out at the edge of an abyss, the topographical and psychological detail of a shattered continent is suggested.[42] At the same time, the stage world's fictional location and physical circumstances form metaphors eloquent of the psychic costs of the exhaustion of a national dream of a better life. For Vladimir and Estragon, it has become too painful even to remember the dream itself:

> **Estragon**. (*restored to the horror of his situation*). I was asleep!
> (*Despairingly.*) Why will you never let me sleep?
> **Vladimir**. I felt lonely.
> **Estragon**. I had a dream.
> **Vladimir**. Don't tell me!
> **Estragon**. I dreamt that –
> **Vladimir**. DON'T TELL ME![43]

In a European frame, in the context of World War II as a moment when the modern dream of human fulfilment in the triumph of reason and technology has produced unspeakable horror, the terror is that any dream may turn out again to be a nightmare. In the wasteland of the spirit that is Independent Ireland's moment of limited decolonization, the terror is that the dream may reformulate a vision of a better life, to which one will never be able to respond in action. In either case, the possible world generated by dreaming must never again be named. Vladimir will play the role of surveillant, of voyeur, of bystander, but he will not accept the responsibilities that attend the role of witness:

> **Estragon.** Who am I to tell my private nightmares to if I can't tell them to you?
> **Vladimir.** Let them remain private. You know I can't bear that.[44]

Sleep, which comes easy to Estragon, preoccupies Vladimir as he struggles to piece together his definitive statement. To sleep is to dream, to enter into a state in which the vicissitudes of the world may be evaded, at the cost of one's human duty to engage with them:

> **Vladimir.** Was I sleeping, while the others suffered? Am I sleeping now? Tomorrow, when I wake, or think I do, what shall I say of today? That with Estragon my friend, at this place, until the fall of night, I waited for Godot? That Pozzo passed, with his carrier, and that he spoke to us? Probably. But in all that, what truth will there be?[45]

The crisis remains one of an overwhelming duty to remember, to enunciate truths drawn from 'a long encounter with reality', in circumstances in which to essay such an encounter is to court physical and psychic disaster. And yet, the imperative to ethical memory remains. Reality must be reconstituted, re-membered, from among the debris of past efforts. It cannot be constituted, as the miraculous *fiat* of a deity, *ex nihilo*. In this light, *Waiting for Godot* resonates with Yeats's resolve to seek creative response to a world which exhausts the spirit, in the careworn products of lived experience themselves:

> Now that my ladder's gone,
> I must lie down where all the ladders start,
> In the foul rag-and-bone shop of the heart.[46]

Beckett's engagement with the failed project of Irish independence privileges the existential crises to which it gives rise, but this strategy is not an end in itself, the destination of 'absurdist' interpretations of his work. As his fictional figures struggle with increasing desperation to escape the bewildering dystopia of an emerging late modern order, they forge and embody metaphors for an ongoing twentieth-century struggle specifically Irish, for all its broader resonances.[47] In a striking parallel to Synge's Christy Mahon and Martin Doul, the centrality of performance as a means of self-actualization is vividly enacted by Beckett's *dramatis personae*. And the specificity which marks that project is the central promise of Irish nationalism: that Independent Ireland will liberate its people into a long postulated dream of a republic of equal citizens. Cultural products, and the representations they mobilize are at the centre of that vision. If the poetic *aisling* or idealized dream of the seventeenth and eighteenth centuries is its purest form of expression, then its most consistent critical questioning is to be found in the plays and the films of the twentieth-century, even if, in some cases, it is necessary to read such artefacts against the grain in order to reveal the social critique they include.

The film *Mise Éire*[48] was produced at a time of profound cultural change in the Republic of Ireland. Eamon De Valera was about to relinquish executive office to his successor as leader of Fianna Fáil, Seán Lemass. Lemass, with T.K. Whitaker, was embarked on the First Programme for Economic Expansion, the economic logic of Fianna Fáil's abandonment of the pieties of republican nationalism. In place of national unity – that grail of the Lemass/De Valera generation – would come a new compact with capitalism itself. The nation would be fulfilled, not in the achievement of independence for the national territory and universal citizenship for the people of the Republic, but in the plenitude of resurgent global capital. Needless to say, this interpretation of 'our' new pragmatism was not publicly promulgated in so many words. It had, however, long been available to consciousness at the lived level of individual, family and, although barely acknowledged as such, class experience.[49]

Mise Éire's triumphalist account of Irish nationalist progression amounted to an almost unchallengeable hegemonic narrative until the North exploded in 1969.[50] It functions as a kind of historical and cultural fulcrum for the period from the aftermath of World War II until the early 1970s. The film contains one sequence which is of particular interest to this discussion of contemporary Irish theatre:

> A hoist camera pans across a city street crammed with heaving humanity assembled to greet Constance Markievicz on her return in 1918 from incarceration in a British jail. At the height of its ecstatic celebration, the image of the popular mass is dissolved into Atlantic waves beating against the 'timeless' western coast of Ireland – a key site and trope of nationalist desires. Immortal nature gives way in seconds to the averted gaze of a piece of neoclassical statuary featured on a bridge

over the river Liffey, which runs through the heart of Dublin city. The detour into storied western seascape facilitates the sublation of radical popular desire into the impassive patrician demeanour accompanying the newly appropriated accoutre- ments of empire. In the city of Dublin, the streets will be avoided in favour of the ornamental traces of a departed elite.

Raymond Williams points out that 'there is no such thing as the masses, only ways of seeing the masses,'[51] and the uncritical reception of *Mise Éire* reveals that not looking is also a way of seeing. Plays written in and about the 1950s in Ireland are functions of the not looking/seeing dynamic of social blindness exposed by reading this film against the grain of its propagandist intentions. Resistance to a detour away from popular liberationist aspiration toward the consolidation of social elites is a key imperative in Irish playwriting during the latter part of the twentieth century.

The period between *Purgatory* and *Waiting for Godot* (1938- 1956) encompasses global social rupture on a scale which makes the designation of World War I as The Great War seem quaint. I argue that Beckett's work brings the aesthetics of Yeats's drama of the frustration of anti-colonialist aspirations in Independent Ireland, to the edge of the abyss opened up by global conflict and European devastation. There is, however, a profound change in the stance toward the dilemma gripping the *dramatis personae*, their capacities to act on the world, and their relationships to the past- present dynamic. The problematics of these relationships dominate the drama of Independent Ireland in the 1950s and 1960s. This period encompasses the fullest articulation of the Independent state's recapitulation of the social dynamics of colonialism, the unerring sign of which was the haemorrhage of mass emigration. It also sees the gradual re-emergence of local resistance, and, in Irish theatre, of postcolonial dreaming. If Yeats's *Purgatory* is a theatre in which refusal is an act of despair, and in *Waiting for Godot* a gesture of exhaustion, M.J. Molloy and Tom Murphy forge dramas of postcolonial resistance, and reinscribe practical utopianism as a resource in their dramatic worlds.

Both Molloy and Murphy specifically stage and explore desires for postcolonial subjectivities. In Molloy, the motivating desire is for a future for one's own people in one's own place. In Murphy, a version of a viable future has been secured, for some. The postcolonial question has to do with the extent of the psychic risks involved, either in being excluded from such a future on the terms offered, or opting into it on those terms. As the analysis offered in Chapter Three demonstrates, Molloy's *The Wood of the Whispering*[52] takes up the dramas of persons' struggling to act on the world, and foregrounds questions of dramatic content, representational strategies and transformative potential. The immobilizing force at the centre of Molloy's dramatic world is rural depopulation by means of mass emigration. For Murphy, in *Famine*,[53] the threat of starvation, leaving flight or death as the stark choice facing a people abandoned, functions as a powerful metaphor for the betrayal of Independent Ireland by the political heirs of the revolutionary generation. These plays mark another shift in Irish theatre – from the dramas of the (Protestant) Ascendancy class to those of the (Catholic) peasantry.[54]

M.J. Molloy and Tom Murphy both come from east Galway, of farming and working class backgrounds, respectively. The emergence of their dramas in the 1950s and 1960s takes Irish theatre all the way along the road from Synge's critical visions of the pristine western peasantry to the enunciations of the heirs of the models for such persons themselves. It is as if Christy Mahon's declaration of intent to go romancing through the wide world from a fictional western point of departure is made good in the emergence of playwrights whose fictions of an actual west of Ireland extend Synge's prophetic critique.[55] The landscape may remain the same, the *dramatis personae* are clearly related, but it is in the specificity of the questions faced in the dramatic worlds that the gulf between the vision critiqued by Synge, Gregory and Yeats, and the reality to which it gave rise, is made visible. Ragged figures, such as Sanbatch, Sadie and the King brothers, Paddy and Jimmy, suggest a continuity of wretchedness with Beckett's tramps, but in *The Wood of the Whispering* there is a reawakening of a sense of historical purpose. This enables the elaboration of a dramatic world in which witness emerges as an alternative to bystander, and the possibility exists for the assumption of agency by the human subject in his own community. Where Beckett's tramps are confounded by a real world, in which unquestioning people are dominated by idiotic 'versions' of the truth,[56] Molloy's marginal figures insist on fashioning another version of Ireland's story.

Murphy's first play was produced by an amateur drama group,[57] and Molloy's works were staples for what was then a hugely popular, and frequently oppositional cultural movement. The well-documented resistance to social critique of Ernest Blythe's Abbey

Theatre[58] had a cultural counterweight in plays produced in rural communities, for whom Molloy and John B. Keane were local laureates. Amateur groups played predominantly to Catholic audiences living out the contradictions produced by independence. Christopher Morash argues:

> We need also to remember that in Tuam, at least, the kinds of plays that amateur companies were choosing to be acted by and for local people were – not always, but often – plays that manifest a completely unexpected form of that 'radical memory' of which Luke Gibbons writes, in that they offer glimpses of a world in which the harsh rigours of hunger or necessity are pushed toward a point of recognition, and hence of transformation – in other words, magic.[59]

Molloy dramatizes the reality that for the people who provide the model for its dramatic world, and who first brought *The Wood of the Whispering* to the stage, via the amateur drama movement's competitive festival circuit, there was an intimacy of thematic content and lived experience:

> The death of a village ... is usually a painful business ... But of this fact our suburban depopulation enthusiasts know nothing. But country people know all about it, and they know the background of this play ... So it was no coincidence that its first amateur performance were (*sic*) by two tiny rural villages: Inchovea in County Clare and Killeedy in County Limerick, which between them won half a dozen festivals with it – before their dramatic societies were shattered by emigration.[60]

Like Yeats in *Purgatory*, Molloy gives us a ruined house as backdrop to *The Wood of the Whispering*, but its significance for the people of his dramatic world, and its dramatic function, is quite different from that of the house in Yeats's play. In 1938, The Old Man, a wanderer, returns to his point of origin to confront his own embodiment of the 'disastrous mingling' of landlord and peasant, and shrinks in horror from past visions of his conception, and from future prospects of his son's fecundity. Aghast at the frustrations born of the playing out of betrayals of hopes engendered in moments of founding and forging, he seeks to bring history itself to an end in a terrible act of murder. By 1950, Molloy's peasants are caught in a Free State, rooted in an impossible home. The Big House is empty, the struggles to overthrow its powerful colonial writ a memory both bitter and sentimental. The moment of limited decolonization has ushered in a robust neo-colonialism, as the project of deferred modernization begins to be thought through. The *dramatis personae* are practical people living through the denial of basic human needs such as shelter, food, and relief from pain and fear. In the refusal of such frugal comforts neo-colonialism inscribes the wretchedness of the neo-colonized. For Molloy's people, the fear of extinction, of erasure in their own place, is as real and in need of excessive acts as the Old Man's terror of the continuity of his adulterated blood line. In Act I, Kitty explains that the peripatetic timberman, Con, has been talking sense to her:

> **Kitty.** He's giving me strong advice to go foreign and not waste my time here.
> **Sanbatch.** (*jumping up in a fury*) He's sending you foreign! The last bright little face that's left in our country? (*He runs for the gun*)[61]

The Wood of the Whispering stages the consequences of the structured betrayals of The Irish Free State by exposing their authorial influences on the lived experiences of the rural poor. I read the play as a central artefact of postcolonial consciousness, a prophetic corrective to the evasions of *Mise Éire*. Such a claim for the play's cultural purpose is supported by M.J. Molloy's explicit identification of the failures of the neo-colonial elite which had assumed office and power in *Saorstát Éireann* [The Irish Free State], in his 'Preface to *The Wood of the Whispering*' (1953),[62] cited in Chapter Three. In an echo of what David Lloyd discerns in the poetry of W.B. Yeats, *The Wood of the Whispering* questions the validity of narratives conjured ahistorically from canonized initiating moments. Lloyd locates the purpose of such narratives in their power to erase whole swathes of human experience from public consciousness. *The Wood of the Whispering* deliberately restores the particularity of experiences common to people erased in *Mise Éire*, and its original production (1953) rages against an official gaze averted from a people exiled in their own country. As my reading of the final episode (Chapter 3) demonstrates, memories of communal desires and public betrayals are inscribed on the bodies of the people depicted, in their physicalities, their words and in their silences. In the face of a lived reality whose contradictions exceed the representational scope of dominant forms of bourgeois theatre, bold and significant dramaturgical choices are made. Specifically, Molloy's disruption of realism in *The Wood of the Whispering* marks it out as a postcolonial work.

Received critical wisdom locates Molloy as a 'folk' playwright, and by this we are invited to agree that his work is of a lesser order of public significance than that of others. Christopher Murray detects a lack of ambition in his dramas:

> Molloy's main interest was as folklorist. He wanted to capture and immortalize the manners, customs, language and people he knew intimately in County Galway... This is a dangerous aim for a playwright, and too often Molloy simply lapsed into quaintness.[63]

By contrast, Welch regards the play as 'a most searching work',[64] and Lionel Pilkington recognizes *The Wood of the Whispering* as 'innovative and theatrically exciting.'[65] Pilkington includes it as a play 'less overtly political'[66] than others of the period, but his use of 'political', in this instance, confines itself to plays shaped by the working through in Independent Ireland of contradictions arising from enduring intranational struggles around the interpretation of the colonial past, specifically Louis D'Alton's *This Other Eden* and Walter Macken's *Twilight of a Warrior*. I argue for a broader reach for the idea of the political, and specifically engage with the significance of intranational contestations of what Pilkington refers to as 'national pieties'.[67] Such contestations derive from and stage desires for postcolonial subjectivities.

Not only does *The Wood of the Whispering* yield profound political significance when read from a postcolonial point of view, but the protagonist engages specifically with the failure of politics in Independent Ireland to engage with the actual needs of the people. The people are alone, betrayed in their communities more comprehensively than in colonial times by remote, unaccountable authority:

> **Hotha.** ...wait till we see what the next election'll do.
> **Sanbatch.** (*fiercely*) Isn't that what we're doing all our lives, and each gang we elected turned out to be worse than the last? Sure, they don't know how we're living at all and how could they? Wance in every five years they come down to draw our votes, halting their cars at crossroads for five minutes, with big detectives all around them, for fear they'd see or hear us.[68]

In evaluating the play from an aesthetic point of view, Murray reads Sanbatch Daly's performance of madness, resulting in multiple marriages, as an unsatisfactory plot resolution, a far-fetched vehicle for narrative closure.[69] In this way, Murray positions the play as a naïve dramatic narrative, calling for crude devices by which a playwright who had essayed an unwieldy theme gets himself off the hook. I argue (Chapter Three) that Sanbatch's performance of madness amounts to a symbolic realization of the regenerative power of communal solidarity, in stark contrast to the simultaneous invocation and betrayal of community by neo-colonial elites. Reluctance to engage with even the possibility of such an interpretation is a pointed example of the sort of critical silences to which Pilkington draws attention, and which the analysis of *Mise Éire* exposes. There can be few clearer instances of criticism disabling the connection between artefact and social context necessary to its ability to intervene in society, and occasion a critical reflection on choices made.

Read against Yeats's Old Man and Beckett's tramps, Sanbatch's excessive actions illustrate both difference and progression in theatrical concerns and social relations: the Old Man, a despairing exile in his own land, can only bring history to an end. His cultural model is tragedy, his reward for monstrous action, the dubious grandeurs of agony and self-destruction. Vladimir and Estragon are both rooted and dislocated, their place both inevitable and strange. No act has any significance for them, except in its confirmation of the insignificance of action itself. For Sanbatch, his own place is a site occupied by small lives to whom even frugal comforts are denied, a home all too real, and all too really at risk of extinction. The only instrument of refusal left to him is his own body, the only strategy, that of Christy Mahon – the power to perform a lie. In playing out his untruth, Sanbatch deploys fiction to enable an epiphany in which the *dramatis personae* reconstitute themselves as a community around his plight. In strategically 'losing himself'[70] he creates space for resistance in a desolate place, and enables the community to imagine futures for itself out of its own human potential. Set against the following dialogue sequence from *Waiting for Godot*, Sanbatch embodies and enacts a sense that, by 1950, the time had come to take whatever action might be necessary, or at least possible, to challenge the deadly consequences of neo-colonial neglect:

> **Vladimir.** We'll hang ourselves tomorrow. (*Pause.*) Unless Godot comes.
> **Estragon.** And if he comes?
> **Vladimir.** We'll be saved.[71]

For Didi and Gogo, all there is to do is to wait for Godot, and suffer the appalling repetitions of a meaningless existence while so doing. Hotha's suggestion that they 'wait till we see what the next election'll do' draws the fierce reaction from Sanbatch cited above (p. 119):

> **Sanbatch.** (*fiercely*) Isn't that what we're doing all our lives, and each gang we elected turned out to be worse than the last?

The contrast illustrates the moment in which the exhaustion detected in *Waiting for Godot*, at the end-point of the frustration of nationalist anti-imperialist aspiration, gives way to a renewed determination to re-commence liberationist projects using whatever limited resources may be available.

Garry Hynes's work on Molloy, Synge and Murphy exposes the inscriptions of economic, cultural and political failure in the homeland of nationalist myth: the rural west of Ireland. Druid's reclamation of Molloy and Synge, and Hynes's staging and restaging of Murphy forces the bodies and experiences of the rural poor into the public domain. In the case of her 1983 production of *The Wood of the Whispering*, Hynes is specific about the importance of actually existing social conditions to the development of the fictional world of the performance text:

> The play is very baroque, sort of a fantasy piece of theatre in some sense, but the production of it arose from a book that was a sociological study of parts of western Ireland in the 1950s. It had nothing to do with the characters but gave a wonderful sense of a community and how that community was breaking up. That absolutely inspired the production of the play that eventually evolved.[72]

The aspirations and sacrifices of the period of anti-colonial struggle haunt the stage world of this play, and the moment of its restaging provides opportunities for realizing metaphors savage in their damnation of the Ireland 'we' have settled for.

This chapter reads *Waiting for Godot* through a postcolonial lens, and places its fictional world in relation to that of Yeats's *Purgatory* and among the catastrophic events of World War II. As an artefact of postcolonial consciousness, it dramatizes the emergent exhaustion of the rhetorical power of the tropes of anti-colonial nationalism in official discourse. The choices made by *dramatis personae* in *The Wood of the Whispering* indicate a movement beyond the inertia of Beckett's tramps, toward active opposition to dystopic circumstances. I will now consider two key postcolonial dramas by Tom Murphy, and argue that they extend the critique offered by Molloy in *The Wood of the Whispering*, as Independent Ireland responds to political attempts to resolve the crises confronting Sanbatch and his neighbours, while leaving untouched the social relations which underpinned them.

---

1 Lionel Pilkington draws attention to Yeats's central role in 'an important alliance between the 'constructive' section of landlord interests in Ireland and a British administration enthusiastically pursuing a policy of Irish national development.' Pilkington, Lionel, *Theatre and the State in Twentieth Century Ireland: Cultivating the People* (Routledge, 2001): 7.

2 W.B. Yeats, 'Easter 1916' in A. Norman Jeffares ed., *W.B. Yeats: Selected Poetry* (Macmillan, 1972): 95.

3 Samuel Beckett, *Waiting for Godot* (Faber and Faber, 1975).

4 David Lloyd, 'Republics of Difference: Yeats, McGreevy and Beckett', *Third Text: Ireland Special Issue*, Vol. 19, Issue 5, ed. Lucy Cotter (Routledge, September 2005): 464.

5 Brian Crow and Chris Banfield, *An Introduction to Post-colonial Theatre* (Cambridge University Press, 1996).

6 Ibid. 169.

7 'In Yeats's and Beckett's drama, for all Yeats's early ideals of a national theatre, there is a shared urge to reach some sort of quick of being, a life of the spirit beyond the specificities of space and culture.' Nicholas Grene, *The Politics of Irish Drama: Plays in Context from Boucicault to Friel* (Cambridge University Press, 1999): 193.

8 See 'Colonial War and Mental Disorders', Frantz Fanon, *The Wretched of the Earth* (Black Cat Books, 1968): 249-310. See also Geraldine Moane, 'Colonialism and the Celtic Tiger: Legacies of History and the Quest for Vision', *Re-inventing Ireland: Culture, Society and the Global Economy*, Peadar Kirby, Luke Gibbons, and Michael Cronin eds (London; Sterling, Virginia: Pluto, 2002): 109-123.

9 '[T]o situate the significance of his writing in relation to Ireland's post-colonial moment and to read his anti-nationalism as a critical political intervention ... involves relocating Beckett in relation to other post-colonial contexts, which cuts against the grain of his reception as a European post-modernist even as it posits a certain questioning of identity as an indispensable element of the decolonizing project' David Lloyd, *Anomalous States: Irish Writing and the Post-Colonial Moment* (Dublin: Lilliput, 1993):4.

10 'There are two distinct but related dramatic texts, *En Attendant Godot* written in French, and *Waiting for Godot* written in Hiberno-English ... [T]he history of literature in Ireland has much to do with ... the sense of English as somehow a language which is not entirely native.' Anthony Roche, *Contemporary Irish Drama from Beckett to McGuinness* (Gill & Macmillan, 1994): 4.

11 Ibid. 6.

12 Beckett (1975): 62.

13 'Beckett's favourite book of the Old Testament: "Two are better than one ... for if they fall, one will lift up his fellow."' (*Ecclesiastes*, Book 4, Chapter 9), cited in Roche (1994): 68.

14 'This need to assemble an identity out of the refractions and discontinuities of exile ... to transform the lyrics of loss into the indefinitely postponed drama of return.' Edward Said, 'Reflections on Exile', *Out There: Marginalization and Contemporary Cultures*, eds Russell Ferguson, et al. (MIT Press, 1991): 41.

15 Beckett (1975): 52.

16 Ibid. 66.

17 Ibid. 53.

18 Ibid. 79-80.

19 For a discussion of the specific significance of the figure of the *attentiste* in post-war France, see Gerry Dukes, "The *Godot* Phenomenon", *Samuel Beckett - 100 Years*, ed. Christopher Murray (New Island Books, 2006): 30-31.

20 Ibid. 80.

21 Ibid. 10.

22 Ibid.

23 Ibid. 53.

24 Ibid. 85.

25 Pozzo: As though I were short of slaves! Ibid. 31.

26 Ibid. 33. In this episode, Lucky is announced as the one who 'taught me all these beautiful things', thus illustrating what Deane identifies as the British desire for the 'fierce, imaginative, poetic' Celtic personality to supplement its own perceived defects. Deane, (1990): 12-13.

27 'Lack-ey or lac-quey: a liveried retainer... a servile follower... to play the lackey; dance attendance; toady; to wait upon; serve obsequiously.' *Webster's Third New International Dictionary – Unabridged* (1993): 1261.

28 Beckett (1975): 23.

29 Ibid. 33.

30 Ibid. 36.

31 Ibid. 89.

32 Vladimir. 'The other, pig!', Ibid. 67.

33 Cited in Vic Merriman, 'Decolonisation postponed: the theatre of Tiger Trash', *Irish University Review*, Autumn/Winter (1999): 307.

34 Ibid. 72-73.

35 Ibid. 73.

36 Ibid.

37 Ibid.

38 Ibid.

39 Ibid. 94.

40 Roche (1994: 6) characterises Beckett's dramatic locations as 'imposed situation(s) in which the characters find themselves and

which they either disguise or subvert through rituals of language, gesture and play.' Eagleton refers to 'a parsimony of gesture which is both theatrically subversive and dramatically engaging'. Eagleton, Terry, 'Political Beckett?' *New Left Review 40*, (July-August 2006): 72.

41 Bill Ashcroft historicises the critical project in which culture is enlisted in the service of imperialist ideology. Culture is presented as that which 'elevates. It is universal, transhuman, unassailable.' Ashcroft, Bill, 'Postcoloniality and the future of English' *Understanding Post-Colonial Identities: Ireland, Africa and the Pacific*, ed. Dele Layiwola (Ibadan: Sefer Books, 2001): 7.

42 'What we see in his work is not some timeless *condition humaine*, but war-torn twentieth-century Europe.' Eagleton (2006): 69.

43 Beckett (1975): 15-16.

44 Beckett (1975): 16.

45 Ibid. 90.

46 Yeats, W.B., 'The Circus Animals' Desertion' in Jeffares ed. (1972): 202.

47 'If the starved, stagnant landscapes of his work are post-Auschwitz, they are also a subliminal memory of famished Ireland, with its threadbare, monotonous colonial culture and its disaffected masses waiting listlessly on a Messianic deliverance which never quite comes.' Eagleton (2006): 70-71.

48 *Mise Éire* (dir., George Morrison, Ireland/1959/Black and White)

49 Pilkington (2001: 4) draws attention to an 'extensive critical reluctance to concede the politically conservative and class-based character of Irish cultural institutions.' This reluctance elaborated throughout the social order, and functioned as a structuring silence.

50 Tony Tracey notes, 'Partisan in its presentation of historical events and decidedly on the side of Pearse's interpretation of the death of the few in the service of the many, (*Mise Éire*) premiered to an ecstatic audience as the closing presentation of the 1959 Cork Film Festival ... Although Morrison has ... claimed that the ... film was a deliberate critique of romantic nationalism, the failure of the sequel, *Saoirse?* [*Freedom?*] would seem to suggest that that was not what was understood, or required by contemporary audiences.' Tony Tracey, 'Mise Éire', *Nationalisms: visions and revisions*, ed. Luke Dodd (Film Institute of Ireland, 1999): 64-65. *Mise Éire* was part of 'school education or university (film) society showings ... throughout the 1960s. Margaret McCurtain, 'Footage from the 1960s' in Dodd ed. (1999): 40.

51 Raymond Williams, *Communications* (Penguin, 1962): 261.

52 M.J. Molloy, *The Wood of the Whispering, Selected Plays of M.J. Molloy*, ed. Robert O'Driscoll (Colin Smythe, 1998): 109-177.

53 Tom Murphy, *Famine* (Gallery Books, 1984).

54 Tom Kilroy engages specifically with the implications of this shift, in Kilroy, Tom, 'A Generation of Playwrights', *Theatre Stuff: Critical Essays on Contemporary Irish Theatre*, ed. Eamonn Jordan (Carysfort Press, 2000): 1-7.

55 For Fintan O'Toole, the link is explicit: 'Synge ... had been followed by M.J. Molloy, a playwright from Milltown, a few miles outside Tuam, to whom Murphy pays a passing tribute in *A Crucial Week in the Life of a Grocer's Assistant* (in) a reference to Molloy's play *The Wood of the Whispering*', O'Toole, Fintan, *Tom Murphy: The Politics of Magic* (New Island, 1994): 34.

56 The tramps argue over discrepancies in accounts of the salvation of two thieves crucified with Christ: Estragon. Who believes him? Vladimir. Everybody. It's the only version they know. Estragon. People are bloody ignorant apes. Beckett (1975): 13-14.

57 'For most people in Ireland in the post-war period, the amateur dramatic movement which burgeoned in the 1950s in festivals and competitions, was their only point of contact with artistic creativity of any kind.' Terence Brown, *Ireland: A Social and Cultural History 1922-2002* (London: Harper Perennial, 2004): 236.

58 Pilkington (2001: 151) refers to 'Blythe's mostly tendentious and formally conservative programme of plays at the Abbey.' See 'Irish theatre and modernization', Ibid. 139-165, for a full discussion.

59 Christopher Morash, 'Murphy, History and Society', *Talking About Tom Murphy*, ed. Nicholas Grene (Carysfort Press, 2002): 29.

60 Molloy (1998a): 112.

61 Molloy (1998b): 133.

62 Molloy (1998a): 111.

63 Murray (1997): 146-147.

64 Welch (2003): 160.

65 Pilkington (2001): 149.

66 Ibid. 148.

67 Ibid.

68 Molloy (1998b): 157-158.

69 'When Sanbatch turns matchmaker in a desperate attempt to counter the social malaise, farce and the grotesque colour the tragic picture.' Murray (1997): 147.

70 In Tom Murphy's *The Sanctuary Lamp*, Harry states, 'I don't mind admitting I keep (madness) as a standby in case all else fails.' Cited in Richard Kearney, *Transitions: Narratives in Irish Culture* (Manchester University Press, 1988): 170.

71 Beckett (1975): 94.

72 Cited in Helen Manfull, *Taking Stage: Women Directors on Directing* (Methuen, 1999): 49.

6 | Them and Us: dramas of a rising tide

The weight of discussion of Irish drama during the 1960s and 1970s emphasizes formal severances, the emergence of a new canon and the stature of the plays of Brian Friel and Tom Murphy. This study is less concerned with such approaches, although they drive the impressive scholarship of Murray, Grene, Roche and others, toward stimulating readings of particular plays, and the *ouevres* of individual playwrights. As Chapter 3 sets out, all too often, critical perspectives on Irish theatre accept the world as an unproblematic given, of which the stage world is a skewed version. If the transformative potential of acts of performance is to be made publicly available, then criticism must acknowledge that dramatic worlds function as metaphorical responses to actually existing conditions. In other words, dramatic action exists in dialogue with the world in which it is staged, and may function mimetically, allegorically or analogically as a representation of that world. Postcolonial criticism situates drama among cultural practices produced initially under conditions of colonial domination. My argument is that the dynamics of the actual worlds produced under colonial conditions are reproduced under neo-colonial circumstances, and postcolonial cultural practices enter into dialogue with the neo-colonial along similar lines. As the discussions of *Cathleen Ní Houlihan* and *The Well of the Saints* suggest, dramatic worlds created under colonial conditions speak, in re-stagings, to neo-colonial realities, and the dynamics of human relations in dramatic worlds produced under neo-colonial conditions testify to continuities in the representation both of social alienation and utopian desire. For these reasons, notions of chronological severance are distinctly problematic for postcolonial criticism.

The advent of the new is accompanied both by promise and erasure as it addresses itself to a national community. The break with the past, the eager embrace of a future, encourages escapist fantasies of a people liberated from itself, floating free in a world available to be remade to order. From a postcolonial perspective, declarations of cultural caesura inhibit the project of decolonization, and function in the body politic less as a bracing breath of fresh air than the temporary euphoria of anaesthetic. The material conditions of the society remain, place has not been supplanted by non-place, and problems dismissed as *passé* will return with renewed urgency to demand resolution. It is in this sense that Tom Murphy's work may be read as a series of dramas of neo-colonial relations. Murphy's first play, written in collaboration with Noel O'Donoghue, is called *On the Outside*,[1] and, although set outside a rural dancehall, it is an explicitly urban drama – a play of small town life. O'Donoghue's and Murphy's agreement that whatever else their play would be, 'it's not going to be set in a kitchen'[2] might suggest that they were about the business of cultural caesura. From a postcolonial perspective, *On the Outside* stages an emerging site for the contestation of the betrayals of Independent Ireland, as experienced by those marginal to the dominant narrative of 1960s Ireland. The play stages the condition of exclusion from a dancehall – a site of leisure and sexual opportunity which seemed the very signature of the new in a modernizing Ireland. During the 1950s, rural dancehalls sprang up all over the country, frequently as facilities used by local parishes, sporting organizations and amateur drama societies to stage functions, dances and performances. Informally, the halls functioned as sites where desires central to an emergent bourgeois narrative reworked ideas of Irishness in the service of official nationalism's project of embracing modernity.

On the Outside is a drama necessary to its time, and any sense of innovation or re-making of the world depicted derives from its relationship with the material circumstances of that time and place. Fintan O'Toole's stimulating readings of the play locate it among the socio-economic convulsions occasioned by the publication and implementation of Whitaker's *First Programme for Economic Expansion*.[3] O'Toole is clear about the dramatic achievement of the play, and sees the economy of form and sharpness of content involved as 'a mark of how strategic was the moment at which

Murphy was impelled into playwriting, a moment at which the social tensions of the country were so compressed and stark that they could be encompassed in a one-act play'.[4] Murphy and O'Donoghue's dramatic action turns on a series of doomed strategies adopted by the internal others of the neo-colonial state to include themselves in its social rituals. O'Toole reads the social class of the protagonists as a crucial factor in a play 'immersed in the minutiae of class division and social mobility'.[5] The plight of persons and groups marginalized in a divided society is central to postcolonial theatre, and is a key concern in all of Murphy's work. Of the violent Carneys depicted in *A Whistle in the Dark* (1961), Lionel Pilkington states, 'Ireland is not associated with a home, but with an anonymous middle-class "them" that insists on their sub-ordination.'[6] By 1998, in *The Wake*, the excluded Finbar testifies to the tenacity of 'the authorities in this town … the reason why I say fuck them is because I'm frightened of every single one of them.'[7] O'Toole argues that, in *On the Outside*, the ferocity of class conflict surpasses even town and country antagonisms, which themselves have the force of 'a state of undeclared war within the nation that goes against every assumption of nationalism.'[8]

O'Toole rightly emphasizes the fact that in the Ireland into which Murphy's plays intervened, Fianna Fáil's version of Irish nationalism had achieved the kind of cultural hegemony of which *Mise Éire* is an artefact. However, it is important to bear in mind that, as the reading of *The Wood of the Whispering* suggests, the status of that hegemony as guarantor and medium of Irishness – like the film's prescriptive narrative – was always contested. *On the Outside* stages that contestation, and draws attention to a site of conflict, emerging in tune with the major mutations in the Fianna Fáil/Nation/Capital relation described in Chapter Five. Roland Barthes suggests that the actions of a bourgeois class are experienced as a series of social effects on the lives, bodies and potential of those they dominate, and for Richard Kearney the struggles of Murphy's *dramatis personae* against the indigenous bourgeoisie are truly desperate. His characterization recalls Fanon, Constantino and Freire on the nationalist bourgeoisie: '(It) has contaminated the very air they breathe; it is witnessed in the visible scars of their failure; it is quite simply that faceless omnipresent "they"… (that will) "kill you if you stay"'.[9] In the face of this, in staging persistent desires for subjectivity and citizenship, *On the Outside* dramatizes a reassertion of postcolonial consciousness.

The Wood of the Whispering essays the gulf which opens in front of Yeats's Old Man, and on the edge of which Vladimir and Estragon deflect agony by substituting amnesia and nostalgia for action. Sanbatch Daly determines to confront the barbarities of Independent Ireland with strategies of refusal and a commitment to fashioning a better life, no matter how meagre. Murphy's *On the Outside* stages the condition of postcolonial refusal in Independent Ireland in the early 1960s, of the neo-colonial circumstances that engender that refusal, and of its consequences. It is, as O'Toole suggests, a drama of a 'strategic moment'. While the social fabric of 1960s Ireland manifests obvious changes when compared to Ireland in the 1950s and previously, it is unhelpful to situate the significance of this play or of others written during that time as arising mainly from a perceived newness or, as Murray would have it, indicative of a 'second renaissance' in Irish theatre.[10]

The world depicted in *On the Outside* operates along similar internal dynamics as do the neo-colonial dystopias anticipated by Synge and dramatized by Yeats. These dynamics produce a dramatic world made harsh again by refusing Molloy's recourse to disrupted realism. As in *Waiting for Godot*, the open road is the location of recurrent, unproductive activity, but the *dramatis personae* here know that better times are abroad for some in Ireland. In a development of Molloy's dramatic world, the young are no longer naïve and wistful, prepared to opt eventually for frugal comfort in the interests of social solidarity. Murphy's young people want their share of life's bounty, and will make use of all available means to get it. The dramatic situation which *On the Outside* explores is that of Frank and Joe, short of money to get into a dance organized by the Irish National Teachers' Organization. Frank has arranged to meet Anne, and the play is structured around seven strategies deployed by the two young men to enter the dancehall. As the dramatic action begins, the women are on stage, and *have obviously been waiting for some time*.[11] Kathleen is finding it impossible to get Anne to give up on Frank, and simply go into the dance. She argues and cajoles, and finally plays her trump card: 'Maybe you'll meet someone with a car.'[12] When they enter the hall, the men appear, and we realize that we have just witnessed the playing out of their first strategy – to delay their arrival until the women pay their own way into the dance. Had they met them outside, Frank would have been obliged to pay for Anne.

Their doomed strategies include fawning on the ostentatious car-owning Mickey Forde, coaxing the bad-tempered box office clerk, scrounging 'pass outs' from people leaving the hall early, and even begging from Daly, the local drunk. Forde, who speaks an argot which mimics the dialogue of Hollywood films, offers a blunt image of the indigenous bourgeoisie. He draws his social models from 'masterful images' produced in the homeland of twentieth-century modernity, the United States of America. He mimics the mien of an American self-made man, flaunts his status, and – specifically because of his economic advantage – is successful with Frank's girl. Tellingly, as their desperation intensifies, Frank and Joe hesitate to pool resources so that one party could buy his way in, and strategize then to include the other. The risk of betrayal haunts everyone in a society whose organizing principle is car ownership. When push comes to shove in *Wood of the Whispering*, the *dramatis personae* have it in them to mobilize around Sanbatch's plight, and commit themselves to the possibility of a sustainable society, founded on mutual reliance. In sharp contrast to Molloy's dramatic world, Murphy stages circumstances in which fervent dreams fail to inspire even the thought of self-sacrifice in pursuit of a modest utopia.

The reality of small town life, in a society mutating from aspiration to community to the pursuit of economic growth is devastating for those on the outside, and is vividly apparent to them:

> **Frank**. Aw but – Jesus – this bumming around from one end of the week to the other is terrible! Jesus! Look at us now! ... Look at us in that oul' job with Dan Higgins. The fags we get out of him – just from soft-soaping an imbecile. Ah, yes, we all get a big laugh but – I don't know.
> **Joe**. Did you see Dan Higgins today going into the boss's office? (*Laughs*) He nearly tore the head off himself pulling off his cap.[13]

The image of Dan Higgins links his servility to the coercive practice of 'pitch capping', where eighteenth-century colonial militias placed tar in a cap on the head of a peasant, and removed most of the scalp in tearing it off. Under neo-colonial conditions of servitude, the peasant obliges by mutilating himself, as he confirms his wretched servility.

> **Frank**. But again it's not so funny. No, serious, sham. This old job. Do you know what I think. Do you know what the job is like? Serious sham ... It's like a big tank. The whole town is like a tank. At home is like a tank. A huge tank with walls running up, straight up. And we're at the bottom, splashing around all week in their

> Friday night vomit, clawing at the sides all around. And the bosses
> – and the big-shots – are up around the top, looking in, looking
> down. You know the look? Spitting. On top of us. And for fear we
> might climb out someway – Do you know what they're doing? –
> They smear grease around the walls.
> *They laugh. Pause.*[14]

This second image of desires for subjectivity thwarted by '*them
with the cars and money*'[15] is as vivid and violent as that of Higgins'
self-mutilation. The unspeakable awfulness of life in a vomit-filled
tank is as graphic an account of oppression as one could wish for.
Work, home and the town itself coalesce to create an image, not of
helplessness, or horror at past deeds, but of organized coercion on a
par with that experienced by Martin and Mary Doul in Synge's *The
Well of the Saints*. The awful curbing of human potential, of desire
for self-actualization, is not simply 'happening', it is being visited
upon young people by their neo-colonial betters:

> **Frank.** It's pushing on. We'd better do something quick.[16]

Laughing it off is no substitute for action to address the
awfulness of their condition.

However, Frank and Joe's resolution to 'do something quick'
dissipates in the face of their lack of funds. They are confronted
again with the illusion of opportunity in the shape of the drunken
Daly, ejected from the hall. He has been accused of stealing drink
provided for the band:

> *They ignore* Drunk. Drunk *begins to move away. He tugs up his
> trousers and money rattles.* Frank *and* Joe *look at each other.*[17]

On hearing the rattle of the drunk's money, the pair begin an
elaborate performance of outrage at the indignities Daly has
suffered at the hands of the Bouncer. They will avenge his honour,
for they are his 'pals'. The drunk is nothing if not generous. He
offers them all he has, falls well short of their requirements, and is
dismissed contemptuously. He will return at the *dénouement*, as, in
O'Toole's words, 'a spectre of what they may become.'[18] When all
strategies have failed, and Anne, the object of Frank's desire and his
motivation to scheme his way into the hall, has left in Mickey
Forde's car,

> *Frank rushes over to the poster and hits it hard with his fist. He
> kicks it furiously.*
> **Joe.** Come on out of here to hell.

They exit. The band plays on. Drunk *is giving a few impotent
kicks to the poster as the lights fade.*[19]

In the neo-colonial purgatory of Independent Ireland, impudence
mutates into impotence, and, hope deferred and heaven denied, the
only option is hell.

Ten years later, Murphy excavates the pit itself in an effort to
fashion dramatic metaphors eloquent of the state into which the
country had declined in the years since independence. *Famine*[20] was
produced first at the Peacock in 1968, revived by Druid Theatre
Company in 1984, and by Garry Hynes at the Abbey in 1993. *Famine*
is a drama from the abyss, rich in examples of the doubleness of
experience and desire. In terms of Irish dramaturgy, it is formally
innovative, after the manner of Brecht.[21] As an historical drama, the
decision to work within an epic structure makes sense: the material
to be staged takes in the extremes of human experience. The
episodic structure enables the narrative sweep of the historical play
to be accommodated in one evening in the theatre. It also enables
the juxtaposition of human intimacy, as in 'Scene 4: The Love Scene'
and 'Scene 12: The Springtime', with public affairs and the
mechanics of colonial rule and resistance efforts, as in 'Scene 2: The
Moral Force' and 'Scene 5: The Relief Committee'. In keeping with
Brecht's concept of complex seeing, the dramatic action is marked
throughout by a dynamic of doubleness, which produces multiple
ambiguities in the dramatic action.

No other event has left as deep a scar on Irish consciousness as
has the terrible suffering and injustice of The Great Hunger. In
1968, *Famine* was directed in the Peacock Theatre by Tomás Mac
Anna, who had directed a triumphalist nationalist pageant marking
the fiftieth anniversary of the 1916 Rebellion, at Croke Park, the
national stadium of the Gaelic Athletic Association, two years
earlier. One year prior to the eruption of what would turn out to be
thirty years of bloody conflict in Northern Ireland, Independent
Ireland under Fianna Fáil was in expansive mood. With the passing
of the torch of destiny to Jack Lynch, the link with the revolutionary
generation had been broken. There was an economic boom,
television had produced a series of local celebrities who embodied
the attainability of bourgeois sophistication, and there was a sense
abroad of optimism. That was the received narrative of Ireland
Successful. It felt like (another) new beginning, but alongside the
carnival of conspicuous consumption, convened by Church and
State, the reality of emigration, economic and spiritual poverty

endured. Into this social dynamic, Tom Murphy inserted a drama of the ultimate colonial horror.

Twenty-five years after De Valera's invocation of a bucolic idyll centred on the ahistorical rural homestead, *Famine* revisits the peasant cabin, for so long a figure for Ireland itself. Garry Hynes's 1993 production took advantage of the expressionistic features of epic theatre by commissioning a set which spoke directly to images of the ancient provenance of the Irish people. Her dry stone structure modelled on Iron Age ring forts located the site of dramatic action as that of the ancient archetypal nation itself.[22] The Ireland of *Famine* is a house of death, an impossible home, in which lethal forces act upon the people. Those forces appear to be beyond their powers, or the powers of those who lead them, to resist. In the midst of the depopulation of the 1950s, a tramp camping out in front of the ruins of a colonial mansion could summon bodily resources to act oppositionally on the world. In 1968, the bodies of the wretched of the 1840s are summoned like ghosts to speak to an accumulating hunger of the spirit.

At first glance, one of the remarkable features of the dramas of Synge,[23] Yeats, Beckett and Molloy is the absence of the embodied Catholic priest, the single most important controlling force in rural Ireland since the 1880s,[24] and the subject of sentimental nationalist narratives, peaking around the centenary of the Rebellion of 1798. *Famine* stages the clergy, not as functions of the spirit, but as arms of the state, colonial and neo-colonial, charged with regulating civil society. The play interrogates the studied ambiguity of the Catholic Church in relation to the starving people. Oppressor and liberator meet in the figure of Fr Horan; to Fr Daly the role of mediator between the people and the colonizer, simultaneously outraged and accommodating. And herein lies a crucial aspect of the doubleness of *Famine*'s dramatic world: what appears as a history play of the colonial past is always a refusal of the ideological consensus at the core of Independent Ireland.

Famine opens with 'Scene 1: The Wake',[25] a moment of communal devastation in Glanconor, the ancient home of the Connors, the head of which family is still regarded as a local king. John Connor's daughter has died of starvation, and family and neighbours join to wake the corpse in time-honoured fashion. As the child's body awaits burial and her soul hovers between this world and the next, it is clear that the co-ordinates that help this community to locate and make sense of itself pre-date, and perhaps contest Christianity. Visitors entering the dead room observe the salutation, 'The Lord have mercy on the soul of the dead!' and receive in response, 'The Lord have mercy on us all.'[26] The liturgical quality of call and response moves immediately into a pagan register, evoking the dead child as a phenomenon of nature:

> **Dan's Wife.** Cold and silent is now her bed;
> **Others.** Yes.
> **Dan's Wife.** Damp is the blessed dew of night,
> But the sun will bring warmth and heat in the
> morning and dry up the dew.
> **Mother.** But her heart will feel no heat from the sun.
> **Others.** No![27]

The scene is compelling in its awful beauty, chilling in its ancient rhythm. In keeping with epic dramaturgy, individual and communal trauma will be set among the material conditions which produce such effects.

The wake itself is only part of the scene's enactment, and the stage juxtaposes the private interior of the death house with the public gathering of men in an exterior space. On the outside, the men speculate on the prospects for the potato crop, thus providing the broader context for the child's untimely death, and enabling the social and economic forces in contention around the potato crop to be staged. The neighbours are critical of John Connor's decision to plant seed potatoes in the diseased earth, rather than use them as food. Because of his inherited authority, they abide by his leadership in such matters, and acknowledge the repetition or amplification of their individual straits in Connor's wretchedness at the failure of the strategy, and the death of his daughter. Connor's -- and the community's -- commitment to the traditions of waking the dead in the case of a child who died of hunger produces a bitter irony not lost on Liam Dougan, whose own mother has recently died of starvation:

> **Liam.** And now a wake -- Like we done! Flaithuil (*generous*) with food, drink and tobaccy. And cannot afford it for life or death![28]

Scene 1 thus sets the stage for an unflinching engagement with the sharp end of human existence in a land given over to unspeakable suffering by those whose possession drains profit from its people. The wake is both proper and preposterous, the ancestral headman both wise and witless, the people neighbourly and hostile, the priest comforting and contemptuous, at one with the people and an agent of a distant power:

> **Fr Horan.** I saw you late into mass again this morning, Brian.
> **Brian.** Oh –
> **Fr Horan.** (*mimicking him*) Oh! Oh!
> **Brian.** Aaa, I'm a slow sleeper, Father.
> *They laugh.*
> **Fr Horan.**(*leaving them*) Be good, men!
> **Fr Horan** *goes into the house. A silence.*[29]

Fr Horan's purpose is control and quietism, the abiding project of the Catholic Church in 1960s Ireland. On his exit, he is described as an advocate of 'moral force', a position which the men deride as inferior to a commitment to armed insurrection. In a telling exchange, Dan and Liam allude to a grand consensus against peasant militancy:

> **Dan.** And I heard 'tis the Queen herself, and not the Pope, is writing the books for all now.
> **Liam.** (*winks at* Brian) Correct. And doesn't she send a pound to O'Connell every week of the year!
> **Dan.** To 'The Liberator' is it?[30]

Fr Horan may perform an easy confidence in his authority among the men, but that authority is resented as yet another manifestation of forces dominating their lives. This is underscored by the sarcastic suggestion that Horan actually serves Queen Victoria, as she is now acting as author to all, including the Pope. The name by which the native political leader, Daniel O'Connell, is known, 'The Liberator', appears hollow indeed if he is experienced by people undergoing terrible privation as nothing more than a paid collaborator with the imperial project which oppresses them.

Late 1960s Ireland was the site of fierce contestation of the power of the Catholic Church, whose hegemony was in the ascendant even as modernization Irish style began to assert itself. The Church had long exercised coercive power over the lives of the people, and legislators set limits to their own social and political horizons, for fear of attracting adverse comment from the clergy, or, in colloquial terms, 'feeling the belt of a crozier.'[31] *Famine's* dramatization of Catholic priests illuminates the power of the Church to control civil society, and regulate social relations in Independent Ireland. The play's epic structure enables the fact and reach of Church power, the complexity of its effects on the body politic, and its mastery of ambiguity to be staged. In thematic terms, the figure of Father Horan, the hot-headed peasant priest, is particularly apt to the task of making disturbing connections between the privations of a colonial past, the aspirations and sacrifices of anti-colonial struggle, and the neo-colonial state which has emerged. The second episode of the play, 'The Moral Force'[32] stages a violent conflict between the word of the priest and the principles of protest and survival. Taunted by the deformed Mickeleen O'Leary, Fr Horan rounds on him for having 'taken the soup' from proselytizing Protestant clergy, the previous winter. He accuses Mickeleen of taking an oath to convert to Protestantism, in return for food:

> **Mickeleen.** And when they gave me their book to kiss -
> **Fr Horan.** And entered into league straightaway with the devil -
> **Mickeleen.** I held it like this -
> **Fr Horan.** And I say here and now -
> **Mickeleen.** But 'twas my thumb I kissed! My thumb!
> **Fr Horan.** (*roars*) And-I-say-here-and-now, that the religion that has to depend on starvation to swell its puny misguided flock is doubly damned!
> *The crowd is angry, pressing forward towards* Mickeleen.
> **Fr Horan.** Keep back there!
> **Mickeleen.** (*above the hubbub*) And I'd take it the same way to stay alive![33]

The issue of strategy in the interests of survival raised here, as Mickeleen protests the duplicity of his performance in front of the Protestant clergy, recalls the tactics of Martin Doul in the face of the Saint, and Sanbatch Daly, in the face of depopulation of the local place. The Church's ambivalence toward violence as a means to an end is staged for the audience in Fr Horan's brutal assault on the lame hunchback. The conflation of Protestantism, blackness, deformity and heresy in Fr Horan's rhetoric illustrates the hysteria with which the newly emancipated religion would seek both to defend and to assert its majority position.

> **Fr Horan.** Keep back I say! Keep-You would! You would!
> *Suddenly, he lashes* Mickeleen *on the legs with his stick.*
> Mickeleen *falls to the ground. The crowd close in, arms and legs working.*[34]

For audiences accustomed to harsh punishment in schools and other institutions run by the Church at the behest of the state, there is much to shock, and to recognize, in the brutal figure in clerical garb, as he thrashes the pitiful hunchback with his stick. What is even more sinister, in terms of the Church's role as a power bloc in

Independent Ireland, is Horan's ability to use theological abstraction and tribal passion to turn the starving people into a mob intent on murder. The consequences for the powerless of the fatal decision of the clerical bureaucracy to position themselves as part of Independent Ireland's ruling elite – predicted in the final scenes of *The Well of the Saints* – are chillingly evident in the violent crushing of Mickeleen's refusal to submit to the Church's rubrics for acceptable social behaviour.

'Scene 5: The Relief Committee'[35] stages a direct conflict between the colonial forces and the Church, as representative of the people. Each participant in the debate over relief for the starving, and the merits of 'resettlement' by assisted passage to Canada, purports to speak in the best interests of 'the masses'. Raymond Williams's comments on the masses as a construct are relevant here, and remind us that *Famine* makes visible those from whom official gazes, of colonizer and indigenous elite alike, have been averted. The Church plays out the role of intermediary with consummate skill, and the dramaturgy exposes the ambiguities of that role. Two priests are present in this scene, Fr Horan – who aggressively asserts his authenticity as a member of the Irish people – and Fr Daly, the Parish Priest, his superior. Fr Daly has a certain urbanity, and maintains a distance between himself and the people, seeing the point of view of the colonial bourgeoisie, and positioning himself to mitigate the cruder ambitions of such as Captain Shine, a local landlord. Fr Daly's appeasing tones derive from more than a sense of diplomacy, or experience in negotiation. His restraint is paternal, his tone embarrassed by Fr Horan's coarseness of temper, accent and pronunciation. The church is figured here as having the capacity to speak simultaneously with two opposing voices. Shine, who elaborates a classically racist discourse in relation to 'the Irish' trades invective with Fr Horan, while acknowledging the appropriateness of Fr Daly's language to this formal, public space.

Father Horan's departure from the meeting is precipitated by an exchange with Shine which turns on the question of identity:

> **Fr Horan.** It's just that you don't understand the Irish yet.
> **Captain.** What? But I am Irish, stupid priest! ... My family goes back several hundred years'.
> **Fr Horan.** To some time of conquest, no doubt, *your honour.*
> **P.P.** (*to* Fr Horan) You have a lot of sick calls to make. I don't think you should waste your time here. Tell them outside to pray.
> Fr Horan *leaves.*[36]

As the meeting resumes, Fr Horan is heard offstage, obeying Fr Daly's instructions:

> **Fr Horan.** (*off; calling to crowd*) Kneel! Kneel! ... Now, pray! Pray! (*hushed murmuring of prayers*) [37]

The anger of the priest functions as a domesticated proxy for rebellion by the people. That anger is ultimately containable by the authoritarian structures of the church, and the habits of mind to which it gives rise. As Horan submits his anger to Daly's authority, the people submit to his will as to that of God. They end up on their knees. This sequence, in which the Church treats with the colonizer in the name of the colonized, has bitter resonances in an Independent Ireland in which the Church's appropriation of the voice of the people was fully articulate. Its influence is evident in the writing of the 1937 Constitution, with its prohibitions on divorce, and its inscription of rights of property and inheritance which underpinned a social system kept in place by emigration, late marriage, and enforced celibacy.[38]

The pairing of personal and public spaces and issues established in the dramaturgy of 'Scene 1: The Wake' is carried through the eleven succeeding scenes. No private moment is ever uniquely intimate to those involved in it, and no public event is without impact on personal subjectivities.[39] The play's commitment to staging the dialectical negotiation of public events and personal possibility enables it to place the dynamics of neo-colonial relations, the interpenetration of the worlds of elites and masses before its audiences. In an echo of the concerns of *The Wood of the Whispering*, 'Scene 4: The Love Scene'[40] stages John Connor's daughter Maeve, and Liam Dougan, two young people of the townland, speculating on their own futures, and that of humanity, in this place of death.

The stage directions specify the awful effects of privation on the bodies of the oppressed:

> Maeve *enters. Her harshness, in the early part of the scene, would be more suited to a bitter old hag.*[41]

Liam Dougan proposes marriage to her, which she rejects. There then follows an episode in which the material transformation of the hungry by food is demonstrated:

> He hands her some nuts. She looks at the apple in one hand, the nuts in the other. She takes a bite of the apple.[42]

> **Maeve.**(*a nervous, involuntary giggle*) It's sour.
> *She eats more of the apple. Progressively, she becomes a sixteen-year-old girl again.*[43]

Even a sour apple can tempt this starving Eve, caught in a parody of Eden, in the kingdom of the dead. In the spirit of one of Brecht's aphorisms, 'Food first, then morals',[44] Liam's wooing may now proceed, and he wins three kisses from Maeve.

> *They laugh. He starts to sing. She joins in singing with him.*
> **Liam.** ... Are you Aurora or the Goddess Flora
> Artimedora or Venus bright –
> *Through the above the moon has come out again, revealing the corpses of a family under a bush. A groan from the prone figure of a man.* Liam *and* Maeve *move apart.*
> **Maeve.** (*whispers*) Chris-jays!
> **Maeve** *runs off.*
> **Liam** *sees the corpses of the family and stands there as if transfixed by them.*[45]

The metaphorical content of this dramatic episode is generated by the rich interplay of a variety of double effects, and is a powerful enabler of complex seeing. The ingestion of food, and its effects, speaks to the enduring human capacity to reconstitute the self, even in extremis. The shrivelled bodies of the sorely oppressed, given nourishment, reveal their humanity, their 'sensuous specificity.'[46] Their first action is to celebrate, to create from the fact of their endurance a cultural practice. Their singing recalls the theatrical effect of the Old Woman's song in *Cathleen Ní Houlihan*. It defines a liminality which separates the lovers temporarily from the immediate concerns of their historical situation. There is in this moment also, a specific affirmation of Sanbatch Daly's endorsement of the restorative power of culture, even amid severe conditions of bodily hardship:

> **Sanbatch.** (*putting aside pipe and tobacco*) Still there's some of the gifts of God we didn't lose yet. I'll diddle a tune for you now that'll put the two of us in great humour.[47]

As it plays out in *Famine*, the lovers' rapture is itself the occasion for the lifting of the clouds which enabled their moment of intimacy to come into being. The audience has always been aware of the presence of the dead, the *dramatis personae* have not. Their fleeting experience of the awakening and satisfaction of desire only sharpens the effect of the return of reality. Bodies nourished, physical appetite is awakened, and the possibility of intimacy, and human futures may be countenanced. As that prospect is celebrated, the fate of 'the natural primary and fundamental unit group of society',[48] the Irish family, is laid bare before the young people, and the audience. To eat, to desire, to love and procreate will not be enough. As Liam intimates, earlier in the scene, the matter of survival is primary, and overrides all other considerations:

> **Liam.** What else could I do? He (the Agent) gave me the job because he said he never had anything against my father.
> **Maeve.** My father is saying something good will happen soon.
> **Liam.** And I overheard them saying the word 'demolition'.
> **Maeve.** And saying we'd be different people if someone came along and put the bit in our mouths.
> **Liam.** There's no one thing else I can do.[49]

For Maeve, intoning her father's assurances in continuous present tense, survival appears as a matter of access to food. For Liam, focused on a future beyond the privations of that present, access to a supply of food legitimizes collaboration with the colonial project of rural depopulation. Maeve does not comprehend what he explicitly states during this exchange. His counterpoint to her aspirations is a statement that he has signed up for a small, but necessary, part in colonialism's 'inevitabilities' – the forced resettlement of his neighbours to Canada. Like her father, Maeve's wish is for food to enable the continuity of living to be resumed. Hence the continuous present tense of her enunciations, a reproduction of John Connor's worldview. For the Connors, the food/transformation relation played out earlier in this scene is about restoring parity with a continuous organic present: 'different people' will turn out to be identical with the people they always were, prior to hunger taking hold of their community.

This point of view contrasts sharply with Liam's. His discourse is of implication in a future which may appear morally compromised, but is a future nonetheless. He has opted for a break with the past, for a future discontinuous with a devastated present. Maeve's paradox of difference/continuity is further ironized by Liam's revelations: 'different people' will indeed result from the price to be paid for food in the extremity wrought by these conditions. The context is one of ultimate choice between life and death, but the postcolonial dilemma is that of *On the Outside*: whether inclusion in a future on the terms offered is actually worse than exclusion. Maeve's recognition of the price demanded for such a future is staged in 'Scene 12: The Springtime',[50] in the closing moments of the play:

> Liam *offers the bread to her again.*
> **Maeve** No! There's nothing of goodness or kindness in this world for anyone. But we'll be equal to it yet.
> **Liam.** Well, maybe it will get better.
> **Maeve.** No.
> **Liam.** And when it does we'll be equal to that too.
> *He puts the bread into her hand. She starts to cry.*[51]

This is bitter bread for Maeve, who has, in 'Scene 11: The Queen Dies'[52] witnessed her father accede to her mother's demands that he kill both herself and Donal, their young son, Maeve's brother. Shorn of the voluntary quality of the Old Man's murder of his son in Yeats's *Purgatory*, this act is the ultimate degradation, when, hunger institutionalized by colonial policy as the lot of the colonized, they expedite their own extinction. Once again, what is staged in *Famine* significantly sharpens engagement with neo-colonial relationships set out in *On the Outside*; in this case, the reported elaboration of Dan Higgins' self-mutilation.[53] And yet John Connor survives, to see the long postponed corn meal arrive, to hold bread in his hands: '*In his isolation he is beginning to sense what he has been through and to understand that his family, village and army is gone.*'[54]

Maeve's tears at the promise that better times will in themselves inaugurate conditions of hardship, which will demand yet more struggle, are amplified by the placing of the loaf in her hands. Bread has functioned as a utopian imaginary throughout this play, and its arrival promises bodily sustenance. In this unrelenting dystopia, that sustenance is available at the price of relinquishing struggle, in gratitude to one's oppressor for mercy shown too late, but shown at last. This is a scorching indictment of any social order, and a powerful metaphor for neo-colonial relations in Independent Ireland's divided society.

The Great Hunger has been visited more than once by Irish artists as a metaphor for the national condition since independence. Éibhlís ní Dhuibhne's *Milseog an tSamhraidh* [Summer Pudding] (1994)[55] stages Irish peasants as refugees in Wales in 1848, and shares with Murphy's *Famine* an epic dramaturgy, and an unflinching engagement with ghastly images around family, life and death. Patrick Kavanagh's epic poem, *The Great Hunger*, vividly adapted to the stage by Tom Mac Intyre and Patrick Mason,[56] stages the belief that bread alone will not sustain humanity. O'Casey's praise for James Larkin makes that clear: 'A man who would place a rose as well as a loaf of bread on every table.'[57] Addressing the hunger of the spirit, responding to desires for present utopia is a condition of actualizing the human subject, not a consequence: the bread and the rose go together. *Famine* is true to the practicalities of this utopian dialectic, in that its dramatic world, and the range of meaning of its dramatic actions are wrought, not only of social reality, but of existing dramatic strategies. Kilroy points to Murphy's 'jolting images'[58] which appear as 'a jumble ... a displacement ... in which the suffering of individuals stands in for the shifting of the floor of a whole civilization.'[59] Echoes of Synge in Murphy's dramas are not, for Kilroy, 'simply modish references. They are evidence of a larger awareness ... an ability to lift the purely personal onto a plane of wider implication.'[60]

In 'Scene 4: The Love Scene', Liam has a secret hoard of nuts and apples. Even though the fruit is sour, it transforms Maeve's demeanour from that of a bitter old hag to that of a sixteen year old girl. What transforms Maeve is not food only, but the type of food to which Synge compared the ideal language of drama: 'In a good play every speech should be as fully flavoured as a nut or apple, and such speeches cannot be written by anyone who works among people who have shut their lips on poetry.'[61] Indeed, after eating the apple Maeve joins in singing an eighteenth century ballad, *The Colleen Rua*[62] in which the language is excessive and mellifluous. Metaphorically, it is food specifically linked to 'the imagination of the people ... rich and living'[63] that rejuvenates Maeve, and occasions the only moment of desire for life fulfilled in the entire play. There is another acknowledgement of the necessity of keeping faith with the promise of the good life of utopian dreaming in Maeve's first refusal of bread offered by Liam in the final scene. Her words recall a celebrated phrase of Yeats,[64] as she stands over the dead body of the hunchback, Mickeleen:

Maeve. No! O'Leary is the only name I'd accept anything from.[65]

Romantic Ireland, driven by desire for decolonization, will not survive the distribution of the colonizer's bread by Irishmen recruited to perpetuate colonial relations among their own people. *Famine*, Ireland's drama of the abyss, stages the nadir of Irish humanity, and maps it on to the present day, explicitly so in

Murphy's writing of the clerical figures, and in performance, in the contested design choices made by Garry Hynes for her 1993 production.[66] As an artefact of postcolonial consciousness, *Famine* extends the refusal of *On the Outside*, and deepens the sense of abandonment of the people of *The Wood of the Whispering*. It essays the material of tragedy, as it is understood by Soyinka,[67] and, using epic form, centres the fate of the people of Glanconor, and the forces which produce it, as a metaphor for contemporary Ireland.

Richard Kearney sees Murphy as an iconoclast of 'the consumerist Irish bourgeoisie who resent any deviant flight of creativity, force many of their artists into exile, and ... try to destroy those who remain'.[68] To the extent that the *embourgeoisement* of Ireland negates the egalitarian energy of the anti-colonial struggle, and structures the indefinite postponement of decolonization, Murphy's perceived iconoclasm is a mark of postcolonial questioning, the historical function of the artist in society. Kearney queries the radical potential of what he reads as an 'angry, at times apocalyptic attitude to contemporary Irish society'[69] in Murphy's work. He detects in the playwright a tendency to the position of the *poète maudit*, and finds 'Murphy's heroes' responding to 'the threat of the irrational collective' with a 'fierce individualism.'[70] This is a trope often used in responding to Murphy's work, and its deployment is a marker of the kind of critical conservatism exposed in Chapter 3. This conservatism is revealed and produces analytical contradictions as Kearney attempts to elaborate his point:

> In Murphy's world, the individual is the agent of liberation; the collectivity – and its related idioms of history, tradition, authority, politics, nationalism, etc. – the agency of coercion. Nearly all his plays are centred round an isolated individual's struggle for self-realization over against the oppressive constraints of his/her social environment ... Murphy's plays declare war on the paralysing forces in our society, compelling us to sound out our most hidden frustrations and fears and encouraging us, where possible, to transcend them in humour and faith. For these above all are the characteristic virtues of Murphy's dramatic enterprise – the laughter that emancipates and the leap of faith towards new *possibilities* of experience, more perfect, more creative, more human.[71]

From my critical perspective, this contradictory summary is inadequate both to the dramatic action and the actual cultural significance of Tom Murphy's dramas. *On the Outside* and *Famine* dramatize individuals and collectivities as socially produced relations, in dynamic dialogue with each other. Soyinka comments on the contingency and significance of tragedy in the contemporary world, and warns against critical dead ends produced by pursuing the seductive binary of individual/society: 'The persistent search for the meaning of tragedy, for a re-definition in terms of culture or private experience is, at the least, man's recognition of certain areas of depth-experience which are not satisfactorily explained by general aesthetic theories ...'[72] Such general theories of 'Murphy's world' or 'Murphy's heroes' stand between reader and performance event, their invocation closes down engagement with the complexities of the actually existing drama.

None of the individuals in these plays is 'isolated' as a natural state. Kearney includes John Connor in his account of isolated individuals at war with invisible social forces, but when Connor stands *in his isolation* with the loaf of bread in his hand, he undergoes an epiphany. He is staged, not in a typical, but in a liminal moment. Frank and Joe are a social unit in Brecht's sense: a complementary pair, a couple and a double at one and the same time. So too are Anne and Kathleen. The dramatic pretext animates the staging of crises produced by the baneful influence of poverty on their attempts to re-form into fecund social units: Frank/Anne and Joe/Other. The impossible versions of moments of fecundity staged in *Famine*, 'The Love Scene' and 'Springtime' ironize notions of natural order and romantic aspiration in a struggling social unit, which functions as a metaphor for persons contesting extraordinary historical forces. Those forces render bread bitter and hope impossible, but the struggle to achieve a future, 'more perfect, more creative, more human' continues.

Collective living is the goal here, writ small in narratives of human intimacy, and large in the dramas of public events which occur in the same dramatic space as parallel, interacting dramatic worlds unfold. The real contest, as Synge predicts, and the vicious argument between Mickeleen and Fr Horan demonstrates, is not between an isolated individual and a malevolent collective, but between competing social models, between opposing visions of collective living. That contest goes to the heart of the drama of Maeve's future choices, and her tears attest that she recognizes it, in the stern plenitude of its ambiguities.

Kearney's critical analysis centres the 'tragedy' of John Connor as the dramatic focus of *Famine*, even though Epic form inaugurates spatial and temporal elaborations which critique and position tragedy as an ideological construct in itself. As O'Toole perceives, 'If Murphy's theatre is anything, it is a theatre of "several things happening at once", with the stage full of oppositions and collisions, presenting both a world of actuality and a world of metaphor.'[73]

I read Connor's 'human paradox' as one part of the fabric of *Famine*, and not as the privileged point of engagement for critical interpretations of the play. To the extent that Kearney's perspective can acknowledge the dramatic importance of Maeve's emergence from deep trauma to contemplate the possibility of a future, it is likely to position it as an example of a commitment to 'redemption' cited as characteristic of Murphy's work. Against this, I suggest that Maeve's dramatic significance resides in her enduring scepticism, her capacity to adhere to aspiration for a future worth struggling for in the face of a moment replete with apparent closure.

In the final moment of the play, her clear apprehension that what is now before her is not the possibility of a future, but a finite range of available future possibilities suggests that Eagleton's discussion of subjectivity as 'living through'[74] is a more enabling analytical tool in seeking to read the significance of her struggle to endure. From a postcolonial perspective, the last thing Maeve's struggles represent is a form of encouragement 'to transcend' material circumstances. If humour, faith or any other human resources are to be deployed in the dramatic worlds before us, they will be deployed as strategies to engage with and remake material circumstances as persons respond in action to the gap which exists between lived experience and utopian aspiration. This moment of personal refusal, of bread, and of the notion of ending, recalls Luke Gibbons's observation that 'narratives in Irish culture offer no insulation from history, and are only as resilient as their capacity to articulate the voices of those who have not been heard, rejecting the habits of authority that have enabled some to continually shout down others'.[75] Resistance to a detour away from popular aspiration toward the consolidation of social elites has been a key imperative in Irish playwrighting during the twentieth century. In forcing the condition of those excluded from the bounty of social and cultural capital in the Ireland of the post-independence generation, and in holding individual aspirations at all times in a critical dynamic with social conditions, Tom Murphy's plays may be read as a series of dramas of postcolonial desiring. The act of reading *Waiting for Godot, The Wood of the Whispering, On the Outside* and *Famine* in counterpoint to each other opens up the possibility of a transformative postcolonial poetics, by engaging with Irish drama as a series of critical responses, not only to neo-colonialism, but to postcolonial consciousness itself, as it plays out in Ireland.

O'Toole's work on Murphy is primarily concerned with canonizing Murphy, and establishing definitively the legitimacy of his claim on our attention. His succinct commentaries on the contradictory imagery of *On the Outside*, for instance, take us to the brink of connections with earlier works, and hesitate: 'the mundane story of two young men waiting outside of a rural dancehall which they don't have the money to enter takes on the metaphysical lineaments of heaven, purgatory and hell.'[76] A postcolonial development of this particular interpretation stresses both a linkage backward to Yeats's *Purgatory*, and outward to comprehend the play's staging of the awful doubleness of actuality/desire under neo-colonial conditions. Roche offers interesting accounts of relations between the works of a variety of Irish playwrights against a postcolonial background, while Margaret Llewellyn-Jones's amplification of his project to include writers marginal to his canon, tends to treat the category of the 'post-colonial' as a given. Nicholas Grene reads Murphy's work against that of Brian Friel and finds Murphy more critically engaged with Independent Ireland, and more formally innovative.[77] Form is an issue in the plays read here, as we move from the repetitions in two acts of Beckett, through the three act disrupted realism of Molloy, to the economy of Murphy's one act world, and into the multiple resonances of his Epic theatre, in search of image-metaphors adequate to the range of human experience in Independent Ireland.

It is a commonplace of critical practice to propose lines of descent in Irish theatre, and I acknowledge that such lines exist among these plays. It is also true that that is not the particular purpose of these readings. There are clear distinctions to be found in the circumstances of dramatic enunciation to which these plays give witness. In the journey from *Waiting for Godot* to *The Wood of the Whispering*, a movement outward, across the abyss that opens up at the end of Said's nationalist anti-imperialist phase of historical development, appears. This is a moment in which I read the emergence of a form of limited decolonization, the moment of elaboration of neo-colonial hegemony. The primary distinction between Vladimir and Estragon and Sanbatch and Sadie, from a postcolonial perspective, is that the latter, though 'starved and raggedy' so that they 'can't go to mass on a Sunday itself', recognize 'still there's some of the gifts of God we didn't lose yet.'[78] They may have very little, but out of their human resources, in fellowship and solidarity, and at risk to themselves, they will fashion a form of citizenship which can underpin a future in community. This is the principle which supports Sanbatch's tentative steps toward mastery of the abyss of neo-colonial existence. He is a bridge builder, a human conduit for the possibility of social transformation, for whom 'the finest thing in the world is to be a little crazy, and to have great learning.'[79]

This chapter argues that, as the logic of the economic programmes of the 1960s asserts itself, *On the Outside* dramatizes an Ireland developed from the world out of which *The Wood of the Whispering*, on one hand, and *Waiting for Godot*, on the other, sought to forge dramatic action, images and metaphors. The subjects of these plays are, like Vladimir and Estragon no longer 'presentable' in public places.[80] Sanbatch and Sadie, are 'so starved and raggedy'[81] that they cannot be seen at Sunday mass, in a country where absence from mass was a clear sign of social exclusion. Mickeleen O'Leary, Frank and Joe, embody people whose lives are elided by the official gaze exposed in the reading of *Mise Éire*. Their concerns are at the heart of dramas wrought in the period from the end of World War II to 1968, and staged powerfully again during the long 1990s. Chapter 7 argues that, during the 1970s and 1980s, Independent Ireland recapitulated the social relations and the personal dramas of emigration and degradation which marked out the 1940s and 1950s. The drift toward urbanization, specifically around Dublin, produced social conditions which generated cultural production, both responsive and prophetic, as even less visible groups, persons and experiences emerged to appropriate public space and national attention for their narratives and aspirations.

---

[1] Tom Murphy and Noel O'Donoghue, *On the Outside*, in Tom Murphy, *Plays 4* (Methuen, 1989): 165-192.

[2] Noel O'Donoghue, cited in Nicholas Grene, *The Politics of Irish Drama* (Cambridge, 1999): 220.

[3] Fintan O'Toole, *Tom Murphy: The Politics of Magic* (New Island Books, 1994), and Ibid., 'Introduction' to Tom Murphy, *Plays 4*: ix-xiv.

[4] O'Toole (1994): 38.

[5] Ibid. 41.

[6] Lionel Pilkington, *Theatre and the State in Twentieth-century Ireland: cultivating the people* (Routledge, 2001): 164.

[7] Tom Murphy, *The Wake* (Methuen, 1998), Scene 3: 17.

8 O'Toole (1994): 41.

9 Richard Kearney, *Transitions: Narratives in Irish Culture*
   (Manchester University Press, 1988): 170.

10 'It is now generally agreed that with the 1960s Irish drama enjoyed a
   second renaissance.' Christopher Murray, *Twentieth-century Irish
   Drama: mirror up to nation* (Manchester University Press, 1997):
   162.

11 Murphy and O'Donoghue: 167.

12 Ibid.169.

13 Ibid.179-180.

14 Ibid.180.

15 Ibid.170, stage direction.

16 Ibid. 179-180.

17 Ibid. 182.

18 O'Toole (1994): 45.

19 Murphy and O'Donoghue: 192.

20 Tom Murphy, *Famine* (Gallery Press, 1984).

21 '*Famine* is clearly Brechtian in its use of projected (usually ironic)
   titles above each scene, its episodic structure, and, as Fintan O'Toole
   has argued, in its insistence on the link between material and
   economic conditions on the one hand, and the intimate life of the
   mind.' Christopher Morash, *A History of Irish Theatre 1601-2000*
   (Cambridge, 2002): 229.

22 Garry Hynes directed *Famine* at the Abbey (1993). The analysis of
   dramatic action in this reading of the play draws on that production.

23 The priest who features in *The Tinker's Wedding* is an adapted rural
   abbé.

24 '(Cardinal) Cullen transformed the Irish Church from a Latin
   American type institution into one of the most efficiently marshalled
   Churches in Europe ... By 1878 few priests ... were left to disturb the
   Cullen vision of Catholic Ireland as a vast mission field.' J. J Lee,.,
   The Modernisation of Irish Society 1848-1918 (Gill & Macmillan,
   1989): 44. 'Between 1851 and 1911 the number of priests increased
   from 2,500 to 4,000, of monks from 200 to 1,200, of nuns from
   1,000 to 9,000'. Lee, *Modernisation*: 18.

25 Murphy (1984): 11-22.

26 Ibid. 11.

27 Ibid.

28 Ibid. 17.

29 Ibid. 14.

30 Ibid. 15.

31 Fine Gael's *Winning Through to a Just Society* (1965) is in many
   ways a document of radical intent: 'Irish society today denies the full
   realisation of (freedom and equality) for all citizens. It is therefore
   not a just society.' It goes on to set out the limits of its radical vision,
   'The social and economic thought of the Fine Gael party has been

formed and moulded by the social doctrines contained in the papal encyclicals ... It is our responsibility as laymen in politics to learn and appreciate these principles'. 'Introduction', *Winning Through to a Just Society* (Dublin: Fine Gael, 1965), unpaginated.

32 Murphy, *Famine*, 'Scene 2: The Moral Force': 23-31.

33 Ibid. 28-30.

34 Ibid. 30.

35 Ibid. 48-58.

36 Ibid. 51-52.

37 Ibid. 53.

38 'An analysis by Roy Geary of the census of 1946 showed that of males in the 15 to 29 age group, 92 per cent were unmarried. Even in the 20 to 39 age group 72 per cent of men were bachelors ... this was utterly extraordinary.' O'Toole, Fintan, *Black Hole, Green Card: The Disappearance of Ireland* (New Island Books, 1994): 168.

39 A social phenomenon explored in the poem by Durcan cited in Chapter Two.

40 Murphy (1984): 43-47.

41 Ibid. 43.

42 Ibid. 45.

43 Ibid.

44 Bertolt Brecht, *The Threepenny Opera*, trans. John Willett and Ralph Mannheim (Methuen, 1979): 55.

45 Murphy (1984): 47.

46 Terry Eagleton, 'Nationalism: irony and commitment', *Nationalism, Colonialism and Literature*, ed. Seamus Deane (University of Minnesota Press, 1990): 37-38.

47 Molloy (1998b): 136.

48 Article 41.1 *Bunreacht na hÉireann* [The Constitution of Ireland] (Dublin: Government Publications, 2002): 136.

49 Murphy (1984): 45-46.

50 Ibid: 87.

51 Ibid.

52 Ibid. 82-86.

53 Murphy and O'Donoghue: 179-180.

54 Murphy (1984): 87.

55 Éibhlís ní Dhuibhne, *Milseog an tSamhraidh agus Dún na mBan trí thine* (Cois Life, 1997): 1-67.

56 Peacock Theatre 1983 and 1986; Tom Mac Intyre *The Great Hunger: poem into play* (Dublin: Lilliput, 1991)

57 'Larkin ... was insistent that workers should demand flowers as well as bread on the table. O'Casey was in complete agreement.' Murray (1997): 109.

58 Kilroy: 5.

59 Ibid.

60 Ibid.

61 J. M. Synge, 'Preface to The Playboy of the Western World', *J. M. Synge: The Playboy of the Western World and Other Plays*, ed. Ann Saddlemyer (Oxford University Press, 1995): 96-7.

62 Murphy (1984): 47.

63 Saddlemyer, ed. (1995): 96.

64 'Romantic Ireland's dead and gone/It's with O'Leary in the grave.' Yeats, W. B., 'September 1913', *WB Yeats: Selected Poetry* ed. A. Norman Jeffares (Macmillan, 1972): 55.

65 Murphy (1984): 87.

66 These included Mickeleen resembling a homeless figure from the streets of emergent Celtic Tiger Dublin, shod with worn runners, and people smoking roll-up cigarettes.

67 'The past is the ancestor's, the present belongs to the living, and the future to the unborn... the immeasurable gulf of transition ... between and around these temporal definitions of experience ... is the fourth stage, the vortex of archetypes and the home of the tragic spirit.' Wole Soyinka, *Myth, Literature and the African World* (Canto, 1995): 148-149.

68 'Tom Murphy's long night's journey into night' Kearney (1988): 169.

69 Ibid. 170.

70 Ibid.

71 Ibid.

72 Soyinka (1995): 140.

73 O'Toole (1994): 55-56. Note the persistence of an opposition between the actual and the metaphorical. In a semiotic reading of theatre, of which O'Toole is elsewhere a subtle exponent, all stage action is both actual to the dramatic world(s) depicted, and metaphorical in relation to the experience/desire dynamic of the world(s) into which it plays.

74 'It is only ambiguously, precariously, that any of us can experience at once the necessary absolutism of a particular demand – to be freed, for example, from an immediate, intolerable oppression – and the more general truth that no one such demand can finally exhaust or preprogram a political future in which the content will have gone beyond the phrase'. Terry Eagleton (1990): 38.

75 Luke Gibbons, 'Narratives of the Nation: Fact, Fiction and Irish Cinema' *Theorizing Ireland*, ed. Claire Connolly (Basingstoke: Palgrave Macmillan, 2002): 75.

76 O'Toole 'Introduction' in Murphy, *Plays 4* : xi.

77 'Tom Murphy did not write the Irish plays that an Irish playwright should. Brian Friel did.' Grene (1999): 218. He develops his argument in chapters on Friel, 'Versions of Pastoral' and Murphy, 'Murphy's Ireland' in Nicholas Grene, *The Politics of Irish Drama: Plays in Context from Boucicault to Friel* (Cambridge University Press, 1999): 194-218, and pp. 219-241, respectively.

78 Molloy (1998): 135-6.

79 Ibid. 136.
80 Beckett (1975): 10.
81 Molloy (1998): 135.

7 | Countering Hegemonies: Wet Paint Arts and Calypso Productions

The period from the first Oil Crisis (1974) to the fall of the Berlin Wall (1989), was one of deepening malaise and reaction in Ireland. Statistically, emigration figures rose to levels reminiscent of the haemorrhages of the 1950s. Culturally, reactionary political movements[1] sought to reinstate the spiritual destitution of those times. When they encountered a tougher, more widely-distributed native liberalism than would have been possible thirty years previously, the stage was set for cultural warfare which endures, more than twenty years later, on battlegrounds such as the question of legislating for abortion. During the 1980s, mainstream Irish theatre engaged with such issues hardly at all, and the focus of a developing 'alternative' or 'independent' theatre sector turned decisively towards the exclusions of contemporary Ireland.

Where small-scale rural or regional amateur theatres had embraced J.B. Keane and M.J. Molloy in the 1950s and early 1960s, models of popular theatre more familiar to audiences in Britain and the developing world began to appear in the 1980s. John Arden and Margaretta D'Arcy developed agit-prop skits in response to the repressive tone of the National Coalition government of 1973-1977.[2] The Project Arts Centre saw stagings in the late 1970s of plays by Jim Sheridan and Peter Sheridan, which wore their class affiliations on their sleeves.[3] The Centre walked a thin legal line by showing John McArdle's *Jacko* (1978),[4] which problematized the role of the Church and clergy in childcare – raising, by means of a sentimental narrative, issues which would engulf the Catholic church at the beginning of the next 'beginning', the era of the Celtic Tiger. Actors Garrett Keogh and Vincent McCabe, who had worked with Arden and D'Arcy, formed Red Rex in 1983, to challenge established ways of making and experiencing theatre. Companies and initiatives such as Moving Theatre, in Dublin, Waterford Arts for All and Wexford Theatre Workshop began 'taking theatre to the people', creating works in non-standard venues[5] and by co-operative means.[6] Waterford Arts for All's claim to progeny such as Red Kettle Theatre Company, Waterford Youth Drama and Waterford Spraoi Street Festival notwithstanding, by far the most significant of these movements was Wet Paint Arts in Dublin.

Founded in 1984, Wet Paint Arts began challenging the reach and potential of drama with young audiences in the wastelands of Dublin's new suburban housing estates. David Byrne, founder-director of Wet Paint Arts, had worked as an actor, and wanted to restore the intelligence and accomplishments of the actor's performing body to the centre of theatre-making. As a performing artist, he was dissatisfied with the dominance of the writer of plays and the cult of the star actor then evident in Dublin theatre. Plays, he felt, should be wrought from the creative collaboration of actor, director and writer. Content struggled for in this way would make unavoidable formal demands on the producers as well. Wet Paint Arts was actually to go further in its collaborative processes, and work would eventually include audiences as critical creative partners in playwrighting as well as in theatrical experiences. In terms of critical cultural engagement, Wet Paint Arts' project would prove to be as significant as Garry Hynes's work on Molloy, Synge and Murphy. Where Hynes exposed the inscriptions of economic, cultural and political failure in that homeland of nationalist myth, the rural west of Ireland, Byrne and Wet Paint sought to interrogate the dynamics of inner city decay and suburban alienation in the capital city. As has been shown, plays such as Molloy's *The Wood of the Whispering*, Murphy's *Famine* and Synge's *The Well of the Saints* are formally innovative, and are marked by the use of heightened language and radical performative gestures as constituents of their fictional worlds. Similar formal characteristics accompany the most significant chapter in Wet Paint Arts' own history: the commissioning, development, and production of Dermot Bolger's first play, *The Lament for Arthur Cleary*.[7]

Just as *The Wood of the Whispering* staged the disappointments and inequities of rural Ireland betrayed, *The Lament for Arthur Cleary* is an urban drama of intranational betrayal. It is also a drama of Ireland's complex relationships with Europe.[8] Formally, *The Lament for Arthur Cleary* develops modes of address in keeping with a key dramaturgical decision by David Byrne: 'When we were working on the production, I kept in mind the requirements, and the skills, of what I felt would be mainly a young audience, maybe not very patient with – or used to – large amounts of dialogue, but very adept at reading meaning from visual material.'[9] Byrne's comments have implications for any attempt to position this play in terms of aesthetics, politics or cultural practice. The play's episodic structure foregrounds narrative as opposed to plot. It is structured as a montage, and makes use of strategies such as repetition of scenes, direct address to the audience, and heightened poetic language. All of these devices are deployed in order to enable the significance of key actions to emerge in production. From the point of view of performance, the convention of actors playing multiple roles clearly serves the needs of narrative over plot, privileges the representation of role over the assumption of character, and lays the ground for a type of complex seeing, threatening to received ways of staging who 'we' are.

The Lament for Arthur Cleary began life as a narrative poem of the same name,[10] a creative response by Dermot Bolger to *Caoineadh Airt Uí Laoire*,[11] the eighteenth century lament by Eibhlín Dhubh ní Chonaill for her murdered husband Art Ó Laoire. Bolger's play was commissioned by Wet Paint Arts for performance to audiences in various locations in the many Dublin suburbs which subsist as economic, social and cultural wildernesses. Touring to a series of what Fintan O'Toole refers to as 'places without history'[12] the play tests the poem's fictional Dublin against the responses of audiences for whom dispossession, exile, and fruitless return are experiences first, and metaphors second. *The Lament for Arthur Cleary* forces audiences to look at an Irishman as he is looked at as an alien in the 'common European home'. There is a relentless demand for engagement with his condition, exemplified in the play's return on four occasions to Arthur's experience of harassment and disorientation at a border checkpoint. As the dramatic action develops, the menacing checkpoint encounters become familiar, both as enactments of exile and forebodings of calamitous return. The border crossings reveal their significance in the gathered juxtapositions of the final enactment. They become the site, not only of memory's revisitations, but of a prophetic glimpse of the future. This is made explicit in Arthur's final conversation with the Frontier Guard:

> **Frontier Guard.** So many trains run through here, day and night, in all directions, all times, coming and going.
> **Arthur**. Who's on that one? Where's it going?

(*Looking down at platform*)
Frontier Guard. Europe ... The future ... Her children.[13]

Arthur, born into a generation of 'stateless persons, undocumented aliens in their own country',[14] contemplates an image of future generations as wandering diaspora. Stateless in his own home, his lover's children will be stateless, as Synge might have it, 'facing hog, dog or divil on the highway of the road.'[15]

The Lament for Arthur Cleary, like its source, *Caoineadh Airt Uí Laoire*, gives voice to the woman's narrative. When the lyrics of her desolation emerge in the spoken language of the play, that voice is positioned as a key organizing element of the drama. The moment of Arthur's death is densely narrated in choric verse by Kathy, before it is played out in the temporal experience of the audience. His relationship with her begins on his return to Dublin. It proves impossible to sustain, not least because the fifteen years which separate them encompass a cultural change so great as to appear to be a complete break with history. Having left behind the contradictions of the 'new beginning' of the 1960s, Arthur returns to face their consequences in the imploding social conditions of 1980s Dublin, 'the heroin capital of Europe.'[16]

Arthur Cleary is at once fully present and tightly bound to the historical figure of Art Ó Laoire, and this doubleness enables him to play an important critical role. Rooted in a Gaelic past, he restores a sense of the participation of historical experience in contemporary narratives of identity. While in Germany as a 'guest worker', the Dublin mapped out in the veins of his arm is an enabling fiction, a necessary talisman to protect and direct his wanderings. Arthur's memorial Dublin was actually a dislocation – a fantasy domesticated to the requirements of the state of exile. His 'Dublin' was fixed, unalterable, because it was never examinable against the changing circumstances of the actual city. Affirmed on his return by the continuities suggested by the presence of so many familiar signs, his drama begins when he superimposes the images generated by personal myth on real streets, among the people Dubliners of his class had become during his absence. In a savage intensification of Murphy's ironies, Dubliners have indeed become 'different people' since 'someone came along and put the bit'[17] in their veins.

The persona of the returned exile, displaced in an Ireland which has changed out of all recognition, is a familiar device in Irish cultural production, and is found even in the myths of a Gaelic society so ancient as to appear prehistoric. The legend of *Tír na nÓg*

[Land of the Young] gives rise to a phrase descriptive of the state of mind of the returned exile, *mar Oisín i ndiaidh na Féinne* [like Oisín after the Fianna][18] in which the returned emigrant experiences home as a familiar place more thoroughly foreign than a place of actual exile; home regained is the site of absence of friends, of emptiness and loss. The historical past of *Caoineadh Airt Uí Laoire* is never fully present in *The Lament for Arthur Cleary*, but it is never absent. The past maintains a presence which shadows the contemporary drama, and yet Arthur Cleary is a truly new figure in Irish theatre, in Homi Bhabha's sense of 'the new as an insurgent act of cultural translation.'[19] He is a marker of radical discontinuity between the historical circumstances of the 1980s, and the formal strategies of Irish theatre of the time. As one force at the centre of a dramatic world produced and exhibited by Wet Paint Arts for what Bennett calls 'non-traditional audiences',[20] he marks out the company's challenge to exclusions naturalized in established practices of theatrical exhibition in Ireland.

Arthur's double presence – driven by emerging struggles and residual contests – filters actually existing conditions through images of an idealized 'then', exposing the failures, omissions and exclusions of Independent Ireland now. In this sense, the present/absent quality of Arthur Cleary counters the appetite cultivated among Abbey audiences for nostalgic 'return(s) to nature and the simple life',[21] a legacy of the meeting of Blythe's programming and the indigenous bourgeoisie's need for reassurance of its achieved modernity. There can be no question of diverting engagement with Arthur's significance by recoding it as a familiar trope of 'them then'. The heroin economy into which Arthur returns is staged in complete implication in the overt economy, driven by commodity consumption, accelerating in range and quantity. The business of this play is 'us now', and as it confronts its audience, so its audience must confront its reading of this present as not just immediate, but strange.

The Lament for Arthur Cleary is a radical text of late twentieth-century Irish theatre, and an important site of negotiations around contemporary mutations of Irish identity. While its status as an act of theatre has been the chief concern of the discussion to now, the choices made by Dermot Bolger, as a writer, need to be examined, because his gesture in appropriating and reworking a canonical narrative of the Gaelic world in the service of the concerns of contemporary Dublin is of considerable significance. Here, in

Amkpa's terms, is a postcolonial act, in which the artist writes back, not to empire, but in the spirit of the wretched of the earth, to the canonized source of official nationalist iconography itself. In Said's schema, *The Lament for Arthur Cleary* is an artefact of liberationist anti-imperialism, in which the radical recalcitrance of Ireland's urban margins to official narratives is made visible. The stage of the National Theatre did not generate this work of auto-critique, but it becomes its destination. By mapping a moment from the long narrative of colonial oppression onto the struggle for self-actualization in 1980s Dublin, Bolger's gesture recalls Murphy's association of the famine of the 1840s with the betrayals of the 1950s and 1960s. There is no margin for misreading Bolger, however – as Hynes found audiences sought to do with *Famine* – as his social palimpsest layers reality, not on to historical fact, but on to poetry and a mythic past, so clearly the repository of images mobilized to narrate Ireland's continuities to itself. Further to this, by centring Arthur's experience in the play, Wet Paint Arts involves the audience in acts of identification with the experience of wandering. In this way, *The Lament for Arthur Cleary* exposes to critical view the assumptions underlying notions of home and experience which authenticate official narratives of a homogenized Irish identity.

Perhaps the most significant achievement of Wet Paint Arts' staging of *The Lament for Arthur Cleary* was registered at the level of cultural politics: the play includes its audience. In pre-production and development, the company of five actors would hold open workshops and response sessions with people in areas to which it was intended to tour the finished play. In the circumstances of performance, the class whose experiences it stages, which is also the play's primary point of address, occupies its place on the cultural map, and must be considered as part of the public sphere. In this way, *The Lament for Arthur Cleary* extends both the dramaturgical strategies and intranational critique of Molloy and Murphy, and occupies and extends Luke Gibbons's category of 'resilient narrative'.[22] In the wake of this play, Irish cultural production which does not envision this public as constituting part of its audience is obliged to acknowledge this choice and to address the reasons why.

The arrival of *The Lament for Arthur Cleary* at the Peacock Theatre in 1989, as the winner of an Edinburgh Festival Fringe First Award, simultaneously announces and problematizes a moment emergent at the beginning of the 1990s. This was the occasion of an apparently more generous willingness on the part of Independent Ireland to at last examine critically all aspects of the socio-cultural complex it had become. The defining event of that time is the election of Mary Robinson as President of Ireland. Public endorsement of Robinson's rhetoric of inclusion, elaborated in her careful handling of symbols, amounted to a political and cultural watershed. As with other instances of historical circumstances exceeding established conventions of representation, the election, not only of a woman, but of a champion of the liberal/left, appeared to many as an example of historical caesura.[23] The official rhetoric of state nationalism, as it mutated into the cultural camouflage of neo-colonialism signally failed to articulate an aspiration to inclusive democracy. The principal victims of this development were the mass of the people and the integrity of the public sphere. Robinson's achievement was read by some of her supporters as a breakthrough to a kind of post-nationalism, in which the people of Independent Ireland shook off the need to define themselves in relation to the tropes of a nationalism whose ultimate purpose was not to be British. While acknowledging the cultural urgency underpinning such feelings, I caution against the notion of 'post-' as the bearer of yet another 'new beginning' that becomes all too readily a false dawn. In Richard Kearney's rhetorical utopianism, the 'post-' as caesura appears to qualify both the nation and modernity itself. From a postcolonial perspective, Robinson's significance resides in her embodiment, at the heart of the state's institutional structures, of a form of critical public consciousness. Her election results from and exposes a commitment to 'living through': 'to undo this alienation, you had to go ... somehow all the way through it and out the other side.'[24]

Living through the contradictions of Independent Ireland was a critical stance all but disabled by the ideological projects of the post-revolutionary elites. The tone of the 1940s and 1950s, as M.J. Molloy's preface to *The Wood of the Whispering* argues, was set by power configurations which eschewed practical decolonization in favour of socio-economic conservatism, and metaphysical contemplation of the essential qualities of Irishness. Gerry Smyth, Lionel Pilkington and others have shown how the state's obsessive regimes of canonization and codification produced coercive structures of exclusion and alienation. The impact of such structures is vividly attested to in Austin Clarke's, 'The Envy of Poor Lovers' (1955):[25]

Lying in the grass as if it were a sin
To move, they hold each other's breath, tremble,
Ready to share that ancient dread – kisses begin
Again – of Ireland keeping company with them.
Think, children, of institutions mured above
Your ignorance, where every look is veiled,
State-paid to snatch away the folly of poor lovers
For whom, it seems, the sacraments have failed.[26]

At the level of political choice, metaphysics and nostalgia substituted for developmental programmes: 'De Valera yearned for a self-sufficient, bucolic, Gaelic utopia ... The Irish people were not prepared to accept the level of frugality that a primarily agricultural society imposed upon them. The result was sustained emigration.'[27] For those who stayed – a generation schooled to the task of inheriting De Valera's 'ideal Ireland' – the brief boom of the 1960s was presented as manifest confirmation of the achievement under native government of the God-given right of Irish people to prosperity on their own soil. This rhetoric withered in the face of the economic, political and social convulsions of the 1970s and 1980s. In 1989, in one of the merciless ironies of history, Mary Robinson defeated, against all the odds, the Fianna Fáil candidate Brian Lenihan, model for the rhetoric of Bolger's smug Politician: 'We know we cannot all live on this one island.'[28]

De Valera's cosy homestead, a generation on, was full. Or had some rooms been boarded up? As a summary of the betrayals of neo-colonialism, Lenihan's phrase is remarkably efficient, a point not lost on Dermot Bolger, when he incorporated and elaborated it in the Politician's speech in *The Lament for Arthur Cleary*:

> We in government are realists first and foremost. We know we cannot all live on this one island. But we are not ashamed. Young people are to Ireland what champagne is to France! Our finest crop, the cream of our youth, nurtured from birth, raised with tender love by our young state, brought to ripeness and then plucked! For export to your factories and offices. Fellow European ministers ... we know you will not turn your backs on them.[29]

The journey from the hegemony – even as a residual social force – of De Valera's symbolic Ireland to the emergence of that of Mary Robinson has a parallel in the development in Irish drama visible in the distance travelled from *Famine* to *The Lament for Arthur Cleary*. Bolger, and his director, David Byrne, developed epic dramaturgy in the light of indigenous representational strategies –

setting out to activate aspects of the past in the service of present desires. Their work also shifts the co-ordinates of Irish identity away from the binary inaugurated by colonial relations, toward a more nuanced, more difficult and more promising engagement with intranational problems in a European context. In Lenihan's remark, and Bolger's deft elaboration on it, the European ideal, attractive to the mass of Irish people for its developed concept of citizenship, is reduced to the status of a waste disposal unit for surplus humanity. On the journey from 'small open economy' to 'small island', a senior Fianna Fáil figure takes us through the heart of neo-colonial cynicism, and announces the bankruptcy of indigenous nationalist elites in terms recognizable to Constantino[30] or Fanon.[31]

The affront to such elites which Mary Robinson represented may be grasped in her announcement of an alternative cultural model in her inaugural speech:

> My primary role as President will be to represent this state. But the State is not the only model of community with which Irish people can and do identify. Beyond our state there is a vast community of Irish emigrants extending not only across our neighbouring island – which has provided a home away from home for several Irish generations – but also throughout the continents of North America, Australia and of course Europe itself. There are over 70 million people living on this globe who claim Irish descent. I will be proud to represent them. And I would like to see Áras an Uachtaráin, my official residence, serve – on something of an annual basis – as a place where our emigrant communities could send representatives for a get-together of the extended Irish family abroad.[32]

This holds out the possibility of an engaged, decolonizing independence, an opening of the present beyond geographical frontiers, and a willingness to engage with a diaspora whose very existence embodies many of the contradictions, injustices and failures of colonial and neo-colonial policies and practices. Ireland, beyond and within itself, is offered as a series of points of identification to those for whom the homesteads of nationalist myth-making were never big enough in the first place. In another sense, Robinson appeals here to 'the people' over the state, but with a different end in prospect than that envisaged by De Valera. She invokes the numerical weight of 'Irish people' globally distributed, primarily to reinvigorate the role of civil society in Independent Ireland. Robinson's role is a symbolic one, but she understands the importance of symbols in the matter of the plurality of identifications which underpin identities.[33] Her interpretation of the 'old concept of the Fifth Province'[34] amounts to a move, in striking contrast to De Valera, to place metaphysics at the service of the people, as a power for reformulating political discourse:

> Ancient legends divided Ireland into four quarters and a 'middle', although they differed about the location of this middle or Fifth Province. While Tara was the political centre of Ireland, tradition has it that this Fifth Province acted as a second centre, a necessary balance. If I am a symbol of anything I would like to be a symbol of this reconciling and healing Fifth Province ... The Fifth Province is not anywhere here or there, north or south, east or west. It is a place within each one of us – that place that is open to the other, that swinging door that allows us to venture out and others to venture in.[35]

In an interesting echo of Bolger's strategy in *The Lament for Arthur Cleary*, Robinson appropriates an ancient myth, with a knowing nod to the propensities of cultural nationalism to do just that. The difference is that she does so in the service of people living in the here and now. Not alone that, but she chooses a myth which is the very figure of indeterminacy, and points – as in my reading of *Cathleen Ní Houlihan* – to the radical ambiguity immanent in all moments of real change and new beginning. For all her exultation in the symbolic, and in spite of her official designation as being 'above politics', Mary Robinson is acutely sensitive to the responsibilities and to the opportunities of elected office. This 'second centre' of necessary balance is far from an attempt, as with populist politicians, to posit an existence for themselves outside of failed institutions and unpopular policies. It represents a practical attempt to think into existence a broader, richer public sphere.

The practical nature of this thinking is elaborated in her remarks on:

> Another level of community which I will represent ... the local community. Within our State there are a growing number of local and regional communities determined to express their own creativity, identity, heritage and initiative in new and exciting ways ... As President I will seek to the best of my abilities to promote this growing sense of local participatory democracy, this emerging movement of self-development and self-expression which is surfacing more and more at grassroots level. This is the face of modern Ireland.[36]

These words stand in contradiction to the exclusions so corrosive of democracy which had come, for many people, to typify lived experience in 'our' State. In Mary Robinson's attempt at definition, the land is bright with the energy of human diversity, not with the flickering lamps of cosy, drowsy homesteads. The ideal Ireland is not a matter of hopeful archaeology, but of deliberate, goal-directed becoming of ourselves with others.

The vigour of debates around the terms of relationships within Ireland itself, and with Europe and the broader world, testifies to the rapidity of change in Independent Ireland at the end of the 1980s. For some, Ireland was ready to take its place among its peers as a modern member-state of the European Union. For others, taking that place was a mixed achievement, compromised by the history of such peers as colonial oppressors and neo-colonial apologists for global inequality.[37] In keenly felt ways, the closing dialogue of *Famine* echoes even as Robinson is inaugurated. The sense of the times was that Irish citizenship, whether expressed in Robinson's postcolonialism or in the 'new realism' of capitalist opportunism, was now experienced in local, European and global terms. If Wet Paint Arts, less than ten years previously, had begun projects of intranational critique in Dublin's housing estates, these times drove some artists toward the problematics of staging fictions enacted in emerging relationships between nation-states, Europe and its others, or globalization.

Calypso Productions[38] emerged in response to that challenge. The company's mission statement of 1995 is about as far as you can possibly travel from the blandness of the genre:

> Calypso's mission is simple, practical and humble. We want to change the world ... the change we want to effect is small, significant and possible ... By our future world family, we will be remembered in one of two ways. We will either have been caring guardians who nurtured their inheritance – social, political, artistic, environmental and sacred – or we will have been the parasites who depleted some of the hope and possibility from their lives. We are all world citizens. Some of us are lucky enough to have inherited life saving rights, life enhancing social opportunities and life affirming creative possibilities. With those rights and privileges comes a responsibility to defend them for ourselves and for others.[39]

The company was formed in autumn 1993 by playwrights Dónal O'Kelly and Kenneth Glenaan, with Charlie O'Neill. Unusually, one writer was based in Dublin, and one in Glasgow. Although this arrangement was to prove too difficult to sustain over time, it culminated significantly in O'Kelly and Glenaan's jointly written *The Business of Blood* (1995), which played in both Scotland and Ireland. 'Calypso' was attractive to the founders because it evoked the creole music of the Caribbean islands, where music became the voice of the voiceless. The decision to describe themselves as 'Calypso Productions' rather than 'Calypso Theatre Company', is a deliberate reflection of their commitment to developing educational programmes and resource materials, alongside theatre, site specific and street performances. The educational materials are circulated widely, and especially to legislators, to whom they are intended as a challenge.

Calypso Productions is funded by *An Chomhairle Ealaíon* [The Arts Council], and seeks dedicated funding from other agencies as appropriate to its various projects. For instance *Cell* by Paula Meehan (1999) attracted funding from the Department of Justice, Equality and Law Reform because it addressed the issue of women's experiences of imprisonment. In its focus on partnerships and its dedication to using 'theatrical narrative to tell stories and to raise awareness about people whose lives are shaped by dramatic events',[40] Calypso is very much a phenomenon of 1990s theatre and society in the Republic of Ireland. This is borne out by its production history between 1993 and 1999: *Hughie on the Wires* by Dónal O'Kelly (1993), *Trickledown Town* by Dónal O'Kelly (1994), *The Business of Blood* by Dónal O'Kelly and Kenneth Glenaan (1995), *Rosie and Starwars* by Charlie O'Neill (1997), *Féile Fáilte* – a street festival celebrating cultural diversity – directed by Declan Gorman (1997), *Farawayan* by Dónal O'Kelly (1998) and *Cell* by Paula Meehan (1999). *Hughie on the Wires* places a young Derry man in El Salvador, achieving multiple resonances between Northern Ireland and Central America; *Trickledown Town* is set in the Caribbean, where an Irish-born functionary of the World Bank comes face to face with the ironies of his dual identity as citizen of a former colony and agent of neo-imperialism; *Féile Fáilte* is a street carnival featuring a fire-breathing Celtic Tiger, repressive border guards, frightened refugees and a newspaperman with the slogan 'Before you open your mind, poison it – with the Daily Lie.'[41]

The Business of Blood by Dónal O'Kelly and Kenneth Glenaan[42] stages the story of Chris Cole, a Christian pacifist who broke into British Aerospace Stevenage and destroyed components of the nosecones of Hawk jetfighters. He acted in order to draw attention both to their use against civilian populations in East Timor, and to what he saw as the hypocrisy of a British government which publicly announces that it does not sell arms to regimes known to be involved in human rights abuses. The deliberate, uncompromising selection of incidents which illustrate lethal double standards in high places and in the population at large characterizes the episodes dramatized in *The Business of Blood*. The consequences of such contradictions in western *realpolitik* are stark and final for peoples of other worlds. It is Calypso's particular concern to expose the extent to which strategic blindness and amnesia at government level have immediate and long-term consequences within western democratic regimes themselves. Recognizably related to British and American workers' theatre of the 1930s, the play provoked sharp dispute in the columns of *The Irish Times*. It was dismissed in David Nowlan's review as follows:

> It has been said, inter alia, that drama is comprised of conflict and change, yet within this work there is no dramatic conflict and there has been no significant change at its conclusion. This is theatre being used to make a point rather than a point being used to create drama.[43]

The message is clear, this is not dramatic art. Fintan O'Toole responded:

> There is a strong tendency to patronise such writing, to see it as at best a lesser form of art, at worst a corruption of aesthetic purity ... The question posed by *The Business of Blood* – whether civilisation can be said to exist at all while complicity with mass murder is treated as a legitimate business – is a question that addresses the very possibility of art itself.[44]

It is clear that when art begins to address the terrain of geo-politics it opens up the question of its own topography as well.

Calypso's engagement with lives lived on globalization's dangerous margins raises questions of dramatic form and audience positions, and this is especially evident in the company's programme for 1997-1998: *Rosie and Starwars* by Charlie O'Neill, directed by Garrett Keogh, *Féile Fáilte*, directed by Declan Gorman and *Farawayan*, written and directed by Dónal O'Kelly. In O'Neill's case, the broad issues were the implications of cultural representation for the lived experience of marginal groups – specifically travellers – and audience composition for theatre events. Both Gorman's production and O'Kelly's play take up these priorities, with *Farawayan* marking a major departure for the company and a signpost toward futures both for the political agency of cultural workers, and for developments in Irish theatre practices in the twenty-first century:

> Too often art and artists travel a journey where the landscapes they move through and the people they encounter become mere observations, ideas to be used. Other artists travel as participants in their landscapes. Their work is about, and comes from their interaction with their fellow world citizens ... Our landscape covers the planet. Our family is global. Our creativity is a critical one.[45]

This assertion of artists' implication in, as opposed to detachment from, the world is central to Calypso's cultural project. Calypso consciously addresses the actual/virtual dynamic of late twentieth-century globalization in ways clearly different from John Crowley's *True Lines*[46] or *Double Helix*[47] for instance. Crowley's work stages young Irish people at large in a shrinking world, engaged with – even embodying – contemporary technology. Formal innovation here foregrounds individual experiences as isolated phenomena elaborated in a global playground. It is of some significance, perhaps, that Calypso's intervention in *The Business of Blood*, along with Donal O'Kelly's *Asylum! Asylum!*[48] addresses a public which had to have issues of race, neo-imperialism and oppression presented to it as if from afar. Even five years on, such an Ireland no longer existed. Ostentatiously prosperous under late capitalism, by 1997 Independent Ireland corresponds to what Ben Agger describes as a 'capitalist, racist and sexist'[49] society, with stark examples of the inequities and exclusions typical of globalized socio-economic orders. Between 1995 and 1998, Calypso Productions exposes the local elaboration of the new international paradigm in its focus on intranational betrayals: of travelling people, refugees and asylum seekers, and a poor, criminalized 'underclass' – the latter a most appalling designation, even in 'a betrayed republic'.[50] This stance aligns Calypso with Cornel West's category of 'new cultural worker'[51] whose central task is the demystification of the seemingly bewildering configurations of globally elaborated economic, social, cultural and political coalitions which characterize lived experience in the western world, as the 1990s draws to a close.

Rosie and Starwars, by Charlie O'Neill, is Calypso's principal contribution to the European Year Against Racism (1997). O'Neill's strategy of refiguring an apparently known material world as a problem is achieved principally by means of that great trope of bourgeois entertainment: boy meets girl. The boy is the ludicrous-but-likeable Seánie 'Starwars' Whelan. The girl is Rosie Joyce, a settled traveller and single parent. *Rosie and Starwars* is set in Ennis, the capital of County Clare. It is 1995 and Clare are about to win the All-Ireland Hurling championship for the first time in over eighty years. In the words of 'Starwars' – a member of the county Under 21 panel – 'The whole county was goin' apeshit on skates!'[52] The play derives its narrative force from the coincidence of success on the hurling field – with its accompanying protestations of the natural superiority of Clare identity – and a crisis involving the occupants of an unserviced halting site for travellers on the outside of the town. Seánie's father, Tom Whelan, is involved in a consortium which plans to develop land which includes the halting site. A local reporter, Jim Furlong, becomes involved when another member of the clandestine consortium, Councillor Larry Hartigan, declares at a Council meeting that traveller men should be clinically castrated. Rosie Joyce, who meets and begins an intimate relationship with Seánie, lives in nearby Limerick city where she works at a Travellers' Resource Centre. Rosie lost part of her leg in an accident when she was four, the details of which are unresolved between herself and her father, Paddy, in whose company she was at the time. After the accident, she was taken from her family on the halting site and placed in care. Rosie's mother, Chrissie Joyce, is involved in agitation to have the unofficial site provided with services.

The play's narrative reaches a climax on the night the Clare hurling team brings home the Liam McCarthy Cup. Seánie and his pals celebrate wildly on a night that 'Ennis was like Rio!' At the same time, Hartigan and a gang of masked thugs attack the traveller families and burn their caravans. Rosie's son, JoJo is trapped in a caravan consumed in flames. In the confusion, Paddy emerges with the child, safe and sound. Police and media extol his heroism. In a final twist, Paddy's revelation that it was a masked attacker who retrieved JoJo from the flames and handed the child to him is blurted out in the course of an interview on national radio by Rosie, infuriated at the construction being placed on the events of that night by a man she had trusted, Jim Furlong. The play foregrounds questions of identity, entitlement and power relations. It attempts to contextualize travellers' difference by deliberately situating traveller experience in relation to the assumptions of the sedentary population, both privately held and publicly promulgated by the communications media.

Members of the Cork Travellers' Visibility Group (TVG) attended a performance of *Rosie and Starwars* on 25 March 1997. During a follow up reflection two days later, the women generated a number of content areas central to my concerns:

> the significance of representation in the construction and delimitation of Travellers' citizenship;
> the mismatch between Traveller experience and the representation of Travellers in cultural production;
> the role of representation in social change.[53]

As travellers see it,[54] there are two categories of traveller in Ireland: actually existing people with specific life histories and experiences, and a textual fantasy, communicated through mainstream cultural production. Let us call the one, traveller, and the other Traveller. As a mediated text, a fiction in which the life experiences to which it claims to refer are often submerged, if not repudiated, Traveller is overwhelmingly constructed in pejorative terms. It is an affront to bourgeois social norms, in opposition to which it is structured in the first place. The authorship of that text is to be found outside traveller society, in the dominant group. Traveller embodies all of the features of stereotype in its quality of being frozen in time, simultaneously childlike and sinister. In a country where many people no longer have day-to-day contact with travellers, familiarity is a function not of lived experience, but of the conventions of cultural production, notably those of film and television.

Stuart Hall points out that

> How things are represented and the 'machineries' and regimes of representation in a culture do play a *constitutive*, and not merely a reflexive, after-the-event role. This gives questions of culture and ideology and the scenarios of representation – subjectivity, identity, politics – a formative, not merely an expressive, place in the constitution of social and political life.[55]

Film is a fiction, but with formidable power to constitute private and social realities. The classical narrative paradigm with its trajectory of norm – disruption – crisis – resolution in return of norm, is particularly socially influential. Travellers who attended showings of *Rosie and Starwars* were acutely aware of this, and criticized *The Field*[56] and *Trojan Eddie*[57] – films popular around the time *Rosie and Starwars* was being written, for figuring the people and the worlds depicted in them as fixed, known and closed to critical questioning. In contrast to the play, both films depict Traveller families in essential terms, especially in relation to gender roles. *Trojan Eddie* stages a physically powerful patriarch, *The Field* a shifty conspiratorial one. Mothers are resigned, survival-driven. Daughters are sexually alluring, their desires leading men into conflicts resulting in a range of outcomes, from role-reversal to ruin and death.

The travelling people, the tinkers, are a key presence in *The Field*. In narrative terms, Bull McCabe's ultimate desolation is figured as their revenge for his son's (Tadhg) killing their stallion donkey which had wandered into the eponymous field. Symbolically, their presence is a constant, fearsome reminder of dispossession and exile. The Travellers amount to a tangible repudiation of, and threat to, Bull's dream of permanent respectability rooted in ownership of the land. In terms of the shattering of his father's hopes, Tadhg's spectacular fall to his death is actually superfluous. The event in itself is necessary to the conventions of tragedy on this scale, and enables closure of the film's narrative. Thematically, Tadhg's death erases the victory won in taking possession of the field; visually, his tumble into the sea maps on to the opening sequence, the dumping of the tinker's donkey. The narrative loop has been closed, but for Bull it is the image of Tadhg setting off down the road in a barrel-top caravan which is decisive. His struggles for the field – in toil, thrift and eventually murder – underpinned by his craving to pass on a viable inheritance – are foreclosed in this image. By taking to the road to wander as a man of no property, Tadhg evokes in Bull a terror he had worked night and day to avoid. The son appears in his father's eyes as an accretion of the spectres of history, a cancellation of the future of the race. Linked forever to the traumas of famine and exile, he will carry into the future the terrifying ghosts of the past and the horrifying insecurities of the Irish diaspora, a living negation of the pure community of blood of which Bull dreams.

As in Sheridan's film, Travellers are a central presence in *Trojan Eddie*. Richard Harris portrays John Power, the patriarch of a settled Traveller family. Brendan Gleeson plays his thuggish son Ginger, enforcer of his father's writ and overseer of Eddie and the other 'buffers'[58] who grind out a living under licence from Power. Even though Power's trading activities are above board and legal, the depiction of the family members and the business operation participates in the grammar of crime films. Scenes in which Power, his hands heavy with rings, is encountered seated in chiaroscuro in an inner room behind a solid writing desk, specifically recall film depictions of mafia figures. This genre choice positions aspects of Traveller life which underpin their social cohesion – uncompromising adherence to family ties, and respect for elders and tradition – as sinister and threatening to sedentary society. Thus, what might be regarded in other groups as social strengths, are coded as introverted, primitive and dangerous. The extensive coverage of the Traveller wedding, with its undercurrent of ghoulish possession, by the lustful old man, of both the body and the dowry of the young woman participates in this construction. On the other hand, Eddie and his associates are actual petty criminals, prepared to exploit Power and his wealth. The choice of Stephen Rea to play Eddie and the construction of a harmless fecklessness as his defining characteristic enables the audience to exonerate him from criminality and to side with him as retribution, in the shape of Power, looms. Read in this way, the text exhibits the double effect of racism at the heart of its narrative structure: the internal strength of Traveller family structures is constructed as socially deviant; the behaviour of the sedentary petty criminal eludes censure by means of its participation in the sympathetic iconography of 'the little guy'.

Many members of the TVG had attended the first screening of *Trojan Eddie* at the Cork Film Festival (October 1996), and their appreciation of *Rosie and Starwars* was often expressed in terms of its difference from the film. 'Mary' was insistent that because sedentary people had little or no contact with travellers, their lives and culture, the apparent verisimilitude of *Trojan Eddie* would result in the development and perpetuation of constructs of traveller life both durable and injurious. She spoke of the trepidation with which she had entered the theatre to see *Rosie and Starwars*, following her experience at *Trojan Eddie*. 'Eileen' agreed that she had wanted the ground to open up and swallow her as she left the cinema. In this light, the depiction of the Joyce family and their life experiences in *Rosie and Starwars* was warmly endorsed by the women. One of the younger women present offered an instructive comment on the positive nature of that depiction:

> I didn't mind the settled people in the play saying we was knackers. We laughed too because of the people who said it, and because you could see the real life of the travellers on the stage as well. We don't want to pretend that travellers are saints. We just want both sides of the story.

A principal objection to *Trojan Eddie* concerned the sexualized representation of the young Traveller woman, the object of John Power's attentions. The group took exception to a scene in which she removes her clothing and dives naked into a river in front of Power, his grandson and Eddie. Asserting that this was unthinkable in traveller culture, 'Eileen' referred to the use of a similar scene in *The Field*. 'No Traveller woman would pick up her skirt and dance around a fire and look at a man – especially a settled man – like that. And in front of her father? At that time the women would have been in the background, in the shadows.' This comment maps on to Jim MacLaughlin's reading of *The Field*, a work in which he detects Keane's 'deep dislike for the poorest of the rural poor'.[59] He continues:

> Thus, in *The Field*, the 'tinker woman' is at once a 'dirty tinker' and a 'dirty whore'. In Jim Sheridan's film adaptation of the play she is a red-haired girl who uses her alluring sexuality to entice Bull McCabe's only son off the land ... the 'tinker woman' was an affront to all patriarchal values ... the very survival of the Travelling way of life (affronted) the hegemonic ideals of the petty bourgeoisie ...[60]

Taken together, Eileen's objection and MacLaughlin's reading draw attention to the fact that, in a narrative otherwise redolent of verisimilitude, Travellers appear as exotics: their milieu is a liminal world within a world. Loud with music and intoxicated by seductive dancing, the camp to which Tadhg is attracted is a place of desire, licence and release.

MacLaughlin situates this representation of Traveller life in Romantic Orientalism, a matrix of discourses of nostalgia and desire: 'Romanticizations of gypsies and nomads, common in Oriental and Western *fictions* in the nineteenth century, are in sharp contrast to the vilification of nomadic peoples and travelling cultures in Western *society*.'[61] European Romanticism's 'exoticization of Gypsies and the nomadic Romany is particularly evident in Prosper Merimée's novel *Carmen*, and in Bizet's opera of the same name. In *Carmen*, the Gypsy woman is an exotic 'other' who is the opposite to the staid Victorian image of motherhood.'[62] The Carmen figure is of Mediterranean origin and MacLaughlin points out that Mediterranean gypsies 'were largely sedentary'[63] interacting intimately 'with settled society and with other nomadic groups'.[64] Irish travellers conform to the more nomadic northern European pattern. These facts notwithstanding, it is the widely distributed Carmen figure which informs the Traveller woman depicted in *The Field*, a figure in which the category Traveller undergoes a double emptying. Travellers neither recognize nor endorse the association with sexual licence. Neither does the degree of intimacy with the sedentary population map on to the reality of many Irish Travellers. Emptied of referents in lived experience, the figure of the Traveller woman is a free-floating signifier available for attachment to a range of fears, desires and prejudices constructed in conformity with the dominant, sedentary perspective. The 'tinker woman' thus constructed recalls Homi Bhabha's discussions of the colonial stereotype.[65]

In Charlie O'Neill's play, Rosie Joyce exudes independence and worldly wisdom. She differs radically from the young women in the films in her assertiveness and independence. What she shares with them is her sexual availability, albeit without the edge of disaster which accompanies it in the film roles. Not only is Rosie available, she is a sexually confident young woman. She openly acknowledges the fact that her son JoJo embodies her deviance from traveller mores. In entering into a sexual relationship outside marriage and outside the group, Rosie disappoints her mother, now raising JoJo as her own son, and earns her father's opprobrium. *Rosie and Starwars* stages one moment of sexual advance, in which Rosie announces her intention to stay overnight with the ludicrous Starwars, in his home in his father's absence. At a level of narrative, it enables her to be found there the following morning by Tom Whelan, and initiates another episode in which racial hatred is expressed – sharpened in this instance by the fear of miscegenation reminiscent of Bull McCabe's horror in *The Field*. Other dramatic devices would have served equally well in enabling Whelan to vent similar invective. The episode might have deepened an emergent love story which might have taken the play into the dynamics of other tales of star-crossed lovers. That it doesn't do so prompts the question as to why this representational option is taken in a play which sets out to rewrite the text, Traveller? The members of the Cork TVG argued that the scene was necessary to the unfolding story, and that in the context of the construction of Rosie's life history offered in the play, her behaviour made sense. The women accepted the behaviour as a regrettable, and predictable consequence of her having lived among settled people, due to her having been taken into care in her formative years. She wouldn't have done that 'if she had been raised as a traveller.'

The Traveller family depicted in *The Field* functions in the film's narrative as a trope, a closed figuration on which the final word has already been spoken. Associated with magic, curses, misfortune and the evil eye, it resonates within the dynamic of attraction and repulsion which underpins dominant accounts of the subaltern body. The tinkers, the tinker woman are emptied of associations with lived experience, and appear before mainstream audiences as categories to be filled with terror and longing. The Travellers depicted in *Trojan Eddie* are more complex. At one level, and especially in the figure of the young woman as object of desire, they conform to the construction of Traveller identified in my reading of *The Field*. At another, they disappear as fact and re-emerge only as a form of behaviour. Power's family are settled travellers, and are not readable as a depiction of travelling people, pure and simple. Neither are they readable as sedentary people, however, and the film opts to locate them in a liminal world, aligned with that of Travellers. Accordingly, the Powers are assigned characteristics which confirm their status as Travellers in all but name: violence and lust. Though well-to-do, the Powers continue to deal in scrap, and to maintain bonds with nomadic Travellers, strongly emphasized in the wedding sequences. These characteristics point to an essential Traveller nature in which they will always function, and against which their actions and attitudes make sense. While Ginger may live in a house, socialize and conduct relationships like any working class male, his principal contribution to the narrative is made in acts of intimidation and murder. It is in these moments that the film marks him out as a Traveller man. The nomadic Travellers depicted in the film are figured as functions of the world controlled by John Power. They are found in, and emphasize, the film's predominantly squalid locations. In summary, both films construct the text Traveller in pejorative terms. 'Traveller' appears in these films as an affront to the metropolitan norms with which it is placed in conflict, and which the films' representational strategies endorse as the appropriate one for its expected audience. Their lived experiences distorted and erased on screen, the presence of travellers as citizens is simply not envisaged.

Rosie and Starwars deliberately problematizes the mediation, by the text Traveller, of relationships between travellers and the sedentary population. In setting the action at the time of the Hurling Championship, *Rosie and Starwars* situates sedentary people in discourses of excess, exuberant tribalism and drunkenness –

conditions typically associated with stereotypes of Traveller. Chrissie Joyce differs from the careworn Traveller mothers of the films in her espousal of organized political action as a means of bettering her family's circumstances. Neither childlike nor sinister, the traveller patriarch, Paddy Joyce, is a working man on whose life the tide has gone out: 'Once the skill in me hands was a blessing, now it's a disease.' O'Neill's careful depiction of the Joyce family as rounded human beings – grounded in his detailed research into traveller experience, and the warmth of his lively script – entitles them to a legitimate call on audience understanding as they attempt to make their way in the world, and is particularly effective in debunking stereotypical fantasies. Rosie herself deliberately opts for action in response to a sharp and thoughtful analysis of the needs of her family's situation. As protagonist and chorus, actor and observer, she names the racism staged in various episodes. Her stance problematizes the roles, not only of the apparently respectable Tom Whelan, but of the would-be detached Jim Furlong. It is in Rosie's presence also that any escapist impetus to romanticize traveller culture is resisted.

Rosie and Starwars does more than thematize and stage everyday encounters in which racism becomes visible. In naming the perspective which obscures its presence, the play stages the invisible power of racist discourse to structure and marginalize a people. In its explicit interrogation of reporter Jim Furlong's mediation of realities apparent to the play's audiences, *Rosie and Starwars* opens up the question of how content comes in these times to be known. The further question as to in whose interests these constructs of factual events circulate and operate is explicit in the action of the play and in Rosie's words. O'Neill's decision to privilege the life experiences of a young traveller woman results in much more than a novel focus for dramatic narrative. It gives rise to a dynamic of action and reflection, of narrative and ethical questioning which grounds the play's transformative potential. It raises urgent questions of knowledge, pedagogy and power and their relationship to cultural participation and social agency. In this way, it responds to and elaborates the transformative consequences of some of Mary Robinson's key concerns. *Rosie and Starwars* obliges audiences to engage with the role of culture in the social construction of reality, and foregrounds the central issue raised by travellers' life experiences: the effective limits of Irish citizenship.

Rosie and Starwars is a cultural intervention within limitations. While the play is undoubtedly a very different order of cultural production from the films mentioned, left to stand alone it can be marginalized as *The Business of Blood* was dismissed. It is for this reason that Calypso produced an accompanying portfolio, *Information and Action on Racism*. The company also committed itself to a programme of exploratory reflection, seminars and discussions during the tour. These strategies contextualize and problematize the performance text, and the range of possible audience positions it may evoke. The point at issue here is not one of access to commodities. The project is specifically and overtly pedagogical. In its commitment to including travellers in audiences for the play, and as participants in workshops and discussions arising from it, Calypso extends its cultural project in important ways. The company's programme situates audiences in critical sites where difference is textualized as part of, rather than apart from, social and cultural experience. This strategy has significant potential to initiate social development through dialogue.

Rosie and Starwars marks an important attempt to reposition readers because of choices deliberately made in its (re)construction of the text Traveller. This is a highly significant achievement, and one which marks both the radical potential of the project and a real development for Calypso around their understanding of the ways in which traveller experience challenges the credibility of Irish citizenship as a guarantor of fundamental rights and opportunities. Generated on the margins of a culture, and at the limits of theatre as a social form within that culture, the figure of Rosie marks a site of cultural discontinuity, of the breakdown of an Irish 'we' as a point of address. In her capacity to embody and enact the experiences and concerns of persons marginal to an official gaze, Rosie is as necessary to her moment as was Arthur Cleary, or Martin Doul, to his.

Farawayan, a performance in eight scenes written and directed by Donal O'Kelly, extends the focus of the *Rosie and Starwars* project to the experiences of refugees and asylum seekers in late 1990s Ireland. *Farawayan* uses the spectacular potential of theatre form to shift the rigid framing of the texts Refugee, Immigrant and Asylum Seeker in response to cultural imperatives analogous to those dictated by the pernicious implications of the text Traveller. In critiquing *Farawayan* it is important to bear in mind the kinds of editorial perspectives and journalistic tropes which were current in print and broadcast media in the racially-charged atmosphere of 1997/8: a front-page editorial in *The Wexford People*[66] spoke of dubious Romanians who could be found wearing designer clothing and basking on the balconies of brand new apartments while local people went without medical care and adequate housing. Specifically, it alleged that young Romanian men were lurking at the gates of local convent schools for the express purpose of enticing young girls to bear the children who would deliver Irish citizenship to the unscrupulous father. Radio phone-ins and evening newspaper headlines in Dublin were equally, if not more, aggressively committed to demonizing the arrivals in terms drawn from the worst excesses of British and American racism. The race card had been played – successfully – in more than one Dublin constituency during the close-run general election of June 1997.

Farawayan was staged at the Olympic Ballroom, off Camden Street, Dublin in autumn 1998. The play's genesis in opposition to the emergence and proliferation of racist discourse in Ireland fits the Calypso profile precisely. So too does the coalition of funders assembled to bring the project to fruition, and the accompanying resource file, *Information and Action on Racism*. In its genesis as a public project, *Farawayan* affirms and lays claim to the role of dramatic artist as critical cultural interlocutor, and asserts its right to public attention: the play inaugurates a conversation with 'Ireland'. *Farawayan* locates familiar content – experiences of emigration, dislocation and despair – among multiplying narratives and provocative images of community. Irish experiences are staged contrapuntally with the biographies of contemporary exiles from the east and from the south in pursuit of an ethical, historicized critique of emergent Irish society. In his programme note for the production, Andy Storey names the ethical purpose of the project in uncompromising language:

> Despite Ireland's relatively small numbers of asylum seekers, it seems to be beyond the capacity of this state to deal with them in a decent manner ... Asylum seekers and immigrants are not burdens to be borne or invaders to be repulsed. They are human beings with life stories and human rights, with abilities and energies, and with a range of contributions to make. They are to be welcomed.[67]

The Ireland staged in *Farawayan* is stark cold, and brutal, as are the questions this piece of work poses to those who live and work within it. As in the case of *The Lament for Arthur Cleary*,

Farawayan's ethical questioning destabilizes stage/audience relationships and inaugurates an exploration of the languages of theatre itself. Donal O'Kelly touches on values central also to *The Lament for Arthur Cleary* and *Rosie and Starwars*, and to Mary Robinson's postcolonial political programme.[68] He situates the creative purpose of *Farawayan* in a vision of theatre's uniqueness as communal experience, and invokes its capacities to forge connections between people, practices and life histories atomized in an increasingly distanced, privatized and mediated stance toward others.

Farawayan is above all an audience experience. Queuing outside the Olympic Ballroom, people receive a programme on admission which is a replica of an Irish/EU passport. This document is stamped, and will be demanded throughout the evening by masked figures who control admission to the balcony, from where the first two episodes will be viewed, and the ground level – vantage point for episodes 3 to 8. The audience is held outside on the street until it reaches a critical mass, and the business of entering the performance space contrasts with the efficiencies expected in standard theatre venues. There is a breakdown in turn-taking, and a sense of disorder. 'Passports' in hand, people begin a slow progress upstairs, to the balcony level, which affords standing room, and a panoramic view of the full sized ballroom floor space. As they jostle to move, or claim vantage points, Faraya is discovered by audience members, held in a dimly lit cubicle off the balcony, guarded by the functionaries, Belt and Buckle.

The play stages Faraya's escape from the hell of Farawaya through a long sea voyage on a makeshift raft, arrival in Ireland, participation in Maud's glittering ball, unmasking as an outsider, bureaucratic assessment, terrified flight and disorientation, physical brutalization and enforced return from whence she came. Throughout the experience, *Farawayan* explores the sensual immediacy of live theatre, the suggestive powers of dynamics of light/darkness, sound/silence, music/cacophony, stillness/-movement. Crucially – in terms of its formal innovations and adaptations – *Farawayan* addresses the dynamic actual/virtual. It does this on a number of levels, including its embodiment of the horrors of contemporary warfare, exile and wandering: horrors available only through virtual contact to most of the people in the audiences for *Farawayan*. Equally, the traumatic disorientations of enforced exile, which completely defeat and are reduced by theatrical realism, are given form in Faraya's experiences at 'Maud's glittering ball' (Episode 4), in 'The Forest of Hatches and Flares' (Episode 5) and during 'The Assessment' (Episode 6).

Episode 6 finds an unmasked Faraya in flight from Maud's dogs, *Costas*[69] and *Airgead*,[70] lost and wandering in the Forest of Hatches and Flares. The audience, now standing or sitting at ground level, witness Faraya's encounter with animate trees containing hatches which open to reveal terrifying flare explosions. This episode takes place on the terrain of folk tale and dreamscape, where ghastly references to the mutilating power of landmines and the psychic wounds of oppression and enforced migration proliferate. Faraya's youth, innocence and exhaustion are vividly staged in a theatre of spectacle and physicality which seeks to implicate the audience in her disorientation. This search for implication over explication marks a significant deepening of Calypso's application of theatrical imagination to contemporary problems, and characterizes a remarkable artistic journey for Donal O'Kelly as a playwright.

In 1994, O'Kelly wrote *Asylum! Asylum!* for the National Theatre. It was staged at the Peacock Theatre, in a proscenium format, where the pull of the conventions of theatrical realism diluted its impact as a cautionary statement to a social order awakening to the potential pleasures of flirtations with advanced consumer capitalism. The 1997 production of the play[71] drew on Patrick Murray's in-the-round design in order to open up the theatrical playfulness of the script's African/Irish encounters, and to enable the magic realist ending to emerge more fully. The second production played directly into the kind of society it had anticipated only four years earlier. If the typical audience comment on *Asylum! Asylum!* in 1994 was 'Interesting play ... couldn't happen here',[72] the 1997 version evoked similar objections from bourgeois audiences as did *The Business of Blood*: 'I don't like being told what to think.'[73] Following that second production, the playwright felt that the content, having become more urgently visible in Irish experience needed not so much to be rewritten as rewrought. In what is almost a unique artistic revisitation in a culture dedicated to the idea of the play as completed literary text,[74] he committed himself to a new engagement with theme, space, actors, exiles, musicians and dancers. Reflecting on the centrality of interrogating form to the representation of unprecedented realities, he wrote:

> *Farawayan* is about the feeling of being faraway and unwelcome. In it, I want to use a non-Irish form of theatre. Or

be part by proxy of generating a new Irish form of theatre. We want to celebrate our barely-happening-but-there-nevertheless multi-cultural diversity. So I want to use Farawayan theatre techniques. And even if I didn't have that excuse, I just find naturalistic theatre ... well, boring a lot of the time ... the form is a bit musty at this stage. It's had its century. Now is the time to shake it off. Maybe. Leave it to the close-up focus-pullers.[75]

The artist states his commitment to an ethical vision, and announces theatre as a site of public conversation on the kind of Ireland emerging in the late 1990s. This stance toward theatre-making is avowedly utopian, and it is also critical, and practical. In marked contrast to contemporaneous productions emanating from Galway or Dublin, but with both eyes set on commercial success on Broadway or in London's West End, it embraces Irish drama's historical responsibility to critique who constitutes an Irish 'we', how they – and those excluded from that consensus – are in the world, and how they, and those excluded, would like to be. In making a claim on public attention as a constituent part of the broad spectrum of endeavour that is Irish theatre at the beginning of the twenty first century, Calypso Productions asserts the diversity and unequal valorization of narratives and images underpinning a mutating social order.[76] It also demonstrates that experiences from the edges of the western mindset and social order cannot be represented in forms developed with the representation of lives lived close to the centre in mind. Notwithstanding the tone of the times, choices remain to be made in these areas, and ethical considerations will either inform the choices made, or will return to judge them. This is a significant public intervention, and testifies to the durability in Irish drama of the values that inspired a group of artists, in an act utopian, critical and practical, to declare a high ambition to a national theatre.

This chapter argues that the postcolonial position articulated by President Mary Robinson emerged in Ireland in response to the crises of the 1980s. Oppositional theatre practices emergent in the 1970s began to cohere in the counter-hegemonic projects of Wet Paint Arts and Calypso Productions. Chapter 8 will address mainstream theatre practices in which such projects are ignored or subverted, often by means of representational strategies around the past, and the poor.

---

[1] See Emily O'Reilly, *Masterminds of the Right* (Attic Press, 1996), for a full discussion of these groups.

2 See John Arden and Margaretta D'Arcy, and group collaboration, 'Immediate Rough Theatre' in Arden & D'Arcy, *Plays One* (Methuen, 1994): 371-432.

3 *Inner City/Outer Space*, by Jim Sheridan, was produced at Project, in association with TEAM Theatre in Education (1979). *The Liberty Suit*, by Peter Sheridan and Gerard Mannix Flynn, was produced by Project at the Olympia Theatre (1977).

4 John McArdle, *Jacko, Three TEAM Plays*, ed. Martin Drury (Dublin: Wolfhound Press, 1988): 19-78.

5 Moving Theatre's production of *Legs 11*, a devised play, scripted by Bernard Farrell, took place at Holy Rosary Parish Hall, Harold's Cross Road, Dublin, in 1979; Waterford Arts For All made regular use of public houses, such as Norris's of Morrison's Road, for a variety of theatre performances.

6 Wexford Theatre Workshop's repertoire included contributions from Billy Roche, among others. The devised play, *Forlorn Point* (1986) was scripted by four company members, including the author.

7 Dermot Bolger, *The Lament for Arthur Cleary, A Dublin Quartet*, (Penguin, 1992): 7-68.

8 See Vic Merriman, 'Centring the Wanderer: Europe as Active Imaginary in Contemporary Irish Theatre', *Irish University Review* 27. 1, Autumn/Winter (1997): 166-187.

9 Interview with David Byrne, August 14, 1994.

10 'The Lament for Arthur Cleary', Dermot Bolger, *Internal Exiles* (Dolmen, 1986): 69-79.

11 Eibhlín Dhubh ní Chonaill, 'Caoineadh Airt Uí Laoire', *An Duanaire/Poems of the Dispossessed*, eds, Kinsella, Thomas, and Seán Ó Tuama (Dolmen, 1981): 200-219.

12 Fintan O'Toole, 'Introduction: on the frontier', Bolger (1992): 1.

13 *The Lament for Arthur Cleary*, Ibid. 67.

14 O'Toole (1992)': 6.

15 J. M. Synge, *The Playboy of the Western World, J. M. Synge: The Playboy of the Western World and Other Plays*, ed. Ann Saddlemyer (Oxford University Press, 1995): 106.

16 O'Toole (1992)': 3.

17 Tom Murphy, *Famine* (Gallery Press, 1984), 'Scene 4: The Love Scene': 46.

18 'after' includes the notion of permanent pursuit or searching after the ghosts of comrades and times past.

19 Homi Bhabha, *the location of culture*, (Routledge, 1998): 7.

20 'With so much theatre activity operating outside recognized cultural institutions, the boundaries of culture are undoubtedly challenged, and the feedback of non-traditional audiences has changed, above all else, the product which we recognise as theatre.' Bennett, Susan, *Theatre Audiences: a theory of production and reception* (Routledge, 1990): 182.

21 Luke Gibbons, *Transformations in Irish Culture* (Cork University Press, 1996): 85. Gibbons positions this as a manifestation of 'the abiding influence of rural ideology on Irish literature.'

22 Gibbons, 'Narratives of the Nation: Fact, Fiction and Irish Cinema', *Theorizing Ireland*, ed. Claire Connolly (Basingstoke: Palgrave Macmillan, 2002): 75.

23 '...the story we are telling ourselves and others in electing you President is that we are not just natives of an ancient land, but citizens of a new society. We have come of age. We have performed a rite of passage from past to future.' Richard Kearney, 'Letters on a New Republic' *Letters from the New Island*, ed. Dermot Bolger (Raven Arts Press, 1991): 309.

24 Terry Eagleton, 'Nationalism: irony and commitment' *Nationalism, Colonialism and Literature*, ed. Seamus Deane (University of Minnesota Press, 1990): 23.

25 Austin Clarke, 'The Envy of Poor Lovers', *Irish Poetry After Yeats*, ed. Maurice Harmon (Dublin: Wolfhound Press, 1979): 39.

26 Ibid.

27 J.J. Lee, *Ireland 1912-1985: Politics and Society* (Cambridge University Press, 1990): 187.

28 Bolger (1992): 14

29 Ibid. 14-15.

30 Renato Constantino, *Neocolonial Identity and Counter-consciousness: Essays on Cultural Decolonization*, ed. István Mészárós (Merlin, 1978).

31 Frantz Fanon, *The Wretched of the Earth* (Black Cat Books, 1968).

32 Fergus Finlay, *Mary Robinson: A President with a Purpose* (O'Brien Press, 1990): 156.

33 'I shall rely to a great extent on symbols. But symbols are what unite and divide people. Symbols give us our identity, our self-image, our way of explaining ourselves to ourselves and others. Symbols in turn determine the kinds of stories we tell, and the stories we tell determine the kind of history we make and remake.' Ibid. 159.

34 'The recent revival of an old concept of the Fifth Province expresses this emerging Ireland of tolerance and empathy.' Ibid.156.

35 Ibid.

36 Ibid.

37 See the range of essays in *Across the Frontiers: Ireland in the 1990s*, ed. Richard Kearney (Wolfhound Press, 1988) for expositions of important arguments around these issues.

38 http://www.calypso.ie

39 Calypso Productions, *Information and Action on Arms*, educational resource materials accompanying *The Business of Blood* (Dublin: Calypso Productions, 1995), unpaginated.

40 Ibid..

41 This played on the contemporaneous advertising slogan of Independent Newspapers, 'Before you make up your mind, open it.' This newspaper group's titles – which include *The Wexford People* - are very widely read, and its editorial lines are aggressively involved in cultural projects, including what Kevin Whelan describes as 'raucous revisionism'. Kevin Whelan, 'Between Filiation and Affiliation: The Politics of Postcolonial Memory', *Ireland and Postcolonial Theory*, Clare Carroll and Patricia King, eds (Cork: Cork University Press, 2003): 96.

42 For a detailed discussion of this play, see Vic Merriman, 'Cartographic Connections: Problems of representation in Calypso Theatre Company's *The Business of Blood*, *The Irish Review: Special Issue on Contemporary Irish Theatre*, ed.Frank McGuinness (Spring 1998): 28-36.

43 David Nowlan, 'Polemic driven to a foregone conclusion', *The Irish Times*, 15 September 1995.

44 Fintan O'Toole, 'Second Opinion: A powerful gesture', *The Irish Times*, 26 September 1995.

45 Calypso Productions, *1995 Mission Statement* (Dublin: Calypso Productions, 1995), unpaginated.

46 John Crowley and others, *True Lines*, (Kilkenny: Bickerstaffe Theatre Company, 1994) unpublished.

47 John Crowley and others, *Double Helix*, (Kilkenny: Bickerstaffe Theatre Company, 1995) unpublished.

48 Donal O'Kelly, *Asylum! Asylum!* (Peacock Theatre, 1994). Published in *New Plays from the Abbey Theatre*, Christopher Fitz-Simon and Sanford Sternlicht, eds (Syracuse University Press, 1996): 113-172.

49 Ben Agger, *Cultural Studies as Critical Theory* (Falmer Press, 1992): 10.

50 'Michael D. Higgins 1993', Jackson, Joe, *Troubadours and Troublemakers: Ireland now – a culture reclaimed* (Blackwater Press, 1996): 212.

51 Cornel West, 'The New Cultural Politics of Difference', *Out There: Marginalization and Contemporary Cultures*, Russell Ferguson, et al., eds (MIT Press, 1992): 19.

52 Charlie O'Neill, *Rosie and Starwars* (Calypso Productions, 1997), unpublished.

53 The structured reflections on *Rosie and Starwars*, facilitated by the author, led to the development of a devised play, *An Unsettled Country* (1998). Charlie O'Neill gave permission to include a soliloquy for Chrissie Joyce, which had been cut during rehearsals for *Rosie and Starwars*. Bríd McCarthy, who played Chrissie in *Rosie and Starwars*, performed the soliloquy in *An Unsettled Country*, which was performed at the Granary Theatre, Cork.

54 All comments by traveller women arose during structured reflection on *Rosie and Starwars*.

55 Stuart Hall, 'New Ethnicities', *Stuart Hall: Critical Dialogues in Cultural Studies*, David Morley and Kuan- Hsing Chen, eds, (Routledge, 1996): 443.

56 Jim Sheridan, *The Field* (Ferndale Films, 1990).

57 Gillies McKinnon, *Trojan Eddie* (Intacta Films, 1997).

58 A Traveller word for a sedentary person.

59 Jim MacLaughlin, *Travellers and Ireland: whose country, whose history?* (Cork: Cork University Press, 1995): 33.

60 MacLaughlin, *Travellers*: 33-4.

61 Ibid. 7.

62 Ibid.

63 Ibid. 16.

64 Ibid.

65 'This conflict of pleasure/unpleasure, mastery/defence, knowledge/disavowal, absence/presence, has a fundamental significance for colonial discourse.' Homi Bhabha, 'The Other Question: the stereotype and colonial discourse', *Screen* 24. 6 (1983): 27.

66 'Refugees: It's Time To End This Fiasco', *The Wexford People*, 29 July 1998: 1.

67 Andy Storey, Programme note to *Farawayan* (Calypso Productions, 1998).

68 Donal O'Kelly, 'Strangers in a Strange Land' in *Irish Theatre Magazine* 1. 1; Autumn 1998: 6-12.

69 *Costas* is the Irish word for 'cost' or 'price', as in the cost of a commodity

70 *Airgead* is the Irish word for 'money'

71 Directed by the author, Granary Theatre, Cork (September 1997). The play ran for two weeks in association with *The Scattering*, an international conference inaugurating The Irish Centre for Migration Studies.

72 In conversation with the author, April 1997, Donal O'Kelly observed that such a comment summarised audience reaction to the Peacock production.

73 Comment made by an audience member during a forum on the play at *The Scattering*.

74 Tom Hickey, Patrick Mason, and Tom Mac Intyre, *The Great Hunger*.

75 O'Kelly, 'Strangers': 12.

76 'Ireland is not one story any more, and we cannot expect single theatrical metaphors for it ... there are stories that no longer assume a single country underlying the drama, a single social world to which the action refers.' Fintan O'Toole, 'Irish theatre is making itself in new ways', in 'The 35th Dublin Theatre Festival: A supplement to *The Irish Times*', 21 September 1994: 5.

8 | Contested Spaces, Competing Voices: Irish theatre 1990-1998

Mary Robinson's presidency (1990-1997) began with a commitment to confronting the accumulated silences and exclusions of Independent Ireland, by means of the mobilization of civil society around a postcolonial democratic project. Even if the state must answer for systemic failure since independence, she asserted the undiminished potential of her inclusive vision of the Irish people. On the occasion of her inauguration in 1990, Mary Robinson announced, 'I shall rely on symbols.'[1] Her presidency stressed the constitutive importance in the social order of people's ability to tell their own stories about themselves, to themselves and to others. For many people on the margins of Independent Ireland, Robinson's presidency marked a new-found affirmation of the rich material potential of the symbolic. Robinson aspired to a 'pluralist, open Ireland within Europe'[2] and 'was not arguing for the replacement of one set of power structures by another but for willingness on the part of each to learn from the other, so that men and women have an equal chance to make their contribution and find their creativity in a society which neither owns and both share'.[3] Such sentiments specifically anticipate the emergence of a decolonized Ireland as a community of aspiration, response and action in the interests of a diverse citizenry. The projects of Calypso Productions (Chapter Seven) respond deliberately to this imperative, and seek to exploit the 'formative ... place in the constitution of social and political life (of) questions of culture and ideology and the scenarios of representation – subjectivity, identity, politics.'[4] The response of the theatrical mainstream to Robinson's open invitation, 'Come dance with me in Ireland' was ultimately more conflicted, but was apparently instantly attuned to the moment, with the huge local and international success of Brian Friel's *Dancing at Lughnasa* (1990).[5]

In returning to the Abbey in 1990, ten years after the first Field Day play – *Translations*[6] – was staged in Derry, Brian Friel acknowledged, symbolically, the enduring status of the stage of the National Theatre as a site of interrogation of the nation and its core questions. In one of the more glaring contradictions attending on the play's success, it inaugurated, arguably, the end of Field Day Productions, the theatrical vehicle of the most coherent attempt at a sustained contemporary project of critical cultural nationalism. Field Day emerged, at least in part, as an attempt to reinvigorate a progressive idea of nation at a time when state repression and republican militancy in Northern Ireland had become locked into a spiral of violent attrition. With state repression and cultural partitionism typifying society in the Republic, the time appeared to those involved to demand that the problematic fiction of the modern nation be seen to respond critically and imaginatively to contemporary circumstances. Implicit in this stance was a conviction that, in the Republic, the national conversation had turned inward, away from the unresolved issues of British colonialism, and from that broader engagement with ideas which characterizes anti-colonial consciousness-raising and nationalist utopianism.

Within two years of its premiere, the director of *Dancing at Lughnasa*, Patrick Mason, succeeded Garry Hynes as artistic director of the Abbey and Peacock theatres, or – as he deliberately reminded everyone – the National Theatre Society. Mason read the mood of the postcolonial moment announced by Mary Robinson astutely. He programmed challenging repertoire from the Abbey's past, staging a brilliant reinterpretation of Frank McGuinness's *Observe the Sons of Ulster Marching Towards the Somme* and Part One of Tony Kushner's *Angels in America*. He gave young directors their head, and entered into partnerships with some of the exciting new theatre companies which emerged in towns and cities outside Dublin during the early 1990s. Mason also initiated the Abbey Outreach Programme, and played a central role in the debates around culture, citizenship and public policy which marked Michael D. Higgins's period in office as Minister for Arts, Culture and the Gaeltacht (1993-1997). His subtle accentuation of the homoerotic in the homosocial in McGuinness's play responded to and amplified the emergence of gays and lesbians into full – decriminalized –

formal citizenship. His sampling of international repertoire, and his commitment to touring the work of the Abbey and Peacock to other countries made a statement about the status of the national theatre and its role as a public intellectual force. In short, Mason's directorship of the National Theatre reasserts some foundational questions about both drama and nation: why would one found a stage for a nation's stories; who can narrate such stories, and how; for whom, and to whom are they to be told?

These questions resonate at the very core of *Dancing at Lughnasa*.[7] The question of narrative voice is highly problematic in all Friel's work, and generates extraordinary energy in his best plays. In *Dancing at Lughnasa* it is most obviously inflected in gender politics as the narrator constructs the remembered world of the Mundy sisters around events of significance in his own life. He is a member of the bourgeoisie, and his memorializations of poor rural women are themselves a form of amnesia, as subtly achieved as in the sequence alluded to in *Mise Éire*. Where the film's editor uses seascape to disengage from the plenitude of human experiences, Friel's Michael deploys distance, an acknowledged partiality in one's ability to remember, and a nostalgic tone, to avert the gaze from the relationship between the socio-economic predicament of the Mundys and the enduring inequalities of 1990s Ireland. In 1936 – the year in which the remembered action of *Dancing at Lughnasa* takes place – De Valera's draughtsmen were busy refining *Bunreacht na hÉireann* [The Constitution of Ireland].[8] That document inaugurated a social order that drastically limited the life opportunities available to the rural poor in Independent Ireland. The play selects out the signatures of that encroaching local reality and frames them as specifically personal difficulties – like Kate's with the local priest. The contradictions around Father Jack's involvement with British Imperialism in Africa are obfuscated by his quirky infirmity, and in Gerry's presence the gathering clouds of European fascism are reduced to a foolish, if exotic pretext for reckless adventure.

In the very fabric of Friel's writing there is, not for the first time, an aversion of the gaze from the *realpolitik* involved and encapsulated in the daily struggle to live an ordinary life in Independent Ireland. This is repeated in popular reception of the metaphorical dance at the play's centre, which has tended to misrecognize it as a celebration. Joe Cleary challenges this misreading:

> Audiences usually perceive this dance ... in wholly positive
> terms as a liberating outburst of repressed energy that
> expresses the pent-up protests of the sisters against De Valera's
> Ireland ... The dance is a sensual frenzy, then, but its rapture is
> not a wholly positive one: there are suggestions of a disfiguring
> surrender to cruelty and pain as well.[9]

This crucial error, disabling the critical aspect of the play's pivotal moment, is compounded in Frank McGuinness's screenplay.[10] McGuinness moves this most private frenzy out of doors, and frames it as an affirmation of sisterhood rather than a cry of pain. From my perspective, the dance is a frenzied 'Yes!' to life desired: a physicalization of the terrifying recognition that postponement of desire has institutionalized conditions in which it will never be fulfilled.

Dancing at Lughnasa is haunted not only by the boy's remembrances of his aunts, but by the spectre of modernization itself. The social costs of modernity with a native bearing are embedded in the threat to cottage-based piece work posed by the opening of a knitting factory, and in reports of the attraction of young people in the village to consumer goods and places far away. They are also present in the absolute power of the priest to determine the staffing of the local school: this will be progress with a peculiarly Irish accent, in which the inchoate and apparently benighted will coexist with, and will be mobilized to domesticate and endorse 'the latest thing'. Gerry's response to reception problems with the radio set is to climb an ancient tree in which to embed its aerial. While aloft, he declares, 'You can see the future from here!'[11] This moment brings together, with great economy, the notion of rooted indigenous features requisitioned in the service of technological devices which arrive announcing a new beginning once again. In this respect, *Dancing at Lughnasa* is a useful matrix for reading, not only the 1930s, and the fictional 1960s, in which Michael's narration is situated, but the 1990s, in which it is produced. In its own silences, hints and tracings it reveals the signatures of a profound cultural change which would engulf Independent Ireland before that decade was out.

By the opening of Act II, the world of Act I has been dismembered, and each of these poor women has, in her own way, met change with self-sacrifice. Living at the margins of the national ideal, their only recourse as the body politic shrank to fit an acceptable vision was to servitude or flight. *Dancing at Lughnasa* does not end with the fulfilment of personal tragedies, but returns to the homestead as a memorial site from which meaning may still be drawn. The question as to what meanings are enabled by that ending is a crucial one. For Cleary, the play's impact is reactionary:

> Unable to identify substantive historical options, the narrative consigns the sisters to their doom, settles for a kind of postmodern playfulness (the music of 'Anything Goes' plays out the piece), and seeks no positive value outside art or the formal order of ceremony.[12]

This is a sobering point, as the invitation to dance issued by Robinson was grounded in a resistant, critical analysis of Irish society. It was not in any sense an invitation to enter and enjoy the transcendent realm of art, which Cleary argues is the net effect of the most successful Irish play of the 1990s.

Mary Robinson articulated, as a major theme of her presidency, her sense of the potential of 'new energies and real creative forces which still remain outside the power structures of the established order.'[13] In 1992, even as she enunciated these ideas for the development of civil society, other forces were at work, which would, within a short space of time, make the period 1990-1997 look like a false dawn indeed. The economic conditions for the Celtic Tiger were emerging, along with their own logic in cultural production. The latter produced alternative glosses on Robinson's utopian discourses, and appropriated her rhetorical style to the advancement of social and cultural objectives whose purposes could hardly have been more different. As Independent Ireland resounded to the first roars of the Celtic Tiger economy, and artists such as Donal O'Kelly and Patrick Mason began reading the signs of the times and developing responses to them, the organs of public legitimation and social pedagogy began to busy themselves offering to the people new stories, new myths, new accounts of who might now constitute a national 'we'.

John Horgan's biography includes an example of how clearly Mary Robinson's challenge was perceived on the wilder shores of the neo-colonial elites:

> Just before polling day, the *Sunday Telegraph*'s Stan Gebler Davies penned a diatribe against the person he described as 'this horrid woman', and reflected with undisguised alarm on the prospect of 'spending the next seven years 'giving out', as we say in Ireland, on such subjects as single-parent families, the plight of the homeless or jobless or itinerant, and the

necessity of introducing into our comfortable but somewhat ramshackle society some element of the compassionate and caring society. Such is the pliability of the Irish people and so deep-seated the desire to please, at whatever cost to others, that some of what she advocates may well get enacted, if only to get her to shut up. The suffering which is the consequence of all liberal legislation would be widespread, devastating and almost entirely confined to the lower orders.'[14]

Such views, fairly typical of the position of the newspaper that printed them, became more publicly acceptable during Robinson's time, as those elites set about making sure that the office of President would find less contentious issues than decolonization as a focus for its symbolic acts.

Mary Robinson left office in 1997, and was replaced by Mary McAleese, a complex figure, combining sharp intellectual ability, social conservatism and gut-level Catholic nationalism. Adept at co-opting and inflecting Robinson's commitments to ideals such as inclusivity and empowerment, McAleese proved most acceptable to contemporary elites. Fergus Finlay, chronicler of Robinson's presidential election campaign observes:

> When President Mary McAleese addressed the Dáil, on the last sitting day of the (twentieth) century, her otherwise moving speech gave me at least an insight into her education and background. She listed off the major events of the beginning of the last century in describing how a 'new generation's bid for freedom from the grip of colonialism gave us the Easter Rising, the War of Independence and a bitter civil war. Along with the forgotten dead in Flanders, each left behind a legacy of success and failure, of pride and contempt, the scarring inheritance, the unfinished business of the next generation.' I wasn't surprised in a way that the President's vision of the new generation's bid for freedom failed to include one other seminal event – the 1913 lock-out. Like most people of my generation, I was taught nothing of that event in school ... But in its own way, it left just as much of a scarring inheritance, just as much unfinished business for the next generation to complete.[15]

In this address, McAleese collapses the multiple constituencies embraced by Robinson, and imagines the nation in homogeneous, monolithic terms which would not have been out of place in the rhetoric of Eamon De Valera, or the cinematic languages of *Mise Éire*. True to her election campaign commitment to 'bridge-building', she now includes in nationalism's version of the island's story 'the forgotten dead' of World War I.

At first glance, this seems to be an ecumenical gesture of a kind associated with Robinson's construct of inclusion. But J.J. Lee is alert to its broader significance in the land of the Celtic Tiger:

> The phrase has often been used that Ireland is a first world country with a third world memory. It is not, I think too fanciful to detect in some of the more ardent advocates of retrospective benediction on the Irish Volunteers in the First World War a desire to equip us now with a first world memory to accompany our newly founded status as an equal partner in Europe, equal with formerly imperialist countries. The dead of the First World War are therefore at risk of being mobilised to show that we too have a respectable imperialist heritage, for it is intriguing to observe the manner in which the three greatest European empires, the British, the French and the Russian, are hailed in revisionist propaganda as the three great defenders of freedom. The layers of motivation in the agendas currently being promoted require the most probing excavation.[16]

McAleese's presence alongside Queen Elizabeth II at a memorial service for those dead at Messines (1998) is clearly defensible on her terms – that in acknowledging the Irishness of those who died 'for the freedom of small nations', Independent Ireland heals a scar. The problem is that the heroism of the dead is a trope of imperialism itself. The focus on heroism evades the reality of the war as a contest within global capitalism, and obscures the social and economic outcomes of the war in ultimately sentimental acts of remembrance. Lee points out that 'It is always possible to tell events *otherwise.* Memory can become an exercise in telling otherwise and in enabling others to tell founding events from their perspectives.'[17] The Messines event is an example of memory as narrative as amnesia. By endorsing historical revision of the role of imperialism in World War I, McAleese colludes with contemporary discourses which resist attempts to critique the economic imperatives of corporate imperialism. Her gesture makes it easier to embrace global capitalism's own account of itself, and endorses the neo-colonial state's turn from the project of decolonization toward a new destination: full absorption into the emergent 'new world order'.

Independent Ireland's mutation into Tiger Ireland acquires a coherent teleology, enabling, among other contradictions, the consummations of consumption to be presented as the highest vindication of citizen rights. In an analysis which points to the mutation of tendencies critiqued by M.J. Molloy, Fergus Finlay remarks:

> Now we are rich beyond our wildest dreams ... rich to the point
> where poverty is beginning to be defined as the absence of a
> second car. We love to consume, to spend, to have ... I couldn't
> help thinking, when the budget caused such a furore last
> month, that at last we were beginning to get a taste of what a
> society without values might look like. That may seem an
> overstatement, but it seems as if something has died along the
> way. To be told that the economy was the priority now, that
> community values had to take second place, and that this was
> official government policy – there was a rude awakening in that
> for a great many people who are concerned about the decline of
> civic life.[18]

In the shadow of the Celtic Tiger, and in the transition from
Robinson to McAleese, mainstream Irish theatre demonstrated
some confusion about how best to engage with its historical
responsibility to critique the canonization of an updated version of
'us now'. Apart from Calypso Productions taking to the streets with
Féile Fáilte (1997),[19] few were able or willing to confront the latest
attempts to construct 'us' at the expense of 'them'. Mainstream Irish
theatre returned instead to the past in order to interrogate the safer
worlds of 'us then'. This 'each way bet' would enable theatre to
harmonize with the project of capitalist reconstruction without
placing actual dramas of Ireland now on the stage:

> The fact that contemporary Irish society continues to rely so
> heavily on invocations of the darkness of the past to validate its
> own sense of enlightenment is not very reassuring. Such a
> society equips itself with neither the imaginative resources nor
> the strategies required to meet the challenges of the future.[20]

And so, myth, grotesque and derivativeness appeared – maybe or
maybe not, in the old Watergate phrase – as parables for the
predicaments of the present.

The Celtic festival of Lughnasa provides a mythic fabric for the
events staged in Brian Friel's play of 1990. The Celtic festival of
Samhain or Hallowe'en is an in-between time, a moment where the
membrane separating this world from that of the dead, of ghosts,
visions and the un-nameable becomes permeable. Unquiet spirits
are said to wander between worlds at this time. Hallowe'en itself
provides a striking example of how the ritual celebration of a
culturally sacred moment can be co-opted and transformed into
another node in the network of conspicuous consumption. Dreamt
and lived out in Ireland as a cultural necessity, it was recognized by
the genius of American capitalism as a unique marketing

opportunity. Its characteristic emblems are distorted, despised grotesques. Hallowe'en 1998 offered a compelling insight into what crucial wanderings, sightings and unsightings might be assembling to dance a new Ireland into being.

As Calypso Productions' *Farawayan* opened at the Olympic Ballroom, off unfashionable Camden Street in Dublin (1998), Marina Carr's *By the Bog of Cats...* (1998)[21] appeared on the stage of the Abbey Theatre. Along with Martin McDonagh, Carr is one of the most celebrated Irish playwrights of the 1990s. In an apparently bold oppositional stance, their successes have been built around plays which stage Ireland as a benighted dystopia. At a time of unprecedented affluence, Carr and McDonagh elaborate a world of the poorly educated, coarse and unrefined. The focus is tight, the performance of violence inhering in the people themselves, grotesque and unrelenting. As in McDonagh's plays, Carr deploys coarseness of accent to signal economic, cultural, emotional and spiritual poverty. *By the Bog of Cats...* and *Portia Coughlan* (1996)[22] take as their point of departure the condition of being poor in contemporary Ireland. It is important to point out that, even when wealthy persons such as Xavier Cassidy (*By the Bog of Cats...*) and Raphael Coughlan (*Portia Coughlan*) are staged, the signifiers by which they communicate are those associated with the Irish past, and with poverty. This effect is produced by the accumulated power of rural settings and rural speech forms to signify poverty, the past, and an overdetermined Irishry to audiences defining themselves as new, cool and 'happening' now.

Both *By the Bog of Cats...* and *Portia Coughlan* travesty the experiences of the poor – urban and rural. Introducing a category of internal outsider known in the United States of America as 'white trash', they posit worlds in which material poverty and moral bankruptcy map on to one another, eerie partners in a dance of death. In McDonagh's case, *The Beauty Queen of Leenane* (1996),[23] *A Skull in Connemara* (1997),[24] *The Lonesome West* (1997)[25] and *The Cripple of Inishmaan* (1997)[26] stage a sustained dystopic vision of a land of gratuitous violence, craven money-grubbing and crass amorality. No loyalty, whether communal, personal or familial can survive in this arid landscape. Death, affection, responsibility appear as meaningless intrusions in the self-obsessed orbits of child-adults. If neo-colonialism repeats the practices of colonialism, these plays demonstrate the cultural logic of such repetitions.

While dystopic visions of Ireland are nothing new in theatre – 'The Love Scene' in Tom Murphy's *Famine* being perhaps the most fully realized – such stagings populated by violent child-adults repeat the angriest colonial stereotypes as a form of communal self-loathing. The *dramatis personae* of these plays specifically mark out figures of the poor which are over-determined in their Irishry, signed by coarse speech, crass behaviour and predilections to violence. Gross caricatures with no purchase on the experiences of today's audiences, their appeal to an emergent consumer-Irish consensus lies in their appearance as ludicrous manichaean opposites – the colonized simian reborn. In each belly laugh which greets the preposterous malevolence of its actions there is a huge cathartic roar of relief that all of this is past – 'we' have left it all behind. The plays' constitution of an apparently homogeneous community around a feared and despised negative exposes the neo-colonial social order as a blatant re-inscription of colonial relations. The problem, from a postcolonial point of view is clear: in the circumstances of their original performances, these plays implicate audiences in particular stances toward the poor, the past and Irishness.

Marina Carr's *Portia Coughlan* and *By the Bog of Cats...* produce tightly sealed dramatic worlds. Their narrative content is overlayered with tropes and conventions of Greek cosmology, as filtered through the pedagogical systems of the Anglo-American world. The nod toward Shakespeare in *Portia Coughlan* goes no further than ironizing the white trash world of Portia against that of the gentle Venetian lady of *The Merchant of Venice*. *By the Bog of Cats ...* is largely a rewrite of concerns staged in *Portia Coughlan*: the troubled outcast woman, the incestuous family, the brutal father, the haunting by dead brother, the corrosive climate of the outcast woman's home. Its frame of reference is that of Euripides' *Medea*, but there is a playful nod toward Shakespeare for good measure. As Act II opens, Carthage Kilbride's mother is found photographing her sequined shoes in deference to the price she paid for them, and the thrift necessary to purchase them:

Mrs Kilbride. I saved like a Shylock for them shoes!'[27]

By the Bog of Cats ... is primarily a play about travellers, the land and rural Ireland. Mrs Kilbride is a monster, even if she has an amusing acquaintance with the Bard of Avon:

Mrs Kilbride. All tinkers understand is the open road and where the next bottle o' whiskey is comin' from.
Monica Murray.You should know all about that, and your own grandfather wan of 'em.
Mrs Kilbride. My grandfather was a wandering tinsmith.
Monica Murray. And what's that, only a tinker with notions?[28]

This episode reveals a double otherness in the Traveller. In a flash of revelation, Mrs Kilbride's excesses are accounted for: two generations on from the roadside, she is by some distance the most uncouth personage on the stage. The best thing Monica Murray can do by way of mitigating the assault on Hester, as a Traveller, is to expose the fact that her most foul antagonist is a Traveller too.

By the Bog of Cats ... specifically grounds Hester Swayne's predilections for violence, deceit and unnatural urges in her identity as a Traveller. Hester appears in a wedding dress, gate-crashing the monstrous petit-bourgeois wedding of Carthage, her daughter's father. At this moment, the mother-in-law's racist epithet, 'Ya piebald knacker!'[29] brought the house down, in the Abbey, the national theatre.[30] In a subsequent scene, the bride's father shoves a loaded shotgun under Hester's skirt in an image of gross brutality so gratuitous that it risks rupturing the boundaries of the fictional world altogether. The play's dénouement sees Hester slit her daughter's throat from ear to ear. Hester Swayne, Traveller, is beyond the pale, a constant figure in a mutating social order desperate for points of otherness against which to imagine its own impossible consistency.

Some commentators claim significance for these dramas on the basis of the perceived boldness of Marina Carr's literary achievement. In his programme note for the Peacock production of *Portia Coughlan*, the playwright Tom Mac Intyre situates Carr's writing in a line of descent from William Faulkner.[31] In commenting on 'a grotesquerie that aspires to the mythic'[32] in *Portia Coughlan*, Mac Intyre observes, 'the Irish sagas come to mind ...'[33] Playwright Frank McGuinness's note in The Abbey's programme[34] for *By the Bog of Cats* ... opens as follows: 'I wonder what Marina Carr believes? I think it might be the Greek Gods – Zeus and Hera, Pallas Athena. She knows what the Greeks know.'[35] He continues, 'She has listened to the stern voice of her true literary ancestor, Emily Brönte.'[36] Turning to the kinds of plays Carr writes, McGuinness declares:

> Her theatre is, in the most brutal sense, heroic. Her brave women look into the face of those who have gone before them – Medea, Hedda Gabler, Miss Julie – and they can hold their own in that tough company who took on their world and tore it to ribbons, for that was their destiny.'[37]

He concludes by returning to his opening question, 'I wonder what Marina Carr believes? I can't say for certain, but I am certain in this play she writes in Greek.'[38]

Mac Intyre embellishes the myth-making, 'Marina Carr is an original. That means, among other things, it's hard to trace the source of her marvels.'[39] In canonizing Marina Carr, these playwrights posit a transcendent lineage of the literary, by means of a discourse of mystification, whose provenance and consequences are discussed in Chapter Three. Joe Cleary's analysis of the cultural meaning of the account of the past staged in *Dancing at Lughnasa* provides an example of their endurance in practices of representation as well as interpretation.[40] In Mac Intyre's and McGuinness's notes, this framing discourse reasserts, in the name of the National Theatre itself, the notion that writers come from a magnificent but perplexing nowhere. Success admits the writer to a loosely defined pantheon of Western literary 'greats'. All distinctions of ethnicity, class, and even gender, disappear during this rite of passage. The works – and the writer – exist outside history, and are encountered as visitations from a timeless, placeless zone of ineffable creativity.

Others seek to canonize Carr for bringing feminist perspectives to the stage. Victoria White enthuses, 'in *By the Bog of Cats...*, (Carr) has recreated the Abbey stage as a national space, and fearlessly put women at the centre of it.'[41] White continues:

> At seven, Hester makes her (First) Communion in a snow-white dress, becomes initiated into a society in which she will have no power, and loses her mother. At seven, her daughter Josie does the same. There are three white dresses around the wedding table of Josie's father (Carthage Kilbride): that of his wife ... his son-adoring mother, and his daughter's Communion dress – a chilling sight. There are still very few Irish women, and almost no little girls, who don't love white dresses ... But Carr spares no feelings in her evocation of the freedom which is sometimes taken away in return for the joy of being a princess for a day. And seeing those terrible rituals being acted out on the national stage has all the "shock of the new".[42]

White's claims around the allure of white dresses expose the essentialism of her discourse. Her summary of the fatal symbolism of the dress on seven year old Josie rests on an unsustainable identity of cultural poverty between Hester and her daughter. The meaning of the text 'Traveller' has changed in the twenty-three years since Hester was seven. Carthage, Josie's father, has not absconded, as Hester's father did. He may have left Hester, but he cherishes Josie, he is a man of property, and has acquired even more means by marrying Caroline Cassidy. White's view of Hester resonates with that of McGuinness, in that neither writer even mentions Hester's identity as a traveller, and both posit essentialized, heroic, female characteristics as her theatrical *raison d'être*. Hester as traveller is unrelentingly the issue in the play, which before the end of Act I has exposed its primary contest as one in which a traveller occupies land owned by a local bourgeois. If *By the Bog of Cats ...* is feminist writing, it is of the kind which has been challenged by those outside the cultural economies of Western bourgeois circulation. Hester Swayne demonstrates in an Irish context the limited egalitarianism of such a cultural stance. Figured as the most fully female of all the *dramatis personae* on show, she is also the most comprehensively damned – in and of herself – for her unnaturalness. In a truly ironic inversion of a powerful feminist slogan, Swayne is obliged to play 'nature' to the audience's 'culture'.

Carr's superimposition of frames of reference drawn from classical and renaissance drama onto contemporary circumstances is particularly problematic. Such explanatory paradigms were contestable even in the cultural circumstances in which they originally emerged. Portia, the Venetian lady, is not at all congruent with Portia Coughlan. So great is the gulf that the incongruity cannot hope to resonate with ironies which might generate a dramatic dynamic.[43] In fact, in her rages and transgressions Portia Coughlan is more like an echo of the figure of Medea. Fintan Goolan's digression on his hatred of 'poetry shite' in school suggests that Portia's name is intended to figure her as someone who was more susceptible to a bourgeois account of the refinements of high art, represented by the literary achievements of William Shakespeare. The Medea figure submerged in *Portia Coughlan* finally makes it to the stage in the person of Hester Swayne in *By the Bog of Cats... .* In Hester and Catwoman (Tiresias), the trope of women made strange by knowledge – of Shakespeare, songs, people and ghosts – which informs *Portia Coughlan* is elaborated. In *By the*

Bog of Cats..., Xavier Cassidy repeats Portia's reference to the small midland community's practice of burning such women as witches, and inaugurates a shorthand reference to intolerance of difference as a generic, gendered response to, in *Portia Coughlan*, the wife of a wealthy man who suffers from depression, and in *By the Bog of Cats...*, to a Traveller woman who has just put a valuable farmhouse, outbuildings and livestock to the torch.

Medea was an aristocrat, and the daughter of a god. She lived in a palace, in a country which was not her own. When supplanted by Jason's strategic marital alliance with a princess, she had actual magical powers, powerful friends, and a safe refuge standing by to which she could resort and claim sanctuary. Ultimately, she could escape the consequences of her murders by means of a chariot supplied by the gods themselves. Hester Swayne is imprisoned in a particularly ugly version of the text, Traveller, analysed in Chapter Seven. She is to be evicted from her home place: 'I was born on the Bog of Cats.'[44] Carthage Kilbride's marriage to Caroline has the character of strategic alliance about it, and is charged with the contemporary social threat of his taking custody of Josie. Hester's lifespan is fatally tied to that of the black swan she drags toward its grave in Act I, Scene 1. Her transgressive drinking and her guilt for her brother's murder function as explanatory 'character flaws' in the dramatic narrative. Like Portia, haunted by her dead twin, Gabriel, Hester is visited by her brother's ghost, and is tortured by neurotic terrors brought on by her mother's desertion. In contemporary terms, Portia's depression, and the catalogue of Hester's 'socio-cultural disadvantage' grounds a chain of cause and effect which damns each of them to inevitable self-destruction. The mobilization of the worlds of the Greeks and the passing references to Shakespeare combine to unproblematically ascribe the inevitabilities of Fate as the explanatory context for the vicissitudes of poor and vulnerable women in these plays. Such a manoeuvre, in which class and entitlement is ignored, and gender defined in reactionary terms, inaugurates at the very centre of the play's dynamic, not questioning but evasion of the social meaning of their positions.

Many 1990s plays stage moments of violence and breakdown of human relations from the deeply intimate to the broadly social, in ways which enable a deepening of audience understanding of the complexities of their conditions. Billy Roche's *Amphibians* (1998)[45] stages a community in turmoil in the shadow of economic change, in which communal values are under fatal strain. The tensions produced cohere in the tortured figure of Broaders, and result in a night of crazed violence, and his flight into exile. By carefully positioning the *dramatis personae* relative to each other, their economic situation and their stance on communal values, *Amphibians* both problematizes and reasserts solidarities around familial relationship, place and labour. In staging the moral emptiness accompanying the first roars of the tiger economy Johnny Hanrahan's and John Browne's *Craving* (1998)[46] elaborates a metaphor of sexual relations as a site for performing class inequities. The play, a problematic but fascinating multi-media event, fictionalizes and occupies Cork city as a liminal space – a site without co-ordinates, but fully implicated in the everyday concerns and projects of what Independent Ireland is becoming. Both *Amphibians* and *Craving* were well received in their places of origination, which they fictionalize, but were staged in Dublin as fringe events. To rework Nicholas Grene on Friel and Murphy, Carr's success at the Abbey, and McDonagh's at Druid, may reside in the fact that they wrote anti-pastoral versions of Ireland and community tailored to the needs of an emerging audience. Hanrahan's and Roche's marginalization may result, in part, from the fact that they did not.

As Lee suggests, the cultural tone of Tiger Ireland is structured around a notion that the past is best forgotten, as its hopes and struggles have lost their relevance now that the appearance of success is everywhere evident. The argument that the apparent ironic playfulness of McDonagh's work marks an ability on the part of the nation to laugh at itself, claims the plays as manifestations of a coming of age, a type of post-colonial maturation.[47] In reality, the expanding elite of a nakedly divided society is confirmed in its complacency, as it simultaneously enjoys and erases the fact that 'our' laughter is at the expense of 'them'. The entirety of McDonagh's *The Leenane Trilogy* stages not one moral voice, save that of the ludicrous Father Walsh ... Welsh, referred to in the first two plays and finally encountered in *The Lonesome West*. His contribution ends in a suicidal walk into the lake at Leenane, leaving the fictional world of the west of Ireland with nothing to counter the craven barbarity of its inhabitants, except the strong possibility that they will one day wipe each other out.

No Syngean anthem to robust paganism this. These plays offer a kind of voyeuristic aperture on the antics of white trash whose reference point is more closely aligned with the barbarous conjurings of Jerry Springer than the continuities of an indigenous tradition of dramatic writing. Importantly, the repellent figures presented turn out to be representations of those most fully betrayed by indigenous self-rule: emigrants, under-educated peasants, bachelor smallholders, women abandoned in rural isolation by economic collapse. In staging peasant life, Synge unambiguously confronted the ideological project to which it had been co-opted: a travesty serving the need felt by a resurgent nationalist bourgeoisie for a foundational myth. The journey from Synge to McDonagh takes us all the way from images which challenge the submerged ideological positions of an emergent neocolonial elite to those which collude in reinforcing them.

The Leenane Trilogy, includes The Beauty Queen of Leenane, A Skull in Connemara, and The Lonesome West. Each play posits a single fictionalized West of Ireland as the locus of its stage world. All the dramatis personae encountered, with the exception of the neutered Father Walsh ... Welsh, are of this world, and their actions conform to its barbaric norms. Norms established at the outset are found to be intact at the end. Neither challenge, change nor redemption are available to the persons of the play. The dénouements to which the audience is led are all signalled in acts of destruction of persons and objects which can be fully accommodated within the terms of this fictional social order. As the lights fade on Maureen's cottage in The Beauty Queen of Leenane, the question as to whether her responsibility for her mother's death will ever emerge is all but negated by the onset of mental illness, and the proposition that, in any neighbouring cottage in this benighted Leenane, a similar set of barbarities is probably in train.

The grotesqueries of A Skull in Connemara, and The Lonesome West confirm this. The plays making up The Leenane Trilogy posit stable worlds wherein the only available conflicts are between competing lusts which must be sated. Complicity can be purchased for 'a Kimberley biscuit'. The murders of dogs and daddies attract only passing comment, and no opprobrium whatever, not to speak of redress or retribution. Against the formal surefootedness of The Lonesome West, the apparent formal naïvety of Molloy's The Wood of the Whispering appears as a heroic attempt to force theatre form to perform modest aspirational possibilities in impossible circumstances. McDonagh's plays parody rural and small town worlds staged in Molloy and Murphy, for the entertainment of metropolitan bourgeoisies. Such closed worlds offer only closed narratives to persons incapable of dreaming a better life into being. For Cleary, the type of representational strategy at work in McDonagh's plays 'clearly acts as a negative validation of the present which, whatever else it might be, is understood as a lucky escape "from all that".'[48]

There is a popular view that McDonagh's work is in some postmodern sense metatheatrical,[49] that the whole project is a wonderful jape in which the jaded repertoire of Boucicault, Synge, and the 'lesser' Abbey playwrights has been plundered as an antique hoard of quirky, dated images. Such theatrical freaks have no currency in an urbane present, so to parade them in all their benightedness is a big joke, in which the laugh is on the naïve drama of a past which really must be left behind. Fintan O'Toole elaborates:

> In (McDonagh's dialogue) Harold Pinter and Joe Orton blend seamlessly with Tom Murphy and John B. Keane to create a vibrantly original mixture of absurd comedy and cruel melodrama. McDonagh's London-Irish background allows him to hold in perfect tension an extraordinary range of elements from both sides of the Irish Sea ... All of this is held together with an utterly 1990s sensibility, in which knowing and playful pastiche becomes indistinguishable from serious and sober intent. The mixture of elements makes sense because the country in which McDonagh's play is set is pre-modern and post-modern at the same time. The 1950s is laid over the 1990s, giving the play's apparent realism the ghostly, dizzying feel of a superimposed photograph. All the elements that make up the picture are real, but their combined effect is one that questions the very idea of reality itself.[50]

From the point of view of the art form itself, one of the casualties here is the radical potential of those theatrical figures from the past. Significant theatre is as much about the reinterpretation of existing work as it is about the creation of the new. Patrick Mason's interpretation of *The Well of the Saints*[51] raises important questions of integrity, truth and spirituality while heightening the pagan rhythms of Synge's language and worldview. If the target is Boucicault, then Garry Hynes' powerful re-appropriation of the colonial textuality of *The Colleen Bawn*,[52] and Conall Morrison's playful clarity with the ironies of the same play,[53] demonstrates that such work, intelligently textualized can perform Amkpa's task of challenging the contradictions of neo-colonialism as it reiterates colonial relations of domination. The easiest target of all, so ruthlessly raided for cheap effect by both Carr and McDonagh, the small town bourgeoisie, can be staged to critical satirical effect, as Gerard Stembridge's production for Barabbas ... the Company of Lennox Robinson's *The Whiteheaded Boy* (1997) demonstrates.

The success in the late 1990s of Carr's and McDonagh's plays has little to do with the loss of relevance of older worlds and their inhabitants. *Portia Coughlan, By the Bog of Cats...*, *The Cripple of Inishmaan* and the *Leenane Trilogy* come from, and perform something else. A neo-colonial society in the throes of globalization is a peculiarly inhospitable location for postcolonial critique. In celebrating the 'new' Irishness of the audience for such spectacles, they simultaneously negate the interrogation of the conditions in which such images are produced and have points of reference. In this way, they point to a turn away from public inquiry, a willingness to settle for a divided society, a fatal refusal of the difficult process of decolonization itself. A spurious post-coloniality of chronological severance institutes a lesser public role for theatre itself, in which its credentials as spectacle overpower its ethical obligation to critique and thus renew the social order.

The resurgent neo-colonialism of late 1990s Ireland is signalled in the renaming, in 1997, of the Department of Arts, Culture and the Gaeltacht, as the Department of Arts, Heritage, Gaeltacht and the Islands. With 'culture' replaced by 'heritage', the state's cultural logic manifests itself in the pursuit of local quietism and international success. In an echo of Fanon, Finlay points out that national elites seek totems of their achievements in the currency of the international bourgeoisie. They also require of that which is identifiably 'Irish' that it perform new cultural tasks, especially in the matter of domesticating wealth and consumption. This can be done directly by constituting reality through the lens of gossip columnists and 'lifestyle' journalism. A new future can also be accomplished by staging the past as a place we're all glad to have left behind; the past must be re-membered, as it were. The question as to how that re-membering is to be accomplished is a central one in the cultural battles of Celtic Tiger Ireland. Mary Robinson used symbols to move beyond the residual oppositions of anti-colonial rhetoric. Mary McAleese uses symbolism to incorporate into national rhetoric facts unpalatable to its assumptions and teleology. Arguing for an ethics of memory, Paul Ricoeur asserts, 'We must preserve traces. We must come to terms with the past, in the interests of justice and ethics in the future.'[54] In the moment of the

Celtic Tiger, ownership of the Irish past is up for grabs again, with competing models of present and future struggling for the power to narrate the nation's future.

When J.M. Synge released his 'playboy' into the civic space opened up by a national theatre, he demonstrated the critical vigour and political significance of performative images themselves. Far from demanding space to express or enunciate a rarefied 'aesthetic' position, and Pilkington's account of the centrality of the National Theatre project to Yeats's concern for continuity of the Anglo-Irish elite notwithstanding,[55] the theatre of Yeats, Gregory and Synge inaugurates a conversation with 'Ireland'. Their use of ambivalent narratives and images of community to critique triumphant nationalism establishes in Irish theatre the commitment of artists to an ethical vision. Irish theatre is thus created as a site of public conversation on the model of social order emerging in anti-colonial nationalism. Such founding principles are uniquely available as the principled basis to interrogate the neo-colonial conditions of contemporary society, and to critique prevailing theatre practices. To put it another way, at the end of the 1990s, choices remain to be made in relation to the Ireland 'we' have settled for.

This chapter argues that Mary Robinson's presidency functions as cultural other to the neo-colonial consensus of Tiger Ireland. As her term of office ended, Robinson's postcolonial project was hotly contested, with liberationist dramas from the margins of Irish theatre countered by resource-rich, globally successful and locally acceptable spectacles of mainstream cultural production. The marginalization of Field Day Productions was not the only contradiction to emerge from the success at the Abbey of *Dancing at Lughnasa*. The elaboration of a kind of negative aesthetic in which to position the past has an important function in a neo-colonial social order, in which conspicuous marginalization and degradation re-inscribe themselves in the bodies of those excluded on the streets of the successor state's towns and cities, as indicators of economic progress. When the future seems set to increase social inequality, the poor are refigured as spectres from a past to which, whatever the shortcomings of the present, or the inadequacy of a future grounded in them, there must be no return. Such an option is a thoroughly false choice, constituted in the main by reactionary strategies of representation and interpretation, and it inverts Bhabha's imperative that art must renew the past, 'refiguring it as a contingent "in-between" space, that innovates and interrupts the performance of the present ... a "past-present" ... part of the necessity, not the nostalgia, of living.'[56] The critical readings of the plays of Friel, McDonagh and Carr in this chapter are intended to expose the performance of neo-colonial relations present in the moment of the Celtic Tiger, which can only be sustained if the past is repositioned as part of the nostalgia, not the necessity of living.

---

[1] Fergus Finlay, *Mary Robinson: A President with a Purpose* (O'Brien Press, 1990): 156.

[2] Ibid.: 143.

[3] John Horgan, *Mary Robinson: an independent voice* (O'Brien Press, 1997): 198.

[4] Stuart Hall, 'New Ethnicities', *Stuart Hall: Critical Dialogues in Cultural Studies*, eds David Morley and Kuan-Hsing Chen (Routledge, 1996): 443.

[5] Brian Friel, *Dancing at Lughnasa*, (Faber and Faber, 1990).

[6] Brian Friel, *Translations* (Faber and Faber, 1981).

[7] Friel (1990). The analysis here refers to the original production by Patrick Mason, Abbey Theatre, 1990.

[8] Bunreacht na hÉireann [The Constitution of Ireland] (Dublin: Government Publications, 2002).

[9] Joe Cleary, 'Modernization and Aesthetic Ideology in Contemporary Irish Culture', *Writing in the Irish Republic: Literature, Culture, Politics 1949-1999*, ed. Ray Ryan (Macmillan, 2000): 124-5.

[10] Pat O'Connor, *Dancing At Lughnasa* (Ferndale Films,1998).

[11] Friel (1990): 53.

[12] Cleary (2000): 126.

[13] Horgan: 198.

[14] Ibid. 141.

[15] Fergus Finlay, 'Unfinished Business', *The Examiner*, 31 December 1999.

[16] Joe Lee, 'Commentary' *Nationalisms: Visions and Revisions*, ed. Luke Dodd (Film Institute of Ireland, 1999): 78.

[17] Ibid.

[18] Finlay (1999).

[19] Assembling on 13 December 1997 in Meeting House Square, Temple Bar - symbolic playground of the Celtic Tiger - the parade routed via Dame Street, Dublin Castle and Christchurch Cathedral, terminating at Dublin City Council, Civic Offices, Wood Quay, for video and fire sculpture presentations on multiculturalism in Ireland.

[20] Cleary (2000): 126-7.

[21] Marina Carr, *By the Bog of Cats ...* (Gallery Books, 1998).

[22] Marina Carr, *Portia Coughlan, The Dazzling Dark: New Irish Plays*, ed. Frank McGuinness (Faber and Faber, 1996): 235-311.

[23] Martin McDonagh, *The Beauty Queen of Leenane*, Martin McDonagh, *Plays 1* (Methuen, 1999): 1-60.

24 Martin McDonagh, *A Skull in Connemara*, Ibid. 61-126.

25 Martin McDonagh, *The Lonesome West*, Ibid. 127-196.

26 Martin McDonagh, *The Cripple of Inishmaan* (Methuen, 1997).

27 Carr (1998): 47.

28 Ibid. 56.

29 Ibid. 54.

30 14 October 1998; author in attendance.

31 Tom Mac Intyre, 'Portia Coughlan' *The Theatre of Marina Carr: before rules was made*, eds Cathy Leeney and Anna McMullan (Carysfort Press, 2003): 80.

32 Ibid. 81.

33 Ibid.

34 Frank McGuinness, 'Writing in Greek: By The Bog of Cats' Leeney and McMullan eds: 87.

35 Ibid.

36 Ibid.

37 Ibid.

38 Ibid. 88.

39 Mac Intyre: 81.

40 Cleary (2000): 126.

41 Victoria White, 'Women Writers Finally Take Centre Stage', *The Irish Times*, 15 October 1998

42 Ibid.

43 As in the contradictions attending the nickname 'Sanbatch', discussed in Chapter Three.

44 Carr (1998): 35.

45 Billy Roche, *Amphibians* (Warner Chappell, 1992), was staged at YMCA Wexford and Andrews Lane Theatre, Dublin (Dublin Theatre Festival Fringe), during 1998.

46 Johnny Hanrahan and John Browne, *Craving* (Unpublished) was staged during 1998 at Everyman Palace Theatre, Cork, Project at the Mint, Dublin (Dublin Theatre Festival Fringe), and Watergate Theatre Kilkenny.

47 Fintan O'Toole sees in McDonagh, 'an utterly 1990s sensibility, in which knowing and playful pastiche becomes indistinguishable from serious and sober intent.' O'Toole, Fintan, 'Introduction', McDonagh, *Plays: 1* (Methuen, 1999): x.

48 Cleary (2000): 108.

49 '(The plays) have a theatrical self-consciousness that has been the hallmark of so much of Druid's work.' Fintan O'Toole, 'The Leenane Trilogy' in Julia Furay and Redmond O'Hanlon eds, *Critical Moments: Fintan O'Toole on Modern Irish Theatre* (Carysfort Press, 2003): 181.

50 O'Toole (1999): x –xi.

51 Abbey Theatre, 1996.

52 Royal Exchange Theatre, Manchester 1995.

53 Abbey Theatre, 1998.

54 Ibid.

55 See Lionel Pilkington, *Theatre and State in Twentieth-century Ireland* (Routledge, 2001), Chapter 1: 'Home Rule and the Irish Literary Theatre: 6-34.

56 Homi Bhabha, *the location of culture*, (Routledge, 1998): 7.

9 | Conclusion. Re-presenting the nation: theatre, utopia and decolonization

The phase of economic development known as the Celtic Tiger is accompanied by a bifurcation of drama itself into a theatre of social critique, and a theatre of diversionary spectacle. The drama of Tiger Ireland includes many mainstream plays which perform a cultural function quite different from that of works staged by Calypso Productions (1993-1999). Marina Carr's *Portia Coughlan* (1996) and *By the Bog of Cats ...* (1998), and Martin McDonagh's *The Leenane Trilogy* (1996-7) restage reductive stereotypes of Irishness itself, whose cultural functioning enables a representation which is also an erasure. A parade of grotesques signals its provenance in the past of Irish theatre, and its dramatic worlds unfold as versions of a national 'we' untenable under current circumstances, sophisticated, urbane and successful. Thus, the present disengages from a national past in which the actual correlatives of such figures presumably exist and make sense. In this way, Celtic Tiger Ireland recapitulates a cultural contest which recalls the moment of nationalist anti-colonialism a century before. Once again, the issue is competing versions of Irishness, and this time the stage of the National Theatre accommodates, not opposition to, but confirmation of the worldview of the indigenous bourgeoisie.[1]

Celtic Tiger Ireland was a strange place to make art. Unprecedented local conditions were accompanied by questions posed for western theatre generally, as the entertainment industry deploys technology to colonize all aspects of human experience. Movement forward was the characteristic trope of the moment, and reflective experiences were rare, if not distinctly unwelcome. Art and artists persisted, and contended daily with silencing strategies which

usurped space available for interpretive stances, as Alice Maher
argues, in the case of the visual arts:

> Television is an important mediation point between artist and
> public, where critical thinking can help move us away from the
> imposition of literary expectations on visual imagery. Irish TV
> starts from the premise that our eyes are not to be trusted when
> it comes to art, and huge efforts are made to explain it away
> rather than to elucidate its existence.[2]

In the Irish homestead, local visitors bearing questions and ideas
were unwelcome, those accompanied by diversions and spectacles
were highly sought after. In this light, it is unsurprising that there is
a persistent doubleness to the *dramatis personae* and the situations
shown on Ireland's stages during the 1990s. Indeterminacy,
ambiguity and contingency are the stuff of dramatic representations,
and both neo-colonial and postcolonial theatre thrive during that
time.

Neo-colonial artefacts prove amenable to the elaboration of a cult
of economic triumphalism which lies at the heart of the Celtic
Tiger's social projects. This is demonstrated in their embodying neo-
colonialism's counter-utopia of international branding and
commercial success. Notably, McDonagh's diversionary spectacles
attract Tony awards on Broadway, and his *The Lieutenant of
Inishmore* (2002) premieres at the Royal Shakespeare Company.
Carr's *On Raftery's Hill* (2000) draws upon the production team
and the stage aesthetics of McDonagh's *The Leenane Trilogy* (1997).
Her *Ariel* (2002) appears at the Abbey as a work aimed squarely at
the international festival circuit, following the exhibition of the 'new
Irishness' of *On Raftery's Hill* in Washington DC, at 'Island: Arts
from Ireland' (2000),[3] a festival of contemporary Irish art.
'Ornamental forms of Irishness'[4] are not only the preferred self-
images of the Celtic Tiger, but they underpin the brand 'Irishness' as
it moves among the circuits of international commodity
consumption. And the ornamental is an ambiguous category,
accommodating representations pretty, grotesque, heroic, base,
contemporary and archaic. Its sundering of linkages between
representations and actually existing conditions in Independent
Ireland align it closely with 'the state's overriding objective [of]
market competitiveness of sectors, not their national ownership nor
their developmental embeddedness in a local society.'[5]

The clash of Mary Robinson's postcolonial purposes and the
triumphalist neo-colonialism of the Celtic Tiger Economy plays out

during the 1990s in a bifurcated national stage: On the one hand are dramas of social critique, plays of those excluded from participation in public discussion in Independent Ireland (Chapter 7). On the other, there are theatrical entertainments in which the past, rural Ireland and the poor are travestied (Chapter 8). Donal O'Kelly and Charlie O'Neill stage dramas of the socially excluded, both international and intranational. O'Neill's *Rosie and Starwars* turns on the fraudulence of journalistic narrative, and draws attention to authoritative popular discourses structuring what is accepted as Irish reality, which are always already exclusive of the life experiences of significant numbers of people. O'Kelly's *Farawayan* disrupts not only the conventions of realism – realist episodes in the play appear completely fantastical – but the critical narrative that Irish drama is founded on a canon of dialogue-driven, singly authored works. The move from disrupted realism to realism as disruption in this work testifies to important mutations in Independent Ireland. As prosperity is visited on a divided society, the official gaze turns away from engagement with social convulsion, in favour of a reinscription of 'economic realism' as the tone and purpose of what Kirby sees as a competition state,[6] which now 'prioritises international competitiveness over social development.'[7]

Fanon predicts that a nationalist bourgeoisie will, for a variety of reasons, opt ultimately for a future among its imagined peers, in an international playground organized on lines which guarantee the satisfaction of its immediate needs. This class sees itself as simply given, formed ahistorically out of overlapping personal narratives of individual endeavour. Concerns for intranational solidarities and the pursuit of a greater distribution of the fruits of the good life appear as diversions from the path of individual and familial gratification. Kirby suggests that 'the new class of internationalized professionals owes less and less allegiance to Irish society and is unlikely to be amenable to any more robust redistributive efforts by the state, if that were to be contemplated.'[8] As it cements its position as a neo-colonial elite, tropes of communal living appear to the indigenous bourgeoisie as merely sentimental images. This turn negates the historical promise of nationalist anti-colonialism, which envisaged the dissolution of the threshold tellingly inscribed in the words of a song widely popularized in Ireland during the 1980s:

> While we seek mirth and beauty,
> And music bright and gay,
> There are pale forms waiting by the door.

Though their voices are silent,
Their pleading looks still say,
'Oh, hard times come again no more'.[9]

By contrast, the cultural tone of Celtic Tiger Ireland emerges as the successor state mutates under globalization, toward 'days of miracles and wonder'.[10] The imbalance in social relations in Independent Ireland in the late 1990s serves as a microcosm of a world dominated by 'a loose affiliation of millionaires and billionaires.'[11] For the first time, Independent Ireland produces a critical mass of indigenous millionaires, and, as in other advanced capitalist societies, the concerns and aspirations of such a group elaborate throughout the social order as the concerns of the nation itself. With the doorway to a haven of 'mirth and beauty' closed on the 'pale forms' of those languishing outside, the narratives of the past are foreclosed, new visions of Irishness emerge, and new futures are posited. The national mood recapitulates Bolger's Politician,[12] not as cynic but as prophet: the Irish are successful, and their destiny is integration in a globalized bourgeoisie moving easily among the organizational arrangements of a triumphant Anglo-American world order. This is neo-colonialism's promise, a counter-utopia to supplant the residual appeal of nationalism's promise of decolonization.

In the hyperactive moment of globalization, mainstream Irish theatre reproduces Irishness as a text for consumption in a series of ornamental spectacles. These 'masterful images' confirm the hegemony of neo-colonialism's counter-utopia by proposing as its other, not decolonization, but the recapitulation of past impoverishment.[13] The signs of the past are the signs of economic failure; those of the present testify to economic success. In the plays of McDonagh and Carr, the past is parodied to the point of travesty, as the repository of an Irishry summoned in order that the distance separating its images from the prosperous beneficiaries of the Celtic Tiger may be established, and affirmed. Against this, in *Famine*, in the 1983 staging of *The Wood of the Whispering* and in *The Lament for Arthur Cleary*, the past is mobilized to reinvigorate a project of decolonization. Bill Gaughran's memorialization of Irish decency and solidarity in *Asylum! Asylum!* obliges and enables him to identify with the humanity of Joseph Omara, Ugandan refugee. *Farawayan* extends the moral imperatives of *Asylum! Asylum!* by staging images of continuity between nineteenth-century Irish emigration and the human flotsam of 1990s globalization.

Postcolonial theatre sees the past, both of historical persons and events, and of cultural strategies and figures, as a libertarian resource to exceed the coercive boundaries set by neo-colonial conditions. Neo-colonial theatre endorses the current moment as a point of arrival, and summons up images of the past for a final, celebratory bonfire.

One of the earliest cultural decisions taken during the Celtic Tiger period was the 'modernization' of the St Patrick's Day Parade in Dublin. This cultural project suggests that Celtic Tiger Ireland may be grasped as an extended public pageant, a kind of victory parade by the national bourgeoisie. The largest floats in the parade pay tribute to ostentatious private wealth, as they pass through streets from which indicators of public squalor have been removed for the duration of the spectacle. This parade is a form of articulation of the ideological valorization of forward movement, as it moves through the centre of Dublin city past sites resonant with struggle, now domesticated to the heritage industry, significant as icons only. Privileging the regal progress of the totems of Ireland Successful, the parade is experienced by anyone who seeks to transgress its trajectory, as a moving boundary to personal journeys, a mobile set of restrictions. The image of the new St Patrick's Day Parade is an eerie travesty of the sequence documenting popular acclaim for Countess Markiewicz, from *Mise Éire*. In the 1919 material, the people, the heroic figure and the streets are one moving mass. At the parade that is the progress of the Celtic Tiger, people line up as inquisitive bystanders, regulated into spectator zones, policed by security personnel, who brook no transgression of the border between the progress of the official exhibits and the space designated for admiring that progress. To combine W. B. Yeats and Alice Maher, a succession of self-images, ornamental and masterful, diverts the gaze and obscures the signs of cultural failure.[14]

And those signs include the parlous condition of Irish drama, as the century draws to a close. State support, which underpinned diverse theatrical contributions to civil society during the 1990s, is systematically withdrawn from theatre in an extension, to a sector which cannot survive without the minimum guarantees provided by public funding, of the neo-liberal *credo* of self-reliance. High rents for rehearsal and performance spaces, especially in Dublin, contribute to a constriction of experimentation driven by ideas and values. Truncation of activity, shorter runs and narrowing ambition prevail across what came to be known as the 'cultural sector' or the 'cultural industries.' Roddy Flynn's conclusion of its effects on broadcasting apply to theatre as well: 'Far from "freeing" broadcasters to be innovative and experimental, the commercialization of broadcasting has had the opposite effect, placing very real limits on the scope for creativity and risk-taking.'[15] The abstract veneration of risk-taking plays out as the fear to do other than conform, and the imperative to celebrate conformity while you're at it. The rhetoric of 'can do' produces the reality of 'don't do,' as Irish theatre falls prey to a pervasive tendency during the Celtic Tiger episode 'to equate the prospects for a small class of international entrepreneurs under the very favourable market conditions which the Irish state has helped create for them, with the prospects for Irish society as a whole.'[16]

It is not unlikely that Irish artists will produce successful theatre in the metropolitan centres of the Anglo-American economic order. It may well be that a trend which re-emerged with Billy Roche's London successes of the 1980s and 1990s will see images of Ireland on the stages and screens of such metropolitan centres. Where Roche and most of his actors commuted from Ireland, however, existing conditions see people gravitate more permanently toward the former imperial centres – a feature of cultural globalization which deserves more rigorous critical attention.[17] In Ireland, for younger artists, crises in the national state are recoded as opportunities in the global village. Emigration mutates into 'working abroad', and lack of opportunity at home is presented as a call to trade one's cultural capital, 'Irishness', on global markets. This trend places at risk the relationship between people and nation, in which place is alive with the contradictions and energies of cultural negotiation, in which a site is a location of culture, in Homi Bhabha's term, and not a space for property speculation and capitalist accumulation. If images are produced elsewhere, at a remove from lived experience, then their resonances are less ample in the actual world on which the fictional world draws. They are likely to be less critical, because their generation is synthetic, rather than organic. The relationship of representations of Ireland to Ireland itself becomes parasitic on earlier representations, rather than critical of, and critical to, the negotiations which characterize lived experiences in a set of existing historical relations.

These trends indicate the extent to which, not least by means of 'arts planning', and the tropes of 'cultural industries' and 'cultural sector', culture has been conscripted in the service of a state project of what Kirby calls an Irish Neo-Liberalism,[18] which sees capitalism 'pursue its market logic with a relentlessness that has not been evident since the first days of the industrial revolution.'[19] Because the historical task of dramatic artists is that of 'living through' antagonistic situations, and turning reifying statements into critical questions, social disengagement is not a morally sustainable option. However, as a society develops languages of justification for economic development which indenture its citizens in perpetuity to the cruelty and caprice of unrestrained 'market forces', it becomes difficult to demand of artists that they undertake critical work, thereby resigning themselves to Tiger Ireland's own version of 'frugal comfort' on the margins of its economies of largesse. There is also the matter of publics for theatre, as opposed to publics for film, and its proliferating technologies of representation and distribution. In the late 1990s, film is positioned as a sectoral competitor for live drama in a daily struggle to maximize audiences. It is abundantly clear that live theatre cannot compete with dramas made for recorded media – nor, I argue, should it bother trying. To the extent that it turns toward spectacle in an attempt to poach audiences from those media, it turns away from the task of renovating theatre's purpose and power to move. Film offers seductively vicarious experiences, and it can also convey a sense of authenticity, by deploying documentary footage of historical events. What theatre can accomplish is engagement with the meanings of such moments, in the sensuous immediacy of performing bodies.

This distinction throws some light, perhaps, on the proliferation of plays for one actor in Ireland in the 1980s and 1990s. Solo performance locates the actor as bearer, in one body, both of identity and difference. Monologue is a means to develop the epic 'I' and create space to assert and enunciate subject positions, however contingent and disjointed. From Dermot Bolger's *The Tramway End* (1990),[20] through Donal O'Kelly's *Bat the Father/ Rabbit the Son* (198)[21] and *Catalpa* (1995),[22] to Marie Jones's *A Night in November* (1994)[23] and Conor McPherson's *The Good Thief* (1994),[24] subjects radically split by the contradictions of personal and national identity (Bolger, O'Kelly and Jones) and crises produced by the interplay of criminality and business (O'Kelly and McPherson), re-member themselves in the process of performance, and organize the fragments of a world imploding under conditions of unbearable pressure, into a multi-voiced narrative. Significantly, all the plays mentioned have enjoyed long runs, revivals and international success, indicating that something of the process of speaking a world into being continues to address human needs among audiences across the Anglo-American world, at a time of the apparently final triumph of technology. There is a frankness and intimacy here which is part, not only of the experience of theatre, but of the experience of narration, the personal account produced specifically for the other. Even among the most bewildering social complexes, those who struggle can speak to others who struggle, and out of such conversations, such testimonies, theatre's functions as critique and prophecy emerge to nourish the social order.

At the end of the 1990s, the question of theatre's economic viability was already an urgent one. The question of its cultural viability, its significance and sustainability as public interlocutor, is perhaps a deeper issue. One of the most shameful icons of the neo-liberal grab for power from the late 1970s on is that of the homeless person, the internal other of the Anglo-American world. The abject body is the focus of a vocabulary of dismissal, its humanity erased by its affront to those ornamental images which attract allegiance and function as desired social models. The abject figure has no purchase on public concern, and cannot even function as it might have in the 1890s, as a reproach to society. The homeless body is a kind of fulcrum for cultural exclusion, intermediary between the native Traveller, and the recently visible Refugee/Asylum Seeker, as a signifier of dispossession and failure. Ireland Successful, a social order definitively organized around profit and loss, winning and losing, has developed and extended its vocabularies of dismissal as it grabs, as of right, at the bountiful products of the New World Order:

> This is an entity – it can hardly be called a society – based on exclusion. It is defined in terms of the exclusion of those who fail to conform to the model of the geographically mobile, who have no need of a sense of place. People exist only as producers and consumers. [There is] no place for the uneconomic.[25]

In such circumstances, counter-hegemonic voices are positioned as those who have lost, or are predisposed to losing. Acknowledging this, David Lloyd proposes such a stance as a point of departure which may enable cultural projects of decolonization. Cultural workers must 'begin to trace alternative histories, histories which may not spell success in terms of the dominant paradigm, and may even ... spell a certain kind of failure.'[26] Lloyd sees in such histories 'a repertoire for what I would call the history of possibilities, thinking, once again, of the ways in which even the defeated struggles and gestures of the oppressed remain in memory to re-emerge as the impulse to new forms of solidarity.'[27] By engaging with 'many, less well-documented memories of other decisions and other affiliations',[28] drama may find a present resource from which to draw critical content. Edward Said's citation of Theodor Adorno's remark 'It is part of morality not to be at home in one's own home',[29] points to internal migration as a strategy by means of which critical engagement may be attempted. In arguing this point, it is worth recalling that Dermot Bolger's poem, 'The Lament for Arthur Cleary' was included in a poetry collection entitled *Internal Exiles*.[30] Perhaps, with the centre crowded out and loud with voices who 'continually shout down others',[31] artists must occupy, or migrate to Independent Ireland's economic margins to generate culturally nourishing narratives and strategies of narration, grounded in testimony and capable of prophecy. In 1991, Cornel West calls for '"prophetic criticism" – the approach appropriate for the new cultural politics of difference – [which] begins with social structural analyses [and] also makes explicit its moral and political aims.'[32] Prophetic criticism is enacted in a critical practice of demystification that, like Deane's 'enabling criticism', sets out to develop terms of engagement which support ethical critique and transformation within differentiated rather than monolithic social realities.

A healthy social order needs imaginative spaces, places in which utopian visions may be created, in which powerful assumptions may be confronted by collectively-held desires for liberation, an emergent movement beyond national consciousness toward social consciousness. To put it another way, such places are sites in which to initiate the advocacy of 'democratic pluralism,'[33] and, potentially, to rehearse and perform the critical potential of a vigorous civil society. Vanguards of elites possessed of intellectual and cultural capital will neither generate nor sustain critical renewal in 'a more divided and less cohesive society.'[34] An ethical failure structured into the state as it was forged, has seen difference definitively emerge as a crucial site of contestation within Independent Ireland. That contest inaugurates new circumstances of struggle: 'the lack of consensus about common values ... the conflictual nature of values and meanings in capitalist, racist and sexist societies ... are powerful initiators as well as symptoms of social change, not to be dispelled or suppressed.'[35]

Kirby and Murphy stress 'the power of the state in constituting civil society and the inadequacy of any view that sees civil society as a discrete entity that firstly constitutes itself and then afterwards establishes relationships with the state.'[36] They conclude that 'civil society needs to organize itself in free space that is designed by and for itself.'[37] To consider how theatre can address the opportunity in this challenge, I will bring into dialogue spatial conceptions of radical, dissenting and transformative cultural action formulated during the 1990s by Homi Bhabha ('Third Space'), Wole Soyinka ('Fourth Stage') and Richard Kearney ('Fifth Province'). This strategy is in keeping with a 'differential analysis'[38] in postcolonial critical practice, which 'marks the rhythmic insistence of cultural singularities that emerge in relation to colonial structures so that the study of one given site may be profoundly suggestive for the understanding of another, without the two sites having to display entire congruence.'[39]

Homi Bhabha sees radical engagement with difference as a prerequisite for, and the motor of, cultural transformation. The struggles that constitute such engagements encompass and stage conflicting positions on the status of memory, the interpretation of the past and its significance for understanding compelling social needs in the present. Reflecting on the contemporary instability of dominant constructs of society, nation and culture, Bhabha proposes a 'Third Space' – a conceptual site in which to enable the truth claims of beleaguered concepts such as society and nation to be articulated in changed circumstances. The wager is that this will release their transformational energies, and animate new and progressive cultural projects. Bhabha interrogates and re-envisages the struggle for subjectivity in light of limits imposed by the socio-economic norms of late capitalism on relations between individuals and groups. Specifically, he draws attention to the central imperative to engage with difference, as a way of generating new cultural life:

> What is theoretically innovative, and politically crucial, is the need to think beyond narratives of originary and initial subjectivities and to focus on those moments or processes that are produced in the articulation of cultural differences. These 'in-between' spaces provide the terrain for elaborating strategies of selfhood – singular or communal – that initiate new signs of identity, and innovative sites of collaboration, and contestation, in the act of defining the idea of society itself.[40]

Bhabha's account of new cultural forms that demand and enable new political forms capable of responding in action to the aspirations they communicate, is very much in tune with my reading of drama as postcolonial desiring. The 'articulation of cultural difference' referred to is not an elite or abstract activity; it occurs in the first place, and every day, at street level. It is an instance of the generation of the raw material for progressive cultural politics among the concrete circumstances of daily living.[41] Ideas, their currency in public discourse and their capacity to enable generative acts of communication in civil society, 'play a crucial role alongside economic power and social institutions in constituting and underpinning a particular social order as well as in challenging it.'[42] Ideas and symbols indicate the extent to which new articulations will be addressed, communicated and encompassed within a mutating social order, as Mary Robinson demonstrated during her postcolonial presidency (Chapter Seven).

Wole Soyinka draws on Yoruba cosmology, neither as a mystifying and timeless source of wonder, nor as a storehouse of originary myths adaptable mainly to the teleology of anti-colonial resistance. He consistently thinks 'beyond narratives of originary and initial subjectivities' in making use of the Yoruba symbolic as a practical resource for negotiating contemporary contradictions. Bhabha argues that 'terms of cultural engagement, whether antagonistic or affiliative, are produced performatively,'[43] and the consequences of a critical performative practice of cultural engagement for the maker of theatre may be grasped in Soyinka's construct of the 'Fourth Stage'. He engages specifically with the vexed question of history, and the representation, in the present, of the past:

> The past is the ancestors', the present belongs to the living, and the future to the unborn ... [T]he fourth area of experience, the immeasurable gulf of transition ... the no-man's land of transition between and around these temporal definitions of experience ... is the fourth stage, the vortex of archetypes and home of the tragic spirit.[44]

The liminal quality of Soyinka's Fourth Stage finds an echo in Richard Kearney's articulation of the Fifth Province, as an enabling site of postcolonial aspiration. This idea draws explicitly on a posited pre-colonial time of self-determined Irishness, but does so in a way which differentiates it from the closed rhetoric of cultural nationalism, whether anti-colonial rhetoric or official state discourse. In a strategy which has rhythmic sympathy with Soyinka,

Kearney deploys an ancestral idea as a means of asserting the constitutive and oppositional potential of acts of imagination:

> The fifth province is to be found, if anywhere, at the swinging door which connects the 'parish' (in Kavanagh's sense) with the 'cosmos'. The answer to the old proverb – 'where is the middle of the world?' – remains as true as ever: 'here and elsewhere'. We are speaking not of a power of political possession but of mind. The fifth province can be imagined and reimagined; but it cannot be occupied. In the fifth province, it is always a question of thinking *otherwise*.[45]

Kearney's Fifth Province, which Mary Robinson appropriates as a figure for civil society,[46] emerges as a liminal space open to the abandoned alternatives cited by Lloyd – those aspirations, identities and subjectivities segregated, marginalized or suppressed in the existing social order. It is a site of recourse, but not of dwelling. Like the theatre, it is a place of generation, emergence and exchange, of radical imagining and performative engagement beyond the limitations of existing social relations.

Bhabha is also alert to the generative potential of liminal spaces – specifically, those political borderlands arbitrarily imposed by modernity:

> To dwell 'in the beyond' is ... to be part of a revisionary time, a return to the present to redescribe our cultural contemporaneity; to reinscribe our human, historic commonality; *to touch the future on its hither side*. In that sense, then, the intervening space 'beyond', becomes a space of intervention in the here and now.[47]

He sees the liminal as a zone of permission and possibility, invisible or recalcitrant to prescriptive psychic maps projected by centres of imperialist power. There is more than an echo of Soyinka's project in his view of the interstices of those maps as sites where signatures of human pasts exist. Recovering and refiguring them may yet enable formerly colonized peoples to see their cultures 'as more than merely damaged',[48] and initiate critical projects which rewrite an atomized, alienated present for a better future in difference.

Bhabha goes on to make explicit the linkage between felt disturbances – which I read as postcolonial desires – the fecundity of the Third Place, and actual political change:

> Political empowerment, and the enlargement of the multi-culturalist cause, comes from posing questions of solidarity and

community from the interstitial perspective. Social differences
are not simply given to experience through an already
authenticated cultural tradition; they are the signs of the
emergence of community envisaged as a project – at once a
vision and a construction – that takes you 'beyond' yourself in
order to return, in a spirit of revision and reconstruction, to the
political conditions of the present.[49]

In this passage, Bhabha forges the link between what Kearney
differentiates as 'political possession', on one hand, and 'power of
mind', on the other. Soyinka's concept of the creative necessity of
transition sharpens engagement with Bhabha's 'beyond': 'to dare
transition is the ultimate test of the human spirit, and Ogun – god of
theatre – is the first protagonist of the abyss.'[50] In this, he
demarcates the territory of postcolonial theatre and alerts us to the
fact that Bhabha's interstices are not only places of opportunity but
also sites of personal danger for those engaged in critical cultural
practices. The corporate boardrooms of late capitalism do not take
kindly to enunciations from dominated positions which seek to
claim a hearing in the marketplace of the global village.[51] Bhabha is
clear on the exposure of the cultural worker as s/he negotiates
Soyinka's abyss: 'The borderline work of culture demands an
encounter with 'newness' that is not part of the continuum of past
and present. It creates a sense of the new as an insurgent act of
cultural translation.'[52] Recalling both Soyinka and Kearney, he
addresses the place of representations of the past in present
historical moments, and their potential for generating better
futures:

> Such art does not merely recall the past as social cause or
> aesthetic precedent; it renews the past, refiguring it as a
> contingent 'in-between' space, that innovates and interrupts
> the performance of the present. The 'past-present' becomes
> part of the necessity, not the nostalgia, of living.[53]

This represents a pointed summary of the interventionist
projects of Wole Soyinka, for whom staging the past is a deliberate
choice, with practical purposes in view. The artist investigates
symbol systems already formed in the abyss of human desiring, in
order to critique the moral dynamics of his social world. In their
critical exploration of past-present relations, and of official
nationalism's deployment (post-independence) of representations of
the past in its performative tropes, the plays I examine parallel
Soyinka's project. During Ireland's long 1990s, the potential of

representations of the past to renew present aspirations to a better future is asserted and problematized in restagings of the seminal works of Synge and M. J. Molloy, in Tom Murphy's *Famine*, and in Dermot Bolger's *The Lament for Arthur Cleary*.[54]

I argue that the historical moment of World War II postpones the reckoning demanded by Yeats's Old Man, and inaugurates a period of paralysis, during which, dreams undone and dreamers derided, there is no constituency for utopian imagining (Chapter 3). I read World War II as a historical rupture which enables a period (1938-1948) during which there is a kind of suspension. With historical process in abeyance, official nationalism regroups and eventually rides out the storm of the postponed reckoning. Reflecting on the rhythms of upheaval, retrenchment and accelerated capitalist neo-colonialism which characterize the history of Independent Ireland, the Celtic Tiger period appears less a moment of economic triumph than a historical hiatus resembling, in its cultural impact, World War II. When J.J. Lee expresses his disgust at what late 1990s Ireland has become, he describes that 'entity' as 'virtually the polar opposite to the dream Ireland of De Valera, which was far more a society than an economy.'[55] This is both an understandable rhetorical gesture, and a rare instance of an outstanding cultural historian invoking a nostalgic version of a problematic past. A more recent past – the postcolonial moment of Mary Robinson's presidency – is even more profoundly antagonistic to that which Lee denounces. De Valera's official rhetoric operated to obscure the dynamics of an unequal society, and both constitutes and exculpates enduring social inequality in Independent Ireland. By contrast, Robinson's presidency offers a range of practical and progressive alternative possibilities, many of which are readily available for recovery. So too, do the *dramatis personae* of what I read as the key libertarian plays of the long 1990s.

In the wake of the Celtic Tiger, the enactment of postcolonial desires in those plays foregrounds the transformative potential of performance as cultural intervention. Critical artefacts reveal currents, feelings and tendencies which actually exist, and can be remobilized, if those who wish to propose a different developmental direction for the state have the will to do so. When Sanbatch Daly mobilizes energies embodied in Martin Doul and the Old Man, he, in turn, embodies the logic of Lloyd's admonition to look to marginalized narratives bearing alternative human possibilities, carefully expunged from official histories and formal narratives of citizenship. For this reason, I claim a powerful role both for performative and interpretive strategies which position drama in Independent Ireland as a utopian cultural provocation, an enactment of desires for decolonization. The concept of performance site as abyss is particularly suggestive in 'an unsettled country'. It demands that the concerns of the nation be performed, not on firm ground, but over a chasm, the gulf between the actual and the aspirational. Between the shores of the abyss is a journey across contradictory desires: for the remembered certainties of the point of departure and the hoped-for promises of the place of arrival. Drama cannot go back, and will never arrive. As an artform whose artefacts play out in real time, it enables a critical present to address the problem that 'it is not the past that needs to be rescued or redeemed, but the future.'[56]

Drama has accompanied public projects liberatory, coercive and celebratory, throughout the twentieth century. Irish drama has been the enduring site of civil conversation on the nature, purpose and meaning of the nation, in itself and in the world. In that sense, it constitutes, at its best, a form of public sphere, without which the state is bereft of the decolonizing aspiration to nation which is its own founding *raison d'être*. Independent Ireland is a narrative upon which, as Luke Gibbons points out, many attempts have been made to speak the final word. In Ireland Successful, communal aspirations and solidarities are distinctly out of step with the triumphal progress of the national bourgeoisie. The public authority of both forum and temple is compromised as never before. The global *agora* is set to colonize all human interactions, refiguring them as transactions, moments in which persons are rewritten as winners or losers. The *teatron* endures, and struggles with the tensions affecting those other institutions, the ideal of whose existence in balance grounds modern notions of democracy and social organization.

As the national state comes more closely to resemble other states assimilated to the Anglo-American model of economic and social organization, the potential for new solidarities across national boundaries emerges. Difference from, and identity with, the dominant accounts of Ireland's economic triumphs are structured as binary opposites, but in the search for critical meaning artists may inhabit strategically Bhabha's 'interstitial' borderlands that appear and dissolve between these categories. In so doing, cultural production may begin to expose to critical view the multiplying contradictions around notions of success and failure which animate or stultify human progress in Independent Ireland. While the reception of such cultural projects may be hostile among the indigenous bourgeoisie, globalization provides outlets also for dissenting narratives produced in response to particular local conditions: 'It is in the concrete circumstances of our struggles that we can begin to speak to each other.'[57] Formally, Drama itself is increasingly understood less as a discrete art form than as a performance practice. The spectrum of performance, as Pilkington and others point out, spans a range including classical drama, applied theatre practices, live art, solo performance and 'traditional public events'. In envisaging performative interventions in civil society, artists and scholars must be open to work done along that spectrum, toward a progressive transformation of public consciousness.

Kirby points out that 'any discussion of social change must address what Halliday has called "the criterion of practicality" namely what is feasible within the limitations imposed by global forces.'[58] The enduring liberationist consciousness of Irish theatre in the 1990s suggests that Drama's practical utopianism can enable projects of communal liberation. It can do so by affirming performance spaces as privileged sites in which to embody and enact present, possible, creative and generous experiences of being, belonging and becoming. *An Unsettled Country*, the project which developed as a creative critical response to *Rosie and Starwars* (Chapter 7) is an example of the generative power of the dramatic artefact. The marriage of the needs of the members of the Cork Traveller Visibility Group and the public commitment of Bríd McCarthy and Charlie O'Neill led to a performance to an audience mainly of travellers, but including social workers and other interested persons. Most importantly, it produced a dialogue, in which the actors publicly narrated their own positions within the protection afforded by the fictional world, and their authority as narrators of their actual world. The innovative work of the Axis Centre in Ballymun, which produced Dermot Bolger's *Ballymun Trilogy* (2004-2008), and the critical projects of the Listen Up! group, in Truagh, Co. Monaghan (2003-2007) provide recent examples of the practical utility of performance in opening up space for challenge, in the hope of enabling space for change.

The cultural history of Ireland's dramas during the long 1990s suggests that if this is again a time of the triumph of the new in Independent Ireland, then the social health of the body politic depends on the capacity to dream new aspirations into being. Those aspirations – the most exciting of which is Peadar Kirby's assertion of the need for a 'second republic' – require a space for articulation, in which responses which do justice to the dream may be enacted. Irish theatre, always locked in contemporary struggles and always capable of exceeding the borders those struggles inscribe, has the capacity and the responsibility to imagine a Decolonized Ireland of solidarity in diverse citizenships. This is the project of J. M. Synge's drama of prophetic witness, and circumstances make such a project more and not less urgent in this historical moment. The figure of the witness is central to liberationist cultural work – this figure stands among the facts and struggles of history, observing, recording and recounting the facts of past experiences as an ethical imperative, so that their materiality and their meanings may be made available to the lived present, and the desired future. The interventionist witness of theatre can enable audiences toward the demystification of contemporary living, in all its exploded complexities. The extent to which it actually does so depends principally on this generation of theatre makers, producers, scholars, commentators and audiences refusing the option of settling for less.

---

[1] For Robert Welch, Marina Carr's plays bring back in the 1990s a rural world, in ways which reveal 'that Irish country life has, in some ways, hardly changed at all in close on a hundred years.' Robert Welch, *The Abbey Theatre 1899-1999: Form & Pressure* (Oxford University Press, 2003): 25.

[2] Alice Maher, 'The Celtic Tiger Has No Eyes', in *The Irish Times*, 28 December 1999.

[3] 'Island: Arts from Ireland' presented *On Raftery's Hill* at the John F. Kennedy Center for the Performing Arts, Washington D. C., from 18-21 May 2000.

[4] Maher (1999)'.

[5] Peadar Kirby, *The Celtic Tiger in Distress: Growth with Inequality in Ireland* (Palgrave, 2002): 143. For an extended and updated review of the literature on the competition state, see Peadar Kirby and Mary Murphy, 'Ireland as a "competition state"', *Contesting the State: Lessons from the Irish case*, Maura Adshead, Peadar Kirby, and Michelle Millar, eds, (Manchester and New York: Manchester University Press, 2008): 120-142

[6] Ibid. 142-144.

[7] Ibid.143.

[8] Ibid. 170.

9 Stephen Foster, 'Hard Times Come Again No More', *Stephen Foster Songbook: Original Music of 40 Songs by Stephen Collins Foster*, ed. Richard Jackson (Dover Press, 1974): 175-6. Recorded by Mary Black on De Danann, *Song For Ireland* (Cara Records, 1983).

10 Paul Simon, 'The Boy in the Bubble', *Graceland* (Warner Bros., 1986). Copyright © 1986, Paul Simon/BMI.

11 Ibid.

12 Dermot Bolger, *The Lament for Arthur Cleary, A Dublin Quartet*, (Penguin, 1992): 14-15.

13 In his speech to his party's 1998 *Ard Fheis* [Annual Conference], Bertie Ahern, who was Taoiseach at the time, declared, 'The cynics may be able to point to the past, but we live in the future.' This peculiar phrase proposes a desirable 'now', in which he held sway, and a return to an awful 'then' of past impoverishment, as the only available political choices.

14 Maher (1999).

15 Roddy Flynn, "Broadcasting and the Celtic Tiger: from promise to practice" *Re-inventing Ireland: Culture, Society and the Global Economy*, (London; Sterling, Virginia: Pluto, 2002): 174.

16 Kirby (2002): 186.

17 Chin-tao Wu finds evidence of enduring imperialist hierarchies, among the consequences of biennialisation for culture from former imperial margins. Chin-tao Wu, 'Biennials Without Borders?', *New Left Review* 57 (May-June 2009).

18 Kirby (2002): 160-163.

19 Falk, cited in Ibid. 162.

20 Dermot Bolger, *The Tramway End: In High Germany* and *The Holy Ground*, in *A Dublin Quartet* (Penguin, 1992): 75-109, and 115-142.

21 Donal O'Kelly, *Bat the Father Rabbit the Son, Far From The Land*, ed. John Fairleigh (Methuen, 1998): 194-234.

22 Donal O'Kelly, *Catalpa* (New Island Books/Nick Hern Books, 1997).

23 Marie Jones, *A Night In November* (New Island Books/Nick Hern Books, 1995).

24 Conor McPherson, *The Good Thief*, *Four Plays*, Conor McPherson (Nick Hern, 1999).

25 Joe Lee, cited in Kirby (2002): 145.

26 David Lloyd, *Ireland After History* (Cork University Press, 1999): 105.

27 Ibid.

28 Ibid.

29 Edward Said, 'Reflections on Exile', *Out There: marginalization and contemporary cultures*, Russell Ferguson, et al. eds, (MIT Press, 1991): 39.

30 Dermot Bolger, *Internal Exiles* (Dolmen Press, 1986): 69-79.

31 Luke Gibbons, 'Narratives of the Nation: fact, fiction and Irish cinema', *Theorizing Ireland*, ed. Claire Connolly (Film Institute of Ireland, 1999): 75.

32 West (1991): 31.

33 David Cairns and Shaun Richards, *Writing Ireland: Colonialism, Nationalism and Culture* (Manchester University Press, 1988): 153-4.

34 Kirby (2002): 68.

35 Ben Agger, *Cultural Studies as Critical Theory* (Falmer, 1992): 10.

36 Peadar Kirby and Mary Murphy, 'State and civil society in Ireland: conclusions and mapping alternatives', *Power, Dissent and Democracy: civil society and the state in Ireland*, Deiric Ó Broin and Peadar Kirby eds (Dublin: A&A Farmer Ltd., 2009): 154.

37 Ibid. 156.

38 David Lloyd, 'After History: Historicism and Postcolonial Studies', *Ireland and Postcolonial Theory*, Clare Carroll and Patricia King eds (Cork University Press, 2003): 48.

39 Ibid.

40 Homi Bhabha, *The Location of Culture*, (Routledge, 1998): 1-2.

41 'Culture does its hegemonic damage at the level of lived experience: that was Gramsci's point.' Ben Agger, *Cultural Studies as Critical Theory* (Falmer, 1992): 193.

42 Kirby (2002): 157.

43 Bhabha (1998): 2.

44 Soyinka, *Myth*: 148-149.

45 Richard Kearney, *Postnationalist Ireland: Politics, Culture, Philosophy* (Routledge, 1997): 100.

46 Fergus Finlay, *Robinson*: 156: 'this Fifth Province acted as a second centre, a necessary balance.'

47 Bhabha, *Location*: 7.

48 Carlos Celdran, radical tour guide, in conversation with the author, Manila, July 2008.

49 Bhabha, *location*: 3.

50 Soyinka, Wole, *Myth, Literature and the African World* (Canto, 1995): 158.

51 As with corporations, so too with the neo-liberal successor state, and Harvey chronicles a series of funding decisions during 'the period from 2002 which [saw] a further reconfiguration by the state of the ... relationship [with civil society actors]. Voluntary, and especially community organisations, were taken aback by the manner and vindictiveness of these actions.' Brian Harvey, 'Ireland and Civil Society: reaching the limits of dissent', Ó Broin and Kirby (eds): 29.

52 Bhabha (1998): 7.

53 Ibid.

54 For a full discussion of Bolger's play, see Vic Merriman, 'Centring the Wanderer: Europe as Active Imaginary in Contemporary Irish

Theatre', *Irish University Review* 27. 1 (Spring/Summer 1997): 166-181.
55 J.J. Lee, cited in Kirby (2002): 145.
56 Joseph Cleary, 'Modernization and Aesthetic Ideology in Contemporary Irish Culture', *Writing in the Irish Republic: Literature, Culture, politics 1949-1999*, ed. Ray Ryan (Macmillan, 2000): 126.
57 Ngugi wa Mirii, speaking at an international conference on Theatre for Development, in which the author participated, at King Alfred's College, Winchester, U.K., June 1995.
58 Kirby (2002): 189.

Works cited

Plays in performance

Amphibians, directed by Billy Roche, YMCA Wexford, and Andrews Lane Theatre, Dublin, 1998.

A Skull in Connemara, directed by Garry Hynes, Town Hall Theatre, Galway, 1997.

Asylum! Asylum!, directed by John Crowley, Peacock Theatre, 1993.

Asylum! Asylum!, directed by Vic Merriman, Granary Theatre, Cork, 1997.

By the Bog of Cats ..., directed by Patrick Mason, Abbey Theatre, 1998.

Cathleen Ní Houlihan, directed by James W. Flannery at The Second Annual Yeats International Theatre Festival, Peacock Theatre, 1990.

Craving, directed by Johnny Hanrahan and John Browne, Everyman Palace Theatre, Cork, 1998.

Dancing at Lughnasa, directed by Patrick Mason, Abbey Theatre, 1990.

Famine, directed by Garry Hynes, Abbey Theatre, 1993.

Farawayan, directed by Donal O'Kelly, Olympia Ballroom, Dublin, 1998.

Purgatory, directed by James W. Flannery at The Second Annual Yeats International Theatre Festival, Peacock Theatre, 1990.

Rosie and Starwars, directed by Garrett Keogh, The Marquee, Meeting House Square, Dublin, 1997.

The Beauty Queen of Leenane, directed by Garry Hynes, Town Hall Theatre, Galway, 1996.

The Colleen Bawn, directed by Garry Hynes, Royal Exchange Theatre, Manchester 1995.

The Colleen Bawn, directed by Conall Morrison, Abbey Theatre, 1998.

The Lament for Arthur Cleary, directed by David Byrne, Dún Mhuire, Wexford, 1989.

The Lonesome West, directed by Garry Hynes, Town Hall Theatre, Galway, 1997.

The Well of the Saints, directed by Patrick Mason, Abbey Theatre, 1996.

The Whiteheaded Boy, directed by Gerard Stembridge, Project Arts
    Centre, 1997.
Waiting for Godot, directed by Walter Asmus, Gate Theatre, Dublin,
    1991.

Published plays:

Arden, John, and Margaretta D'Arcy and group collaboration,
    'Immediate Rough Theatre', John Arden & Margaretta D'Arcy, *Plays
    One* (London: Methuen, 1994): 371-432.
Beckett, Samuel, *Waiting for Godot* (London and new York: Faber and
    Faber, 1975).
---, *Endgame* (London and new York: Faber and Faber, 1976).
Behan, Brendan, *The Quare Fella* (London: Methuen, 1977).
Bolger, Dermot, *The Lament for Arthur Cleary*, Dermot Bolger, *A
    Dublin Quartet* (London and New York: Penguin, 1992): 7-68.
---, *The Tramway End: In High Germany* and *The Holy Ground*,
    Dermot Bolger, *A Dublin Quartet* (London and New York: Penguin,
    1992): 75-109, and 115-142.
Carr, Marina, *By the Bog of Cats ...* (Loughcrew, Oldcastle, Co. Meath:
    Gallery Books, 1998).
---, *Portia Coughlan, The Dazzling Dark: New Irish Plays*, ed. Frank
    McGuinness (London and new York: Faber and Faber, 1996): 235-
    311.
Friel, Brian, *Dancing at Lughnasa*, (London and new York: Faber and
    Faber, 1990).
---, *Translations* (London and New York: Faber and Faber, 1989).
Jones, Marie, *A Night In November* (Dublin: Dublin and London: New
    Island Books/Nick Hern Books, 1995).
McArdle, John, *Jacko, Three TEAM Plays*, ed. Martin Drury (Dublin:
    Wolfhound Press, 1988): 19-78.
McDonagh, Martin, *The Beauty Queen of Leenane*, Martin McDonagh,
    Plays 1 (London: Methuen, 1999): 1-60.
---, *A Skull in Connemara*, McDonagh, *Plays 1*: 61-126.
---, *The Lonesome West*, McDonagh, *Plays 1*: 127-196.
---, *The Cripple of Inishmaan* (London: Methuen, 1997).
Mac Intyre, Tom, *The Great Hunger:Poem into Play* (Dublin: Lilliput,
    1991).
McPherson, Conor, *The Good Thief, Four Plays*, Conor McPherson
    (Nick Hern Books, 1999).
Molloy, M. J., *The Wood of the Whispering*, ed. Robert O'Driscoll,
    Selected Plays of M. J. Molloy (Colin Smythe, 1998): 113-177.
Murphy, Tom, and Noel O'Donoghue, *On the Outside*, Tom Murphy,
    Plays 4 (London: Methuen, 1989): 165-192.
Murphy, Tom, *Famine* (Loughcrew, Oldcastle, Co. Meath: Gallery
    Press, 1984).
ní Dhuibhne, Éibhlís, *Milseog an tSamhraidh agus Dún na mBan trí
    thine* (Dublin: Cois Life, 1997): 1-67.

O'Kelly, Donal, *Asylum! Asylum!*, *New Plays from the Abbey Theatre*, eds Christopher Fitz-Simon, and Sanford Sternlicht (Syracuse: Syracuse University Press, 1996): 113-172.

---, *Catalpa* (Dublin and London: New Island Books/Nick Hern Books,1997).

---, *Bat the Father Rabbit the Son*, *Far From The Land*, ed. John Fairleigh, (London: Methuen, 1998): 194-234.

Roche, Billy, *Amphibians* (Warner Chappell, 1992).

Synge, J. M., *The Playboy of the Western World*, J. M. Synge: *The Playboy of the Western World and Other Plays*, ed. Ann Saddlemyer (Oxford: Oxford University Press, 1995):

---, *The Well of the Saints*, J. M. Synge: *The Playboy of the Western World and Other Plays*, ed. Ann Saddlemyer (Oxford: Oxford University Press, 1995) : 51-94.

Yeats, W.B., *Cathleen Ní Houlihan*, *W.B. Yeats Selected Plays* ed. A. Norman Jeffares, (Dublin: Gill & McMillan, 1991): 2-13.

---, *Purgatory*, *W.B. Yeats Selected Plays* ed. A. Norman Jeffares, (Dublin: Gill & McMillan, 1991): 209-218.

Unpublished plays:

Cork Travellers' Visibility Group, with Victor Merriman, and additional material by Charlie O'Neill, *An Unsettled Country*, Granary Theatre, 1998.

Crowley, John, and others, *True Lines*, Bickerstaffe Theatre Company, 1994.

---, *Double Helix*, Bickerstaffe Theatre Company, 1995.

Gorman, Declan, *Féile Fáilte*, Calypso Productions, 1997.

Hanrahan, Johnny and John Browne, *Craving*, Meridian Theatre Company, 1998.

O'Kelly, Donal, *Farawayan*, Calypso Productions, 1998.

O'Neill, Charlie, *Rosie and Starwars*, Calypso Productions, 1997.

Sheridan, Jim, *Inner City/Outer Space*, Project Arts Centre, in association with TEAM Theatre in Education, 1979.

Sheridan, Peter, and Gerard Mannix Flynn, *The Liberty Suit*, Project Arts Centre/ Olympia Theatre, 1977.

Wexford Theatre Co-op, *Forlorn Point*, 1986.

Publications by playwrights and theatre companies:

Calypso Productions, *Information and Action on Arms* (Dublin: Calypso Productions, 1995), unpaginated.

---, *1995 Mission Statement* (Dublin: Calypso Productions, 1995), unpaginated.

http://www.calypso.ie

Clancy, Annette, Facing Forward: A document commissioned by The Abbey Theatre in partnership with The Arts Council for **abbey**onehundred (Dublin: Abbey Theatre, 2005)

Molloy, M. J., 'Preface to *The Wood of the Whispering*', *Selected Plays of M. J. Molloy*, ed. Robert O'Driscoll, (Colin Smythe, 1998): 111-112.

Storey, Andy, 'Programme note to *Farawayan*' (Calypso Productions 1998), unpaginated.

Synge, J.M., 'Preface to *The Playboy of the Western World*' in *J. M. Synge: The Playboy of the Western World and Other Plays* Ann Saddlemyer ed. (Oxford: Oxford University Press, 1995): 96-7.

Yeats, W. B., 'Preface to *The Well of the Saints*', *J.M. Synge: The Playboy of the Western World and Other Plays* Ann Saddlemyer ed. (Oxford: Oxford University Press, 1995): 52-56.

Poetry:

Bolger, Dermot, *Internal Exiles* (Dublin: Dolmen Press, 1986).

---, 'The Lament for Arthur Cleary', *Internal Exiles,* Dermot Bolger (Dublin: Dolmen Press, 1986): 69-79.

Clarke, Austin, 'The Envy of Poor Lovers', *Irish Poetry After Yeats* ed. Maurice Harmon (Dublin: Wolfhound Press, 1979): 39.

Durcan, Paul, 'Making love outside Áras an Uachtaráin', *The Selected Paul Durcan*, ed. Edna Longley (Belfast: Blackstaff Press, 1982): 85.

ní Chonaill, Eibhlín Dhubh, 'Caoineadh Airt Uí Laoire', *An Duanaire* [Poems of the Dispossessed] eds Thomas Kinsella and Seán Ó Tuama (Dublin: Dolmen Press, 1981): 200-219.

Yeats, W.B., 'September 1913', *W.B. Yeats: Selected Poetry* ed. A. Norman Jeffares (Basingstoke: Macmillan, 1972): 55.

---, 'Easter 1916' *WB Yeats: Selected Poetry* ed. A. Norman Jeffares (Basingstoke: Macmillan, 1972): 95.

---, 'Sailing to Byzantium' *WB Yeats: Selected Poetry* ed. A. Norman Jeffares (Basingstoke: Macmillan, 1972): 104.

---, 'The Circus Animals' Desertion' *WB Yeats: Selected Poetry* ed. A. Norman Jeffares (Basingstoke: Macmillan, 1972): 202.

Prose works:

O'Brien, Flann, *At Swim-two-birds* (London and New York: Penguin, 1968).

---, *Stories and Plays* (London and New York: Penguin, 1977).

---, *The Third Policeman* (London and Glasgow: Picador, 1974).

Songs:

Foster, Stephen, 'Hard Times Come Again No More', *Stephen Foster Songbook: Original Music of 40 Songs by Stephen Collins Foster* ed. Richard Jackson (Mineola, NY: Dover, 1974): 175-6. Recorded by Mary Black on De Danann, *Song For Ireland* (Cara Records, 1983).

Simon, Paul, 'The Boy in the Bubble', *Graceland* (Warner Bros., 1986) Copyright © 1986, Paul Simon/BMI.

Films:

McKinnon, Gillies, *Trojan Eddie* (Intacta Films, 1997).

Morrison, George, Director, *Mise Éire* (Ireland/1959/Black and White).

O'Connor, Pat, *Dancing At Lughnasa* (Ferndale Films,1998).

Sheridan, Jim, *The Field* (Ferndale Films, 1990).

Interviews conducted by the author:

Amkpa, Awam, Massachussetts, 12 August 1999.

Byrne, David, Kilkenny, August 14, 1994.

Hanrahan, Johnny, Cork, 15 September 1998.

Hynes, Garry, Dublin, 24 August, 1994.

O'Kelly, Donal, Dublin, 10 April 1997.

Prentki, Tim, Dublin, June 2002.

Author's annotations of conferences and other public fora:

Public discussion on *The Arts Plan 1995-1997*, Gate Theatre, Dublin, October 1995.

International Conference on Theatre for Development, King Alfred's College, Winchester, U. K., June 1995.

Ricoeur, Paul, 'Memory and Forgetting: The 1997 Agnes Cuming Lecture in Philosophy', Part 2, University College Dublin, April 1997.

Public forum on *Asylum!Asylum!* at Granary Theatre, during *The Scattering*, September 1998.

Gibbons, Luke, 'Nation, Narrative, History', closing address to *Nationalisms: visions and revisions* (Conference organized by RTÉ and the Film Institute of Ireland. Dublin, November 1998).

Amkpa, Awam, *Drama and the Languages of Postcolonial Desires*, was first presented as a paper to The Shaw Arts Festival, convened by the author, Dublin Institute of Technology, 9 April 1999. Dr. Anthony Roche chaired a response session, in which Amkpa elaborated on his paper, and in which the author participated.

Critical works:

Adshead, Maura, Peadar Kirby and Michelle Millar eds (Manchester: Manchester University Press, 2008): 25-49.

Agger, Ben, *Cultural Studies as Critical Theory* (London: Falmer, 1992).

Amkpa, Awam, *Drama and Postcolonial Desires* (London and New York: Routledge, 2004).

Anderson, Benedict, *Imagined Communities* (London: Verso, 1993).

Arts Community Education Committee, *Art and the ordinary: the report of the Arts Community Education Committee* (Dublin: Arts Community Education Committee, 1989)

Badiou, Alain, *Metapolitics* (London and New York: Verso, 2005).

Barthes, Roland, *Mythologies* (London and Glasgow: Paladin, 1980).

Benson, Ciarán, *The Cultural Psychology of Self: place, morality and art in human worlds* (London and New York: Routledge, 2001).

Bentley, Eric, ed. *The Theory of the Modern Stage* (London and New York: Penguin, 1986).

Benjamin, Walter, *Understanding Brecht* (London and New York: Verso, 1992).

Bennett, Susan, *Theatre Audiences: toward a theory of production and reception* (London and New York: Routledge, 1990).

Bhabha, Homi, *the location of culture*, (London and New York: Routledge, 1998).

Boal, Augusto, *Theatre of the Oppressed* (London; Sterling, Virginia: Pluto, 1987).

Breen, Richard, Damian Hannan, David B. Rottman, and Christopher T. Whelan, eds, *Understanding Contemporary Ireland: State, Class and Development in the Republic of Ireland* (Basingstoke: Gill & Macmillan, 1990).

Brown, Terence, *Ireland: A Social and Cultural History 1922-2002* (London: Fontana, 2004).

Bruner, Jerome S., *The Process of Education* (Harvard, 1977).

Cairns, David, and Shaun Richards, *Writing Ireland: Colonialism Nationalism and Culture* (Manchester: Manchester University Press, 1988).

Carroll, Clare, and Patricia King eds, *Ireland and Postcolonial Theory* (Cork: Cork University Press, 2003).

Clancy, Patrick, Shelagh Drudy, Kathleen Lynch, and Liam O'Dowd eds, *Irish Society: Sociological Perspectives* (Dublin: Institute of Public Administration, 1997).

Connolly, Claire, *Theorizing Ireland* (Basingstoke: Palgrave Macmillan, 2002)

Cotter, Lucy, ed. *Third Text: Ireland Special Issue 19.5* (London and New York: Routledge, Taylor Francis, 2005).

Crow, Brian and Chris Banfield, *An Introduction to Post-colonial Theatre* (Cambridge: Cambridge University Press, 1996).

Daly, Mary E., *The Slow Failure: Population Decline and Independent Ireland, 1920-1973* (Madison: University of Wisconsin, 2006).

Dooley, Terence A.M., *'The land for the people': the land question in independent Ireland* (Dublin: University College Dublin Press, 2004).

Fanning, Ronan, *Independent Ireland* (Dublin:Helicon, 1983).

Fanon, Frantz, *The Wretched of the Earth* (Black Cat Books, 1968).

Fine Gael, *Winning Through to a Just Society* (Dublin: Fine Gael 1965).

Finlay, Fergus, Mary Robinson: A President with a Purpose (Dublin: O'Brien Press, 1990).

Freire, Paulo, *The Pedagogy of the Oppressed* (London: Pelican, 1985).

---, *Education for Critical Consciousness* (New York: Continuum, 1992).

Gibbons, Luke, *Transformations in Irish Culture* (Cork: Cork University Press, 1996).

Giddens, Anthony, *The Consequences of Modernity* (Cambridge, Oxford, and Boston: Polity, 1996).

Giroux, Henry A., *Fugitive Cultures: Race, Violence and Youth*, (London and New York: Routledge, 1996).

Government of Ireland, *Bunreacht na hÉireann* [The Constitution of Ireland] (Dublin: Government Publications, 2002).

Grene, Nicholas, *The Politics of Irish Drama: Plays in Context from Boucicault to Friel* (Cambridge: Cambridge University Press, 1999).

Harte, Liam and Yvonne Whelan eds, *Beyond Boundaries: Mapping Irish Studies in the Twenty-first Century*, (London: London; Sterling, Virginia: Pluto, 2007).

Hayward, Katy, *Irish Nationalism and European Integration: the official redefinition of the island of Ireland* (Manchester: Manchester University Press, 2009).

Horgan, John, *Mary Robinson: an independent voice* (Dublin: O'Brien Press, 1997).

Kearney, Richard, *The Wake of Imagination* (London: Century Hutchinson, 1988).

---, *Transitions: Narratives in Irish Culture* (Manchester: Manchester University Press, 1988).

---, ed., *Across the Frontiers: Ireland in the 1990s* (Dublin: Wolfhound, 1988).

--- ed., *Visions of Europe* (Dublin: Wolfhound, 1992).

---, *Postnationalist Ireland: Politics, Culture, Philosophy* (London and New York: Routledge, 1997).

Kiberd, Declan, *Inventing Ireland: The Literature of the Modern Nation* (London: Vintage, 1996).

Kirby, Peadar, *Poverty Amid Plenty: World and Irish Development Reconsidered* (Dublin: Trócaire, 1997).

---, *The Celtic Tiger in Distress: Growth with Inequality in Ireland* (Basingstoke: Palgrave Macmillan, 2002).

Kirby, Peadar, Luke Gibbons, and Michael Cronin, eds *Re-inventing Ireland: Culture, Society and the Global Economy*, (London, Sterling, Virginia: Pluto, 2002).

Lee, J. J., *The Modernisation of Irish Society 1848-1918* (Dublin: Gill & Macmillan, 1989).

---, *Ireland 1912 – 1985: Politics and Society* (Cambridge: Cambridge University Press, 1990).

Llewellyn-Jones, Margaret, *Contemporary Irish Drama and Cultural Identity* (Bristol: Intellect Books, 2002).

Lloyd, David, *Anomalous States: Irish Writing and the Post-Colonial Moment* (Dublin: Lilliput, 1993).

---, *Ireland After History* (Cork: Cork University Press, 1999).

Lonergan, Patrick, *Theatre and Globalization: Irish Drama in the Celtic Tiger Era* (Basingstoke: Palgrave Macmillan, 2009).

Lorde, Audre, *Sister Outsider*, (Berkeley: University of Berkeley Press, 1984): 100.

Manfull, Helen, *Taking Stage: women directors on directing* (London: Methuen, 1999).

Mason, Patrick, *A High Ambition* (Dublin: The National Theatre Society, 1993).

MacLaughlin, Jim, *Travellers and Ireland: whose country, whose history?* (Cork: Cork University Press, 1995).

McGrath, John, *A Good Night Out – Popular Theatre: Audience, Class and Form* (London: Methuen, 1989).

Morash, Christopher, *A History of Irish Theatre 1601-2000* (Cambridge: Cambridge University Press, 2002).

Murray, Christopher, *Twentieth-century Irish Drama: mirror up to nation* (Manchester: Manchester University Press, 1997).

Nightingale, Virginia, *Studying Audiences: the shock of the real* (London and New York: Routledge, 1996).

Ó Broin, Deiric and Peadar Kirby eds, *Power, Dissent and Democracy: civil society and the state in Ireland* (Dublin: A&A Farmer Ltd., 2009).

O'Reilly, Emily, *Masterminds of the Right* (Dublin: Attic Press, 1996).

O'Toole, Fintan, *Black Hole, Green Card* (Dublin: New Island, 1994).

---, *Tom Murphy: The Politics Of Magic* (Dublin: New Island, 1994).

Pašeta, Senia, *Before the Revolution: Nationalism, Social Change and Ireland's Catholic Elite, 1879-1922* (Cork: Cork University Press, 1999).

Pilkington, Lionel, *Theatre and State in Twentieth-century Ireland* (London and New York: Routledge, 2001).

Rebellato, Dan, *Theatre & Globalization* (Basingstoke: Palgrave Macmillan, 2009).

Roche, Anthony, *Contemporary Irish Drama: from Beckett to McGuinness* (Dublin: Gill & Macmillan 1994)

Smyth, Gerry, *Decolonisation and Criticism* (London; Sterling, Virginia: Pluto Press, 1998).

Soyinka, Wole, *Myth, Literature and the African World* (Cambridge: Canto, 1995).

Staniszewski, Mary A., *Believing is Seeing: Creating the Culture of Art* (London and New York: Penguin, 1995).

Szondi, Peter, *The Theory of the Modern Drama* (Cambridge, Oxford, and Boston: Polity Press, 1987).

Tiffin, Chris and Alan Lawson, eds, *De-scribing Empire: Post-colonialism and textuality* (London and New York: Routledge, 1994).

Wa Thiong'o, Ngugi, *Decolonising the Mind* (Athens, Ohio: James Currey Heinemann, 1987).

---, *Moving the Centre: The Struggle for Cultural Freedoms* (Athens, Ohio: James Currey Heinemann, 1993).

Walsh, Martin, *The Brechtian Aspect of Radical Cinema* (London: BFI, 1981).

Webster's Third New International Dictionary – Unabridged (Springfield, Mass.: Merriam-Webster, 1993).

Welch, Robert, *The Abbey Theatre 1899-1999: Form & Pressure* (Oxford: Oxford University Press, 2003).

Williams, Raymond, *Communications* (London and New York: Penguin, 1962).

---, *Marxism and Literature* (Oxford: Oxford University Press, 1977).

---, *Keywords: A Vocabulary of Culture and Society* (London: Fontana, 1989).

Willett, John, (trans.) *Brecht on Theatre* (London: Methuen, 1979).

---, and Ralph Mannheim (trans.), *Bertolt Brecht, The Threepenny Opera* (London: Methuen, 1979).

Wright, Elizabeth, *Postmodern Brecht: A Re-presentation* (London and New York: Routledge, 1989).

Articles:

Amkpa, Awam, 'Drama and the Languages of Postcolonial Desire' *Irish University Review*, 29. 2 Autumn/Winter (1999): 294-304.

---, *Framing narratives of postcoloniality* in http://www.mtholyoke.edu/~aamkpa/ Framing.Questions.html

Ashcroft, Bill, 'Postcoloniality and the future of English', *Understanding Post-Colonial Identities: Ireland, Africa and the Pacific*, ed. Dele Layiwola (Ibadan: Sefer Books, 2001): 1-17.

Breatnach, Pádraig A., 'Crisis in our Universities: the impact on the Humanities', *Studies: An Irish Quarterly Review*, (Vol. 96, No. 384, 2007): 391-406.

Clarke, Jocelyn, '(Un)critical conditions', *Theatre Stuff: Critical Essays on Contemporary Irish Theatre*, ed. Eamonn Jordan, (Dublin: Carysfort Press, 2000): 95-106.

Cleary, Joseph, 'Modernization and Aesthetic Ideology in Contemporary Irish Culture', *Writing in the Irish Republic: Literature, Culture, politics 1949-1999*, ed. Ray Ryan (Basingstoke: Macmillan, 2000): 106-129.

---, '"Misplaced Ideas"?: Colonialism, Location and Dislocation in Irish Studies', *Ireland and Postcolonial Theory*, eds Clare Carroll and Patricia King (Cork: Cork University Press, 2003): 16-45.

Deane, Seamus, 'Introduction' to *Nationalism, Colonialism and Literature*, ed. Seamus Deane (Minneapolis: University of Minnesota Press, 1990): 3-19.

Dukes, Gerry, 'The *Godot* Phenomenon', *Samuel Beckett – 100 Years*, ed. Christopher Murray (Dublin: New Island Books, 2006):

Eagleton, Terry, 'Nationalism: irony and commitment', *Nationalism, Colonialism and Literature* ed. Seamus Deane (Minneapolis: University Of Minnesota Press, 1990): 23-39.

---, 'Political Beckett?' *New Left Review 40*, (July-August 2006).

Frazier, Adrian, 'Introduction: Irish Theatre Scholarship', *The Irish Review* 29 (2002): 1-9.

Fricker, Karen and Brian Singleton, 'Irish Theatre: Conditions of Criticism', *Modern Drama XLVII. 4* (Winter 2004).

Gibbons, Luke, 'Alternative Enlightenments', *1798: 200 years of resonance*, ed. Mary Cullen, (Belfast: Irish Reporter Publications, 1998): 119-127.

---, 'Narratives of the Nation: Fact, Fiction and Irish Cinema', *Nationalisms: visions and revisions*, ed. Luke Dodd (Dublin: Film Institute of Ireland, 1999): 66-73.

Harrington, John P., 'The Irish Beckett', *Modern Irish Drama*, ed. John P. Harrington (New York: Norton, 1991): 545-550.

Harvey, Brian, 'Ireland and Civil Society: reaching the limits of dissent', *Power, Dissent and Democracy: civil society and the state in Ireland*, Deiric Ó Broin and Peadar Kirby eds (Dublin: A&A Farmer Ltd., 2009): 25-33.

Hall, Stuart, 'New Ethnicities', *Stuart Hall: Critical Dialogues in Cultural Studies*, eds, David Morley and Kuan- Hsing Chen (London and New York: Routledge, 1996): 441-449.

Jackson, Joe, 'Michael D. Higgins 1993', *Troubadours and Troublemakers* (Dublin: Blackwater Press, 1996): 205-213.

Kearney, Richard, 'Letters on a New Republic', *Letters from the New Island*, ed. Dermot Bolger (Dublin: Raven Arts Press, 1991): 302-321.

Kilroy, Tom, 'A Generation of Playwrights', *Theatre Stuff: Critical Essays on Contemporary Irish theatre*, ed. Eamonn Jordan (Dublin: Carysfort Press, 2000): 1-7.

Kirby, Peadar and Mary Murphy, 'State and civil society in Ireland: conclusions and mapping alternatives', *Power, Dissent and Democracy: civil society and the state in Ireland*, Deiric Ó Broin and Peadar Kirby eds (Dublin: A&A Farmer Ltd., 2009): 143-159.

Kirby, Peadar, *Village Magazine*, July 2009.

Lee, Joe, 'Commentary', *Nationalisms: visions and revisions*, ed. Luke Dodd, (Dublin: Film Institute of Ireland, 1999): 74-80.

Lloyd, David, 'After History: Historicism and Irish Postcolonial Studies', Carroll and King eds, *Postcolonial Theory*: 46-62.

Mathews, P.J., 'A Battle of Two Civilizations?: D.P. Moran and William Rooney', *The Irish Review* 29, Autumn (2002): 22-37.

McCurtain, Margaret, 'Footage from the 1960s' *Nationalisms: Visions and Revisions*, ed. Luke Dodd (Dublin:Film Institute of Ireland, 1999): 40-43.

McGuinness, Frank, 'Writing in Greek: By The Bog of Cats ...', *The Theatre of Marina Carr: before rules was made*, eds Cathy Leeney and Anna McMullan (Dublin: Carysfort Press, 2003): 87-88.

Mac Intyre, Tom, 'Portia Coughlan' , *The Theatre of Marina Carr: before rules was made*, eds Cathy Leeney and Anna McMullan (Dublin: Carysfort Press, 2003): 80-82.

Merriman, Vic, 'Centring the Wanderer: Europe as Active Imaginary in Contemporary Irish Theatre', *Irish University Review* 27. 1 (Spring/Summer 1997): 166-181.

---, 'Cartographic Connections: Problems of representation in Calypso Theatre Company's *The Business of Blood*, *The Irish Review: Special Issue on Contemporary Irish Theatre*, ed. Frank McGuinness (Spring 1998): 28-36.

---, 'Decolonisation postponed: the theatre of Tiger Trash', *Irish University Review* 29. 2 (Autumn/Winter, 1999): 305.-317

---, 'Seeing Sites: Dramatic images as Representations of the Social World', in *A is for Art: a CIRCA special supplement on arts education* (Dublin and Belfast, 1999): 15-17.

Miller, Toby, 'Culture and the Global Economy', *Performing Hybridity*, May Joseph and Jennifer Natalya Fink eds, (Minneapolis: University Of Minnesota Press, 1999): 35-45.

Morash, Christopher, '"Something's Missing": Theatre and The Republic of Ireland Act', *Writing in the Irish Republic: Literature, Culture, Politics 1949-1999*, ed. Ray Ryan (Basingstoke: Macmillan, 1999): 64-81.

---, 'Murphy, History and Society', *Talking About Tom Murphy*, ed. Nicholas Grene (Dublin: Carysfort Press, 2002): 17-30.

O'Brien, Flann, 'A Bash in the Tunnel', *Stories and Plays* (London and Glasgow: Paladin, 1991): 167-175.

O'Kelly, Donal, 'Strangers in a Strange Land', *Irish Theatre Magazine* 1.1 (Autumn 1998): 6-12.

O'Toole, Fintan, 'Introduction: on the frontier', *A Dublin Quartet*, Dermot Bolger, (London and New York: Penguin 1992): 1-6.

---, 'Introduction' to Tom Murphy, *Plays 4* (London: Methuen, 1997): ix-xiv.

---, 'Irish Theatre: The State of the Art', *Theatre Stuff: Critical Essays on Contemporary Irish Theatre*, ed. Eamonn Jordan ed (Dublin: Carysfort Press, 2000): 47-58.

---, 'Introduction' to Martin McDonagh *Plays: 1* (London: Methuen, 1999): ix-xvii.

---, 'The Leenane Trilogy' in Julia Furay and Redmond O'Hanlon eds, *Critical Moments: Fintan O'Toole on Modern Irish Theatre* (Dublin: Carysfort Press, 2003), : 179-182.

Pilkington, Lionel, 'Theatre History and the Beginnings of the Irish National Theatre Project', *Theatre Stuff: Critical Essays on Contemporary Irish Theatre*, ed. Eamonn Jordan (Dublin: Carysfort Press, 2000): 27-33.

---, 'Recent Developments in Irish Theatre History', *Modern Drama XLVII. 4* (Winter 2004).

Porter, Norman, 'The Ideas of 1798: Do they have any meaning for contemporary unionism?', *1798: 200 Years of Resonance* ed. Mary Cullen (Belfast: Irish Reporter Publications, 1998): 105-111.

Robinson, Mary, with Richard Kearney, 'A Question of Law: The European legacy', *Visions of Europe*, ed. Richard Kearney (Dublin: Wolfhound, 1992): 133-143.

Rowlands, Michael, 'Memory, Sacrifice And The Nation', *Cultural Memory: New Formations* 30: 8-17.

Saddlemyer, Ann, 'Introduction', *The Playboy of the Western World and Other Plays* ed. Ann Saddlemyer (Oxford: Oxford University Press, 1995): vii-xxi.

Said, Edward, 'Yeats and Decolonization', *Nationalism, Colonialism and Literature*, ed. Seamus Deane (Minneapolis: University of Minnesota Press, 1990): 69-95.

---, 'Reflections on Exile', in Russell Ferguson, et al. eds, *Out There: marginalization and contemporary cultures* (Boston: MIT, 1991): 357-366.

Schulte-Sasse, Jochen, 'Foreword: On the difference between a mimetic and a semiotic theory of the modern drama', *Theory of the Modern Drama*, Peter Szondi, (Cambridge, Oxford, and Boston: Polity Press, 1987): vii-xvi.

Shaw, Bernard, 'Preface for Politicians', *John Bull's Other Island*, (London and New York: Penguin, 1984).

Tracey, Tony, 'Mise Éire', *Nationalisms: visions and revisions*, Luke Dodd, (Dublin: Film Institute of Ireland, 1999): 64-65.

West, Cornel, 'The New Cultural Politics of Difference', *Out There: Marginalization and Contemporary Cultures*, Russell Ferguson et al. eds (Boston: MIT, 1992): 19-36.

Whelan, Kevin, 'Between Filiation and Affiliation: The Politics of Postcolonial Memory', *Ireland and Postcolonial Theory*, Carroll, Clare, and Patricia King, eds (Cork: Cork University Press, 2003): 92-108.

Newspaper articles:

Byrne, Jason, 'Not My Cup Of Tea', *The Irish Times*, 1 August 2000: 16.

Editorial, 'Refugees: It's Time To End This Fiasco', *The Wexford People*, 29 July 1998.: 1.

Finlay, Fergus, 'Unfinished Business', *The Examiner*, 31 December 1999.

Maher, Alice, 'The Celtic Tiger has no Eyes', *The Irish Times* (28 December 1999).

Marre, Oliver, 'They're too cool for school: meet the new history boys and girls: Theory is a thing of the past for these hip young historians', *The Observer*, 28 June 2009.

McMonagle, Niall, 'Shiny new texts and new ideas ...' *The Irish Times Weekend*, 26 June 1999.

O'Halloran, Tim, letter to *The Irish Times*, 12 July 2000: 14.

O'Toole, Fintan, 'Irish theatre is making itself in new ways', in 'The 35th Dublin Theatre Festival: A supplement to *The Irish Times*', 21 September 1994: 5.

Scott, Peter, 'Reaching Beyond Enlightenment' (*Times Higher Education Supplement*, 24 August 1990).

The Wexford People, 'Wexford film director has major win in Galway', *Wexford People*, 26 July 2000.

White, Victoria, 'Desperately Seeking Asylum', *The Irish Times*, 26 August 1994.

---, 'Women Writers Finally Take Centre Stage', *The Irish Times*, 15 October 1998.

Zappone, Katherine E., and Peadar Kirby, 'Harney got it wrong about our "inclusive" society', *The Irish Times*, 13 August 1999: 13.

Reviews:

Nowlan, David, '*A Life*, by Hugh Leonard', *The Irish Times*, 14 July 2000.

---, 'On Raftery's Hill', *The Irish Times* 10 May 2000.

---, 'Polemic driven to a foregone conclusion', *The Irish Times*, 15 September 1995.

O'Toole, Fintan, 'Second Opinion: A powerful gesture', *The Irish Times*, 26 September 1995.

Official Publications:

Murphy, Francis, Helen Buckley and Laraine Joyce, *The Ferns Report* (Dublin: Government Publications, 2005).

Report of the Commission to Inquire into Child Abuse (The Ryan Report) (Dublin: Government Publications, 2009).

Index

Carysfort Press was formed in the summer of 1998. It receives annual funding from the Arts Council.

The directors believe that drama is playing an ever-increasing role in today's society and that enjoyment of the theatre, both professional and amateur, currently plays a central part in Irish culture.

The Press aims to produce high quality publications which, though written and/or edited by academics, will be made accessible to a general readership. The organisation would also like to provide a forum for critical thinking in the Arts in Ireland, again keeping the needs and interests of the general public in view.

The company publishes contemporary Irish writing for and about the theatre.

Editorial and publishing inquiries to:
Carysfort Press Ltd.,
58 Woodfield,
Scholarstown Road,
Rathfarnham,
Dublin 16,
Republic of Ireland.

T (353 1) 493 7383
F (353 1) 406 9815
E: info@carysfortpress.com
www.carysfortpress.com

HOW TO ORDER

TRADE ORDERS DIRECTLY TO:
Irish Book Distribution
Unit 12, North Park, North Road,
Finglas, Dublin 11.

T: (353 1) 8239580
F: (353 1) 8239599
E: mary@argosybooks.ie
www.argosybooks.ie

INDIVIDUAL ORDERS DIRECTLY TO:
eprint Ltd.
35 Coolmine Industrial Estate,
Blanchardstown, Dublin 15.
T: (353 1) 827 8860
F: (353 1) 827 8804 Order online @
E: books@eprint.ie
www.eprint.ie

FOR SALES IN NORTH AMERICA AND CANADA:
Dufour Editions Inc.,
124 Byers Road,
PO Box 7,
Chester Springs,
PA 19425,
USA

T: 1-610-458-5005
F: 1-610-458-7103

"Buffoonery and Easy Sentiment":
Popular Irish Plays in the Decade Prior to the Opening of The Abbey Theatre

Christopher Fitz-Simon

In this fascinating reappraisal of the non-literary drama of the late 19th - early 20th century, Christopher Fitz-Simon discloses a unique world of plays, players and producers in metropolitan theatres in Ireland and other countries where Ireland was viewed as a source of extraordinary topics at once contemporary and comfortably remote: revolution, eviction, famine, agrarian agitation, political assassination.

The form was the fashionable one of melodrama, yet Irish melodrama was of a particular kind replete with hidden messages, and the language was far more allusive, colourful and entertaining than that of its English equivalent.

ISBN: 978-1-9045505-49-5   €20.00

The Fourth Seamus Heaney Lectures, 'Mirror up to Nature':

Ed. Patrick Burke

What, in particular, is the contemporary usefulness for the building of societies of one of our oldest and culturally valued ideals, that of drama? The Fourth Seamus Heaney Lectures, 'Mirror up to Nature': Drama and Theatre in the Modern World, given at St Patrick's College, Drumcondra, between October 2006 and April 2007, addressed these and related questions. Patrick Mason spoke on the essence of theatre, Thomas Kilroy on Ireland's contribution to the art of theatre, Cecily O'Neill and Jonothan Neelands on the rich potential of drama in the classroom. Brenna Katz Clarke examined the relationship between drama and film, and John Buckley spoke on opera and its history and gave an illuminating account of his own *Words Upon The Window-Pane*.

ISBN 978-1-9045505-48-8   €12

The Theatre of Tom Mac Intyre: 'Strays from the ether'

Eds. Bernadette Sweeney and Marie Kelly

This long overdue anthology captures the soul of Mac Intyre's dramatic canon – its ethereal qualities, its extraordinary diversity, its emphasis on the poetic and on performance – in an extensive range of visual, journalistic and scholarly contributions from writers, theatre practitioners.

ISBN 978-1-904505-46-4   €25

Irish Appropriation Of Greek Tragedy

Brian Arkins

This book presents an analysis of more than 30 plays written by Irish dramatists and poets that are based on the tragedies of Sophocles, Euripides and Aeschylus. These plays proceed from the time of Yeats and Synge through MacNeice and the Longfords on to many of today's leading writers.

ISBN 978-1-904505-47-1   €20

Alive in Time: The Enduring Drama of Tom Murphy

Ed. Christopher Murray

Almost 50 years after he first hit the headlines as Ireland's most challenging playwright, the 'angry young man' of those times Tom Murphy still commands his place at the pinnacle of Irish theatre. Here 17 new essays by prominent critics and academics, with an introduction by Christopher Murray, survey Murphy's dramatic oeuvre in a concerted attempt to define his greatness and enduring appeal, making this book a significant study of a unique genius.

ISBN 978-1-904505-45-7   €25

Performing Violence in Contemporary Ireland

Ed. Lisa Fitzpatrick

This interdisciplinary collection of fifteen new essays by scholars of theatre, Irish studies, music, design and politics explores aspects of the performance of violence in contemporary Ireland. With chapters on the work of playwrights Martin McDonagh, Martin Lynch, Conor McPherson and Gary Mitchell, on Republican commemorations and the 90th anniversary ceremonies for the Battle of the Somme and the Easter Rising, this book aims to contribute to the ongoing international debate on the performance of violence in contemporary societies.

ISBN 978-1-904505-44-0 (2009) €20

Ireland's Economic Crisis - Time to Act. Essays from over 40 leading Irish thinkers at the MacGill Summer School 2009

Eds. Joe Mulholland and Finbarr Bradley

Ireland's economic crisis requires a radical transformation in policymaking. In this volume, political, industrial, academic, trade union and business leaders and commentators tell the story of the Irish economy and its rise and fall. Contributions at Glenties range from policy, vision and context to practical suggestions on how the country can emerge from its crisis.

ISBN 978-1-904505-43-3 (2009) €20

Deviant Acts: Essays on Queer Performance

Ed. David Cregan

This book contains an exciting collection of essays focusing on a variety of alternative performances happening in contemporary Ireland. While it highlights the particular representations of gay and lesbian identity it also brings to light how diversity has always been a part of Irish culture and is, in fact, shaping what it means to be Irish today.

ISBN 978-1-904505-42-6 (2009) €20

Seán Keating in Context: Responses to Culture and Politics in Post-Civil War Ireland

Compiled, edited and introduced by Éimear O'Connor

Irish artist Seán Keating has been judged by his critics as the personification of old-fashioned traditionalist values. This book presents a different view. The story reveals Keating's early determination to attain government support for the visual arts. It also illustrates his socialist leanings, his disappointment with capitalism, and his attitude to cultural snobbery, to art critics, and to the Academy. Given the national and global circumstances nowadays, Keating's critical and wry observations are prophetic – and highly amusing.

ISBN 978-1-904505-41-9 €25

Dialogue of the Ancients of Ireland: A new translation of Acallam na Senorach

Translated with introduction and notes by Maurice Harmon

One of Ireland's greatest collections of stories and poems, The Dialogue of the Ancients of Ireland is a new translation by Maurice Harmon of the 12th century *Acallam na Senorach*. Retold in a refreshing modern idiom, the *Dialogue* is an extraordinary account of journeys to the four provinces by St. Patrick and the pagan Cailte, one of the surviving Fian. Within the frame story are over 200 other stories reflecting many genres – wonder tales, sea journeys, romances, stories of revenge, tales of monsters and magic. The poems are equally varied – lyrics, nature poems, eulogies, prophecies, laments, genealogical poems. After the *Tain Bo Cuailnge*, the *Acallam* is the largest surviving prose work in Old and Middle Irish.

ISBN: 978-1-904505-39-6 (2009)   €20

Literary and Cultural Relations between Ireland and Hungary and Central and Eastern Europe

Ed. Maria Kurdi

This lively, informative and incisive collection of essays sheds fascinating new light on the literary interrelations between Ireland, Hungary, Poland, Romania and the Czech Republic. It charts a hitherto under-explored history of the reception of modern Irish culture in Central and Eastern Europe and also investigates how key authors have been translated, performed and adapted. The revealing explorations undertaken in this volume of a wide array of Irish dramatic and literary texts, ranging from *Gulliver's Travels* to *Translations* and *The Pillowman*, tease out the subtly altered nuances that they acquire in a Central European context.

ISBN: 978-1-904505-40-2 (2009)   €20

Plays and Controversies: Abbey Theatre Diaries 2000-2005

Ben Barnes

In diaries covering the period of his artistic directorship of the Abbey, Ben Barnes offers a frank, honest, and probing account of a much commented upon and controversial period in the history of the national theatre. These diaries also provide fascinating personal insights into the day-to- day pressures, joys, and frustrations of running one of Ireland's most iconic institutions.

ISBN: 978-1-904505-38-9 (2008)   €35

Interactions: Dublin Theatre Festival 1957-2007. Irish Theatrical Diaspora Series: 3

Eds. Nicholas Grene and Patrick Lonergan with Lilian Chambers

For over 50 years the Dublin Theatre Festival has been one of Ireland's most important cultural events, bringing countless new Irish plays to the world stage, while introducing Irish audiences to the most important international theatre companies and artists. Interactions explores and celebrates the achievements of the renowned Festival since 1957 and includes specially commissioned memoirs from past organizers, offering a unique perspective on the controversies and successes that have marked the event's history. An especially valuable feature of the volume, also, is a complete listing of the shows that have appeared at the Festival from 1957 to 2008.

ISBN: 978-1-904505-36-5   €25

The Informer: A play by Tom Murphy based on the novel by Liam O'Flaherty

The Informer, Tom Murphy's stage adaptation of Liam O'Flaherty's novel, was produced in the 1981 Dublin Theatre Festival, directed by the playwright himself, with Liam Neeson in the leading role. The central subject of the play is the quest of a character at the point of emotional and moral breakdown for some source of meaning or identity. In the case of Gypo Nolan, the informer of the title, this involves a nightmarish progress through a Dublin underworld in which he changes from a Judas figure to a scapegoat surrogate for Jesus, taking upon himself the sins of the world. A cinematic style, with flash-back and intercut scenes, is used rather than a conventional theatrical structure to catch the fevered and phantasmagoric progression of Gypo's mind. The language, characteristically for Murphy, mixes graphically colloquial Dublin slang with the haunted intricacies of the central character groping for the meaning of his own actions. The dynamic rhythm of the action builds towards an inevitable but theatrically satisfying tragic catastrophe. ' [The Informer] is, in many ways closer to being an original Murphy play than it is to O'Flaherty...' Fintan O'Toole.

ISBN: 978-1-904505-37-2 (2008)   €10

Shifting Scenes: Irish theatre-going 1955-1985

Eds. Nicholas Grene and Chris Morash

Transcript of conversations with John Devitt, academic and reviewer, about his lifelong passion for the theatre. A fascinating and entertaining insight into Dublin theatre over the course of thirty years provided by Devitt's vivid reminiscences and astute observations.

ISBN: 978-1-904505-33-4 (2008)   €10

Irish Literature: Feminist Perspectives

Eds. Patricia Coughlan and Tina O'Toole

The collection discusses texts from the early 18th century to the present. A central theme of the book is the need to renegotiate the relations of feminism with nationalism and to transact the potential contest of these two important narratives, each possessing powerful emancipatory force. Irish Literature: Feminist Perspectives contributes incisively to contemporary debates about Irish culture, gender and ideology.

ISBN: 978-1-904505-35-8 (2008)   €25

Silenced Voices: Hungarian Plays from Transylvania

Selected and translated by Csilla Bertha and Donald E. Morse

The five plays are wonderfully theatrical, moving fluidly from absurdism to tragedy, and from satire to the darkly comic. Donald Morse and Csilla Bertha's translations capture these qualities perfectly, giving voice to the 'forgotten playwrights of Central Europe'. They also deeply enrich our understanding of the relationship between art, ethics, and politics in Europe.

ISBN: 978-1-904505-34-1 (2008)   €25

A Hazardous Melody of Being:
Seóirse Bodley's Song Cycles on the poems of Micheal O'Siadhail

Ed. Lorraine Byrne Bodley

This apograph is the first publication of Bodley's O'Siadhail song cycles and is the first book to explore the composer's lyrical modernity from a number of perspectives. Lorraine Byrne Bodley's insightful introduction describes in detail the development and essence of Bodley's musical thinking, the European influences he absorbed which linger in these cycles, and the importance of his work as a composer of the Irish art song.

ISBN: 978-1-904505-31-0 (2008)   €25

Irish Theatre in England: Irish Theatrical Diaspora Series: 2

Eds. Richard Cave and Ben Levitas

Irish theatre in England has frequently illustrated the complex relations between two distinct cultures. How English reviewers and audiences interpret Irish plays is often decidedly different from how the plays were read in performance in Ireland. How certain Irish performers have chosen to be understood in Dublin is not necessarily how audiences in London have perceived their constructed stage personae. Though a collection by diverse authors, the twelve essays in this volume investigate these issues from a variety of perspectives that together chart the trajectory of Irish performance in England from the mid-nineteenth century till today.

ISBN: 978-1-904505-26-6 (2007)   €20

Goethe and Anna Amalia: A Forbidden Love?

Ettore Ghibellino, Trans. Dan Farrelly

In this study Ghibellino sets out to show that the platonic relationship between Goethe and Charlotte von Stein – lady-in-waiting to Anna Amalia, the Dowager Duchess of Weimar – was used as part of a cover-up for Goethe's intense and prolonged love relationship with the Duchess Anna Amalia herself. The book attempts to uncover a hitherto closely-kept state secret. Readers convinced by the evidence supporting Ghibellino's hypothesis will see in it one of the very great love stories in European history – to rank with that of Dante and Beatrice, and Petrarch and Laura.

ISBN: 978-1-904505-24-2   €20

Ireland on Stage: Beckett and After

Eds. Hiroko Mikami, Minako Okamuro, Naoko Yagi

The collection focuses primarily on Irish playwrights and their work, both in text and on the stage during the latter half of the twentieth century. The central figure is Samuel Beckett, but the contributors freely draw on Beckett and his work provides a springboard to discuss contemporary playwrights such as Brian Friel, Frank McGuinness, Marina Carr and Conor McPherson amongst others. Contributors include: Anthony Roche, Hiroko Mikami, Naoko Yagi, Cathy Leeney, Joseph Long, Noreem Doody, Minako Okamuro, Christopher Murray, Futoshi Sakauchi and Declan Kiberd

ISBN: 978-1-904505-23-5 (2007)   €20

'Echoes Down the Corridor': Irish Theatre - Past, Present and Future

Eds. Patrick Lonergan and Riana O'Dwyer

This collection of fourteen new essays explores Irish theatre from exciting new perspectives. How has Irish theatre been received internationally - and, as the country becomes more multicultural, how will international theatre influence the development of drama in Ireland? These and many other important questions.

ISBN: 978-1-904505-25-9 (2007) €20

Musics of Belonging: The Poetry of Micheal O'Siadhail

Eds. Marc Caball & David F. Ford

An overall account is given of O'Siadhail's life, his work and the reception of his poetry so far. There are close readings of some poems, analyses of his artistry in matching diverse content with both classical and innovative forms, and studies of recurrent themes such as love, death, language, music, and the shifts of modern life.

ISBN: 978-1-904505-22-8 (2007) €25 (Paperback)
ISBN: 978-1-904505-21-1 (2007) €50 (Casebound)

Brian Friel's Dramatic Artistry: 'The Work has Value'

Eds. Donald E. Morse, Csilla Bertha and Maria Kurdi

Brian Friel's Dramatic Artistry presents a refreshingly broad range of voices: new work from some of the leading English-speaking authorities on Friel, and fascinating essays from scholars in Germany, Italy, Portugal, and Hungary. This book will deepen our knowledge and enjoyment of Friel's work.

ISBN: 978-1-904505-17-4 (2006) €30

The Theatre of Martin McDonagh: 'A World of Savage Stories'

Eds. Lilian Chambers and Eamonn Jordan

The book is a vital response to the many challenges set by McDonagh for those involved in the production and reception of his work. Critics and commentators from around the world offer a diverse range of often provocative approaches. What is not surprising is the focus and commitment of the engagement, given the controversial and stimulating nature of the work.

ISBN: 978-1-904505-19-8 (2006) €35

Edna O'Brien: New Critical Perspectives

Eds. Kathryn Laing, Sinead Mooney and Maureen O'Connor

The essays collected here illustrate some of the range, complexity, and interest of Edna O'Brien as a fiction writer and dramatist. They will contribute to a broader appreciation of her work and to an evolution of new critical approaches, as well as igniting more interest in the many unexplored areas of her considerable oeuvre.

ISBN: 978-1-904505-20-4 (2006) €20

Irish Theatre on Tour

Eds. Nicholas Grene and Chris Morash

'Touring has been at the strategic heart of Druid's artistic policy since the early eighties. Everyone has the right to see professional theatre in their own communities. Irish theatre on tour is a crucial part of Irish theatre as a whole'. Garry Hynes

ISBN 978-1-904505-13-6 (2005) €20

Poems 2000-2005 by Hugh Maxton

Poems 2000-2005 is a transitional collection written while the author – also known to be W.J. Mc Cormack, literary historian – was in the process of moving back from London to settle in rural Ireland.

ISBN 978-1-904505-12-9 (2005) €10

Synge: A Celebration

Ed. Colm Tóibín

A collection of essays by some of Ireland's most creative writers on the work of John Millington Synge, featuring Sebastian Barry, Marina Carr, Anthony Cronin, Roddy Doyle, Anne Enright, Hugo Hamilton, Joseph O'Connor, Mary O'Malley, Fintan O'Toole, Colm Toibin, Vincent Woods.

ISBN 978-1-904505-14-3 (2005) €15

East of Eden: New Romanian Plays

Ed. Andrei Marinescu

Four of the most promising Romanian playwrights, young and very young, are in this collection, each one with a specific way of seeing the Romanian reality, each one with a style of communicating an articulated artistic vision of the society we are living in. Ion Caramitru, General Director Romanian National Theatre Bucharest.
ISBN 978-1-904505-15-0 (2005) €10

George Fitzmaurice: 'Wild in His Own Way', Biography of an Irish Playwright

Fiona Brennan

'Fiona Brennan's introduction to his considerable output allows us a much greater appreciation and understanding of Fitzmaurice, the one remaining under-celebrated genius of twentieth-century Irish drama'. Conall Morrison

ISBN 978-1-904505-16-7 (2005) €20

Out of History: Essays on the Writings of Sebastian Barry

Ed. Christina Hunt Mahony

The essays address Barry's engagement with the contemporary cultural debate in Ireland and also with issues that inform postcolonial critical theory. The range and selection of contributors has ensured a high level of critical expression and an insightful assessment of Barry and his works.

ISBN: 978-1-904505-18-1 (2005) €20

Three Congregational Masses

Seoirse Bodley

'From the simpler congregational settings in the Mass of Peace and the Mass of Joy to the richer textures of the Mass of Glory, they are immediately attractive and accessible, and with a distinctively Irish melodic quality.' Barra Boydell

ISBN: 978-1-904505-11-2 (2005) €15

Georg Büchner's Woyzeck,

A new translation by Dan Farrelly

The most up-to-date German scholarship of Thomas Michael Mayer and Burghard Dedner has finally made it possible to establish an authentic sequence of scenes. The wide-spread view that this play is a prime example of loose, open theatre is no longer sustainable. Directors and teachers are challenged to "read it again".

ISBN: 978-1-904505-02-0 (2004) €10

Playboys of the Western World: Production Histories

Ed. Adrian Frazier

'The book is remarkably well-focused: half is a series of production histories of Playboy performances through the twentieth century in the UK, Northern Ireland, the USA, and Ireland. The remainder focuses on one contemporary performance, that of Druid Theatre, as directed by Garry Hynes. The various contemporary social issues that are addressed in relation to Synge's play and this performance of it give the volume an additional interest: it shows how the arts matter.' Kevin Barry

ISBN: 978-1-904505-06-8 (2004) €20

The Power of Laughter: Comedy and Contemporary Irish Theatre

Ed. Eric Weitz

The collection draws on a wide range of perspectives and voices including critics, playwrights, directors and performers. The result is a series of fascinating and provocative debates about the myriad functions of comedy in contemporary Irish theatre. Anna McMullan

As Stan Laurel said, 'it takes only an onion to cry. Peel it and weep. Comedy is harder'. 'These essays listen to the power of laughter. They hear the tough heart of Irish theatre – hard and wicked and funny'. Frank McGuinness

ISBN: 978-1-904505-05-1 (2004) €20

Sacred Play: Soul-Journeys in contemporary Irish Theatre

Anne F. O'Reilly

'Theatre as a space or container for sacred play allows audiences to glimpse mystery and to experience transformation. This book charts how Irish playwrights negotiate the labyrinth of the Irish soul and shows how their plays contribute to a poetics of Irish culture that enables a new imagining. Playwrights discussed are: McGuinness, Murphy, Friel, Le Marquand Hartigan, Burke Brogan, Harding, Meehan, Carr, Parker, Devlin, and Barry.'

ISBN: 978-1-904505-07-5 (2004) €25

The Irish Harp Book

Sheila Larchet Cuthbert

This is a facsimile of the edition originally published by Mercier Press in 1993. There is a new preface by Sheila Larchet Cuthbert, and the biographical material has been updated. It is a collection of studies and exercises for the use of teachers and pupils of the Irish harp.
ISBN: 978-1-904505-08-2 (2004) €35

The Drunkard

Tom Murphy

'The Drunkard is a wonderfully eloquent play. Murphy's ear is finely attuned to the glories and absurdities of melodramatic exclamation, and even while he is wringing out its ludicrous overstatement, he is also making it sing.' The Irish Times

ISBN: 978-1-90 05-09-9 (2004) €10

Goethe: Musical Poet, Musical Catalyst

Ed. Lorraine Byrne

'Goethe was interested in, and acutely aware of, the place of music in human experience generally - and of its particular role in modern culture. Moreover, his own literary work - especially the poetry and Faust - inspired some of the major composers of the European tradition to produce some of their finest works.' Martin Swales

ISBN: 978-1-9045-10-5 (2004) €40

The Theatre of Marina Carr: "Before rules was made"

Eds. Anna McMullan & Cathy Leeney

As the first published collection of articles on the theatre of Marina Carr, this volume explores the world of Carr's theatrical imagination, the place of her plays in contemporary theatre in Ireland and abroad and the significance of her highly individual voice.

ISBN: 978-0-9534257-7-8 (2003) €20

Critical Moments: Fintan O'Toole on Modern Irish Theatre

Eds. Julia Furay & Redmond O'Hanlon

This new book on the work of Fintan O'Toole, the internationally acclaimed theatre critic and cultural commentator, offers percussive analyses and assessments of the major plays and playwrights in the canon of modern Irish theatre. Fearless and provocative in his judgements, O'Toole is essential reading for anyone interested in criticism or in the current state of Irish theatre.

ISBN: 978-1-904505-03-7 (2003) €20

Goethe and Schubert: Across the Divide

Eds. Lorraine Byrne & Dan Farrelly

Proceedings of the International Conference, 'Goethe and Schubert in Perspective and Performance', Trinity College Dublin, 2003. This volume includes essays by leading scholars – Barkhoff, Boyle, Byrne, Canisius, Dürr, Fischer, Hill, Kramer, Lamport, Lund, Meikle, Newbould, Norman McKay, White, Whitton, Wright, Youens – on Goethe's musicality and his relationship to Schubert; Schubert's contribution to sacred music and the Lied and his setting of Goethe's Singspiel, Claudine. A companion volume of this Singspiel (with piano reduction and English translation) is also available.

ISBN: 978-1-904505-04-4 (2003)   €25

Goethe's Singspiel, 'Claudine von Villa Bella'

Set by Franz Schubert

Goethe's Singspiel in three acts was set to music by Schubert in 1815. Only Act One of Schuberts's Claudine score is extant. The present volume makes Act One available for performance in English and German. It comprises both a piano reduction by Lorraine Byrne of the original Schubert orchestral score and a bilingual text translated for the modern stage by Dan Farrelly. This is a tale, wittily told, of lovers and vagabonds, romance, reconciliation, and resolution of family conflict.

ISBN: 978-0-9544290-0-3 (2002)   €20

Theatre of Sound, Radio and the Dramatic Imagination

Dermot Rattigan

An innovative study of the challenges that radio drama poses to the creative imagination of the writer, the production team, and the listener.
"A remarkably fine study of radio drama – everywhere informed by the writer's professional experience of such drama in the making…A new theoretical and analytical approach – informative, illuminating and at all times readable." Richard Allen Cave

ISBN: 978- 0-9534-257-5-4 (2002)   €20

Talking about Tom Murphy

Ed. Nicholas Grene

Talking About Tom Murphy is shaped around the six plays in the landmark Abbey Theatre Murphy Season of 2001, assembling some of the best-known commentators on his work: Fintan O'Toole, Chris Morash, Lionel Pilkington, Alexandra Poulain, Shaun Richards, Nicholas Grene and Declan Kiberd.

ISBN: 978-0-9534-257-9-2 (2002)   €15

Hamlet: The Shakespearean Director

Mike Wilcock

"This study of the Shakespearean director as viewed through various interpretations of HAMLET is a welcome addition to our understanding of how essential it is for a director to have a clear vision of a great play. It is an important study from which all of us who love Shakespeare and who understand the importance of continuing contemporary exploration may gain new insights." From the Foreword, by Joe Dowling, Artistic Director, The Guthrie Theater, Minneapolis, MN

ISBN: 978-1-904505-00-6 (2002) €20

The Theatre of Frank Mc Guinness: Stages of Mutability

Ed. Helen Lojek

The first edited collection of essays about internationally renowned Irish playwright Frank McGuinness focuses on both performance and text. Interpreters come to diverse conclusions, creating a vigorous dialogue that enriches understanding and reflects a strong consensus about the value of McGuinness's complex work.

ISBN: 978-1904505-01-3. (2002) €20

Theatre Talk: Voices of Irish Theatre Practitioners

Eds Lilian Chambers, Ger Fitzgibbon and Eamonn Jordan

"This book is the right approach - asking practitioners what they feel." Sebastian Barry, Playwright "... an invaluable and informative collection of interviews with those who make and shape the landscape of Irish Theatre." Ben Barnes, Artistic Director of the Abbey Theatre

ISBN: 978-0-9534-257-6-1 (2001) €20

In Search of the South African Iphigenie

Erika von Wietersheim and Dan Farrelly

Discussions of Goethe's "Iphigenie auf Tauris" (Under the Curse) as relevant to women's issues in modern South Africa: women in family and public life; the force of women's spirituality; experience of personal relationships; attitudes to parents and ancestors; involvement with religion.

ISBN: 978-0-9534257-8-5 (2001) €10

'The Starving' and 'October Song':

Two contemporary Irish plays by Andrew Hinds

The Starving, set during and after the siege of Derry in 1689, is a moving and engrossing drama of the emotional journey of two men.

October Song, a superbly written family drama set in real time in pre-ceasefire Derry.

ISBN: 978-0-9534-257-4-7 (2001)   €10

Seen and Heard: Six new plays by Irish women

Ed. Cathy Leeney

A rich and funny, moving and theatrically exciting collection of plays by Mary Elizabeth Burke-Kennedy, Síofra Campbell, Emma Donoghue, Anne Le Marquand Hartigan, Michelle Read and Dolores Walshe.

ISBN: 978-0-9534-257-3-0 (2001)   €20

Theatre Stuff: Critical essays on contemporary Irish theatre

Ed. Eamonn Jordan

Best selling essays on the successes and debates of contemporary Irish theatre at home and abroad. Contributors include: Thomas Kilroy, Declan Hughes, Anna McMullan, Declan Kiberd, Deirdre Mulrooney, Fintan O'Toole, Christopher Murray, Caoimhe McAvinchey and Terry Eagleton.

ISBN: 978-0-9534-2571-1-6 (2000)   €20

Under the Curse. Goethe's "Iphigenie Auf Tauris", A New Version

Dan Farrelly

The Greek myth of Iphigenie grappling with the curse on the house of Atreus is brought vividly to life. This version is currently being used in Johannesburg to explore problems of ancestry, religion, and Black African women's spirituality.

ISBN: 978-09534-257-8-5 (2000)   €10

Urfaust, A New Version of Goethe's early "Faust" in Brechtian Mode

Dan Farrelly

This version is based on Brecht's irreverent and daring re-interpretation of the German classic. "Urfaust is a kind of well-spring for German theatre… The love-story is the most daring and the most profound in German dramatic literature." Brecht

ISBN: 978-0-9534-257-0-9 (1998) €10